"Offenses will come. It's a given. *Unpacking Forgiveness* wisely prepares us for the aftermath. Grieving the loss of our six children in a van accident and then being reminded of that loss throughout thirteen years of subsequent battles forced us to search the Scriptures concerning the issue of forgiveness. Chris not only has confirmed answers that we had found but has thoroughly sorted out what it takes to be right with God and man. This is a diligent work with heart."
—SCOTT AND JANET WILLIS

"Forgiveness of one another is one of the most important subjects in the Bible, and yet one so often misunderstood. Now Chris Brauns has done a magnificent job in helping us understand the true nature of biblical forgiveness. Every Christian will profit from reading and applying this book."
—JERRY BRIDGES, author of *The Pursuit of Holiness*

"Here is a book that lives up to its title. Forgiveness remains a distant dream for many people precisely because they don't know what it means, where to begin, or what to expect. Blending contemporary stories with the teaching of the Bible, Christopher Brauns unpacks forgiveness so that we can be set free from bitterness. I especially appreciated his emphasis on coming back to the character of God and learning to delight in him as the only way forward when we have been deeply hurt. A book to be read on your knees. It could change your life."
—RAY PRITCHARD, President, Keep Believing Ministries; author,
The Healing Power of Forgiveness, *Credo*, *Discovering God's Will for Your Life*, *The Incredible Journey of Faith*

"Biblical, accessible, thorough, and practical, Rev. Brauns builds from the Scriptures a solid model of forgiveness that is clear, engaging, and convincing. He tackles the issues, answers the questions, and provides the guidance needed to forgive even the hard cases in a Christ-honoring way. Highly recommended!"
—JOHN N. DAY, Pastor, Bellewood Presbyterian Church, Bellevue,
Washington; author, *Crying for Justice*

"There is no more common or urgent pastoral need in the church today than to cultivate the gospel practice of forgiveness. Christians need to know what the Bible teaches and live it out, radically. *Unpacking Forgiveness: Biblical Answers for Complex Questions and Deep Wounds* is an engaging, convicting, but emphatically encouraging treatment of this hugely important (and sometimes mind-bogglingly challenging) part of life. Dr. Brauns writes from the standpoint of a faithful, wise, experienced, and caring pastor who has seen the heartbreak of an unforgiving spirit at work in the lives of people, but also the power of grace in the hearts of Christians who have learned to forgive and be forgiven."
—J. LIGON DUNCAN III, Chancellor and CEO, Reformed Theological
Seminary, Jackson, Mississippi

"There are few things more unnatural and few things more holy than forgiveness. Living as we do in a fallen world, we are given endless opportunities both to extend and to seek forgiveness. In *Unpacking Forgiveness*, Chris Brauns eschews the easy answers and looks to the Bible to provide God's wisdom on how and when we are to forgive. Relying on his experience as a pastor and his deep knowledge of Scripture, he provides what is a logical, well-illustrated book on the subject. With humor at times and appropriate gravitas at others, Brauns leads the reader first to understand and then to apply what the Bible teaches on forgiveness. Because it deals biblically with a subject of universal importance, any reader can benefit from reading *Unpacking Forgiveness*. I recommend that you do just that."
—TIM CHALLIES, author, *The Next Story*; blogger, Challies.com

"Using the parameters 'forgive as God forgives,' this book describes something *other* than a cheapened, 'automatic' forgiveness. Dr. Brauns lays careful gridlines that are 'dripping with Scripture,' as he puts it, for working through complex and deeply painful situations. *Unpacking Forgiveness* offers a tender hand of guidance to those who ache to unpack what life has flung at them and awakens a longing for the happiness that only forgiveness can bring."
—SHANNON POPKIN, Speaker, Freelance Writer, Blogger

"In a culture that all too often embraces oversimplistic remedies for forgiveness and reconciliation, Brauns provides a truly helpful and honest discussion about biblical forgiveness. *Unpacking Forgiveness* will be an essential resource for small groups, students, and ministry leaders (seasoned or newcomers) because it wrestles with the intellectual, emotional, and biblical issues of living in redemptive relationships in a fallen world."
—PETER G. OSBORN, Vice President for Adult Learning, Grand Rapids Theological Seminary

"*Unpacking Forgiveness* is a must-read for every believer. All my life I was told to forgive, and now Chris Brauns tells me how. This practical and powerful book paints a penetrating picture of the forgiving Christ, my model on how to forgive. I cannot escape the bold and beautiful biblical truths within these pages. As a Christ-follower, I know exactly how to respond to those who have hurt me, and each action response sets me free . . . indeed."
—DOUG FAGERSTROM, Executive President and CEO, Marketplace Chaplains USA

unpacking
FORGIVENESS

biblical answers for complex
questions and deep wounds

chris BRAUNS

CROSSWAY

WHEATON, ILLINOIS

Unpacking Forgiveness

Copyright © 2008 by Chris Brauns

Published by Crossway
        1300 Crescent Street
        Wheaton, Illinois 60187

Published in association with the literary agency of Credo Communications, LLC, Grand Rapids, MI 49525

Cover design: Jessica Dennis

Cover photo: iStock

First printing, 2008

Printed in the United States of America

ISBN-13: 978-1-58134-980-1
ISBN-10: 1-58134-980-7
ePub ISBN: 978-1-4335-2140-9
PDF ISBN: 978-1-4335-0484-6
Mobipocket ISBN: 978-1-4335-0485-3

Library of Congress Cataloging-in-Publication Data
Brauns, Chris, 1963–
   Unpacking forgiveness : biblical answers for complex questions and deep wounds / Chris Brauns.
      p. cm.
   Includes bibliographical references and index.
   ISBN 978-1-58134-980-1
   1. Forgiveness of sin. 2. Forgiveness—Religious aspects—
Christianity. I. Title.
BT795.B26   2008
234'.5—dc22   2008009804-

For Jamie,

the grace and truth of Genesis 2:18 in my life

Contents

Acknowledgments

Acknowledging everyone who contributed to this book would amount to writing an autobiography. But several deserve mention.

In addition to being a top flight archery instructor, Shannon Popkin and her husband, Ken, encouraged me to pursue publication in the first place. Joy McCarnan was a special measure of grace. She made me smile, even while she warned me about splitting infinitives or otherwise butchering the King's English. Rick Wells helped me sift through the sand to pick up the right smooth stones.

God has used so many to shape my thinking: the faculty at Grand Rapids Theological Seminary and Gordon-Conwell Theological Seminary including Peter Osborn (who along with Chad Wright was there on Black Monday and a few other dark occasions), Dave Turner, and Haddon Robinson and other friends like Les Flanders, Chip Bernhard, Tom Price, Dave Hills, Tim Johnson, and Jeff Dodge. Thanks to Grand Ledge Baptist Church, where I first began to develop this material, and the "triangular" team of Andrew Ford, Brian McLaughlin, and John Lemke.

Here in Stillman Valley, the Julia Hull District Library cheerfully tracked down obscure titles. Kim at the Post Office welcomed extra mail, even at Christmastime. Our restaurant, The Royal Blue, is the best place around for an author to sit down with a cup of black coffee and a hot plate of food and scribble on a legal pad. I am privileged to serve at the Congregational Christian Church of Stillman Valley, "The Red Brick Church," where Jana Krause, Kevin Glendenning, Leonard and Pat Carmichael, Brad Carlson, Brian Bosecker, Tom Eytalis, and a lot of other "bricks" help build my ideas and support me as a pastor in an ongoing way. We love Stillman Valley.

Thanks to my agent, Tim Beals of Credo Communications, and to Crossway for this opportunity. Allan Fisher, Ted Griffin, Josh Dennis, and Jill Carter have been patient throughout.

While I preemptively deny whatever yarns they might spin about my growing up years, none of this would have happened apart from my parents, Sharon Galloway and William D. Brauns III, my grandparents, my brothers and sisters, my aunts, cousins, and other extended family. I owe a deep debt of gratitude to my in-laws, Helen Baier Limbaugh and the late Jack Limbaugh.

Our children are a wonderful combination. I am thankful for Allison, a sharp thinker who laughs occasionally at my jokes; for Christopher, a sensitive and encouraging conversationalist; for Benjamin, who has had the most passionate faith in how God might use this project; for our four-year-old, Mary Beth, who whispered quietly to her dolls when I was writing and prayed with sweet earnestness that only children can manage.

Most of all, I praise the Lord for my pretty, smiling wife, Jamie. "Many women do noble things, but you surpass them all" (Proverbs 31:29, NIV).

Ultimately, all praise and glory must go to the Lord Jesus Christ, who is before all things and in whom all things hold together (Colossians 1:17).

Introduction:
The Forgiveness Quiz

Open my eyes, that I may behold wondrous things out of your law.
PSALM 119:18

The Forgiveness Quiz

Let's start with a quiz. I know the idea of a pop quiz may trigger unpleasant memories. But quizzes can serve noble purposes. I hope to accomplish two things with this one. First, it is a discussion starter. You probably will not agree with all my answers. That is okay. General Patton said, "If everybody is thinking alike, somebody isn't thinking." Let this pop quiz start some thinking.

The second purpose of this quiz is to anticipate where this book is headed. Think of this forgiveness quiz as an aerial preview. If you are like me and you skip around when you read a nonfiction book, this quiz will help you skip directly to the section of the book that interests you.

See how you do. You should be able to complete this in the time it takes to hum the theme from *Jeopardy!* You are on the honor system. No looking ahead. For the sake of those around you, hum the *Jeopardy!* theme softly.

The Forgiveness Quiz—Questions

1. True or False

Where deep wounds between people are concerned, forgiveness can be unpacked in a moment.

2.   True or False
Personal happiness and joy can legitimately motivate people to live out what the Bible teaches about forgiveness.

3.   True or False
Most Christian pastors and counselors agree about what forgiveness is and how it should take place.

4.   True or False
Forgiveness occurs properly only when certain conditions are met.

5.   True or False
Jesus said little about how people should resolve interpersonal conflict.

6.   True or False
A willingness to forgive is a test of whether or not a person will go to heaven when he or she dies.

7.   True or False
Good people get to the bottom of all their disagreements.

8.   True or False
There are times when it is wrong to forgive.

Where I Come from as an Author

Before we grade your answers to the Forgiveness Quiz, let me share two things about where I come from in writing this book. *First, I write as a pastor involved in people's lives.* I cannot tell you how many hours I have spent working through complex forgiveness questions with people in my churches. On the day I am writing this, I have listened to two different women with broken hearts. I sat across the table and hurt with them and prayed and watched small piles of mascara- and tear-soaked tissues build.

Looking back across the years I can recall images of so many tired, wounded people. I think, for instance, of my friend Deb (not her real name). When I first met Deb, she was grieving the loss of her only son who had died at the age of seven after a long illness. She was devastated.

In the midst of losing her son, Deb discovered that her husband was involved with pornography. His addiction eventually destroyed their marriage, and they were divorced. Soon after, Deb's former husband was tragically killed in an accident.

Can you imagine? Her son died. Her marriage fell apart. Her former husband died. Consider the emotionally charged, complex forgiveness questions that Deb faced.

- Should Deb have forgiven her husband even though he was not repentant?

- How could she know whether he really was repentant?

- If Deb was able to forgive her husband, would that mean she should not have divorced him?

- How about after her husband died? Would it be appropriate or easier then for Deb to forgive him?

- What about her anger and grief over losing her son? No doubt, at points Deb even struggled with anger toward God. How should she have handled her anger? Should Deb have forgiven God?

I believe the answer to the last question, "Should Deb have forgiven God?" is an emphatic no! That God should be forgiven implies that God may have done something wrong. Many disagree and would not hold to my negative view of the idea of forgiving God. Arguably, the most influential Christian book written on forgiveness in the last fifty years contends that it is acceptable and even healthy for people to "forgive God."[1] I will have more to say about this in Chapter 5.

You might ask me, how do you have the confidence to disagree with a book written by a well-known Christian authority? Or, how can a pastor help people when, in cases like Deb's, the wounds are so deep and the questions are so complex? Where is there hope for people who get sick to their stomach when they even begin to think about the abuse they have suffered?

This brings me to the second thing I want to say about my approach to writing this book. And this is the heart of what I have to say: *I write with the firm conviction that only God's Word can unpack forgiveness.* When I talk with people like Deb, what gives me confidence is to know that God is there, and he is not silent. He has spoken clearly and sufficiently through his Word. God has given us all that we need for life and godliness through our knowledge of him who called us by his own glory and goodness (2 Peter 1:3). And his Word is where we find our knowledge of him. God's Word can and does unpack forgiveness. It makes wise the

---

[1] Lewis B. Smedes, *Forgive and Forget: Healing the Hurts That We Don't Deserve* (New York: Simon & Schuster, 1984), 111–123.

simple, giving joy to the heart and light to the eyes. It is more precious than any treasure and sweeter than honey (Psalm 19:7–11).

But Scripture must be understood and applied accurately. I have been careful not to pluck verses out of context or force them into the mold of my position. I do not want to read my own meaning into the text. Rather, my goal has been to *listen* to the Word.

In emphasizing the authority of God's Word, I do not mean to imply that I have not learned from others about forgiveness. Quite the opposite has occurred, in fact. A number of books on forgiveness have sharpened my thinking significantly. I also consult multiple commentaries when I study any given Bible passage. My interaction with these other sources will be evident to the reader. The Bible, however, must always have the final say.

In summary, this is a book written by a pastor who is actively involved in people's lives. And the goal is to shine the light of God's Word on forgiveness. Only God working in and through his Word can help us unpack forgiveness. The wounds are otherwise too deep, the problems too complex. But God working in and through his Word can answer any question and heal any hurt.

Answers to the Forgiveness Quiz
Here are the answers to the Forgiveness Quiz.

The Forgiveness Quiz—Answers
1. False
Where deep wounds are concerned, forgiveness can be unpacked in a moment.

2. True
Personal happiness and joy can legitimately motivate people to live out what the Bible teaches about forgiveness.

3. False
Most Christian pastors and counselors agree about what forgiveness is and how it should take place.

4. True
Forgiveness occurs properly only when certain conditions are met.

5.   False
Jesus said little about how people should resolve interpersonal conflict.

6.   True
A willingness to forgive is a test of whether or not a person will go to heaven when he or she dies.

7.   False
Good people get to the bottom of all their disagreements.

8.   True
There are times when it is wrong to forgive.

Your score?

If you posted a perfect score, don't celebrate just yet. Be humble. It was true/false after all. You may have just guessed. Keep reading.

At the other end of the grading scale, if you missed several, you could interpret your score in a couple of ways. The truly humble and teachable may say, "Wow, I really need to learn more about forgiveness. I am going to keep reading." On the other hand, if you are more like me, you will want to debate. So, let me start making my case. These are preliminary explanations for the debaters; and essentially the rest of the book will flesh out these brief thoughts.

Statement #1: Where deep wounds are concerned, forgiveness can be unpacked in a moment. FALSE.

Here is how I define "unpacking forgiveness."

unpacking forgiveness: (1) To understand biblical truth about forgiveness and the application of that truth to complex problems in life. (2) To unload the burdens we carry because of wounds that we have received from others, and have given to others.

So there are two goals of unpacking forgiveness. The first is to understand biblical teaching. The second is to implement that understanding and to be freed from the burdens that weigh us down.

Neither of these goals is accomplished in a moment. Unpacking forgiveness is like relocating a family. While you may move on a particular day, unpacking takes a lot longer. It's a process. Boxes remain packed for months, years even. My family moved almost two years ago, and we are still unpacking.

But don't be discouraged by that. While it is true that unpacking forgiveness is a process, with God's help it is one that you can work through. The key is to get started. If you have been deeply wounded in life, then you cannot afford to leave the boxes stacked somewhere in the basement. With God's help you need to understand what his Word teaches and how you can find rest and healing by his grace.

Statement #2: Personal happiness and joy can legitimately motivate people to live out what the Bible teaches about forgiveness. TRUE.

Too many people dread learning about forgiveness. They fear they will learn what they ought to do and that what they ought to do will make them miserable. Such a fearful approach is destined to fizzle. We cannot approach a biblical study of forgiveness like we are on our way to get a root canal. If that is where you are at, if you are struggling with a lack of motivation to understand and live what God's Word teaches about forgiveness, then my prayer is that Chapters 1–2 will be a great encouragement to you.

Statement #3: Most Christian pastors and counselors agree about what forgiveness is and how it should take place. FALSE.

In reality, pastors and counselors disagree profoundly about forgiveness. This is just a fact. Go to a website that sells books, type the words "forgiveness" and "Christian" in the search box, and hit enter. You will get hundreds of titles. If you had the inclination to order ten to fifteen of these books, you would find that views range from East to West, and not only among secular or Christian authors. Even among Christian authors, opinions about forgiveness range from Maine to California.

You might respond, "I have no interest in surveying everyone's opinion and listening to a technical argument about forgiveness." I understand. Most of the people I pastor are trying to get their grass cut and their children to baseball practice on time. But you must and actually *do* believe something about forgiveness. And whether you think about it or not, every day you implement those beliefs about forgiveness.

Your convictions about forgiveness will shape how you respond when your spouse complains about how you seasoned the chicken. Your views about forgiveness may determine how you handle a teenager who rolls her eyes, or how you relate to an abusive parent, or whether or not you go ahead and marry your fiancé, or if you should counsel your friend to leave her husband. You do not have to read every book on forgiveness, but you may have to decide whether or not to change churches because of what the pastor or one of the elders did. The forgiveness choices you make will shape much of your life. For that reason, *you must consciously work out what you believe about forgiveness and then intentionally put those beliefs into action.*

Of course, that begs the question, how can anyone decide who is right when there are so many conflicting opinions? The answer is that you must consistently evaluate everything against the gold standard of Scripture. Be like the Bereans Luke wrote about in Acts 17:11:

> *Now [the Bereans] were more noble than those in Thessalonica; they received the word with all eagerness, examining the Scriptures daily to see if these things were so.*

Luke tells us that the Bereans were "more noble" because they were "examining the Scriptures" for themselves. The word translated "examining" was often used in legal settings in the first century. The Bereans judiciously studied the Bible for themselves to see if what Paul said was true.

Be like the Bereans. Resolve that you are going to work out an understanding of forgiveness based on the Word of God. You don't need my opinion or anyone else's. You need to hear from God. When you work through your personal beliefs about forgiveness, be thoroughly biblical. Know where the relevant references are in the Bible. When you pick up any book on forgiveness and read it, ask yourself, does this book plainly set forth the teaching of Scripture? How much is it really interacting with the Bible?

This is for sure: if a book on forgiveness is going to be worth your while, it should be dripping with Scripture.

Statement #4: Forgiveness occurs properly only when certain conditions are met. TRUE.

If you answered "false," you are not alone. Whenever I give this quiz, a number of people give that answer. One author dedicated his book on forgiveness with this phrase: "To God who forgives all."[2] This is an unconditional statement. It says categorically that God forgives all. No exceptions.

Is that how it works? Does God forgive *everyone*?

---

[2]Randall O'Brien, *Set Free by Forgiveness: The Way to Peace and Healing* (Grand Rapids, MI: Baker, 2005). Reading the rest of this book, I assume the author's intent was to communicate that God is *willing* to forgive all. But the way this statement was made is potentially misleading.

Every time I think about that book dedication, I am puzzled. For a while I kept thinking I was missing something. I asked a lot of people, "Is that true? Does God forgive all?"

The answer to that question is decidedly no. Of course, it may feel warm and fuzzy to say that God forgives all, but the reality is that he does not. The Bible is full of true stories about people who were *not* forgiven.

Here is one such grim story that you know. Before I even remind you of it, let me assure you, I am not making light of this. It is a story of awful judgment.

Picture it. Goliath went out every day and talked trash about God. Nine feet tall, cursing, spitting, taunting, he defied God. But soon enough David pulled off the quintessential upset of all time and took Goliath down with one smooth stone.

At the risk of grossing you out, did you ever meditate on what Scripture says David was lugging around when he debriefed with King Saul after the fight? First Samuel 17:57 reads:

And as soon as David returned from the striking down of the Philistine, Abner took him, and brought him before Saul with the head of the Philistine in his hand.

David had Goliath's head because he had severed it with the giant's own sword. And now, rather than dropping the violence from the story, Scripture describes how David dragged Goliath's dripping, discolored, already smelly head around.

After David knocked Goliath down, he did not offer Goliath an ice pack and lean over and whisper, "Goliath, you have really gotten a lot of people upset on the other side of the valley, but we love and forgive you." No, he hacked off his head and dragged it from the battlefield.

Is that not truly awful? Here is the thing. The story of David and Goliath is not in the Bible so we have an inspiring story for undersized children or so we have something to tell our football teams before they play a highly ranked opponent. Nor is it a model of how we resolve interpersonal differences. God included it in the Bible to show us the reality of his judgment and that he does *not* forgive all.

The reality of God's justice is not limited to the Old Testament. Revelation, the last book in the Bible, graphically describes what will happen to those who are not forgiven. In the Gospels, Jesus prophesied weeping and gnashing of teeth for the unforgiven. And John wrote about forgiveness with a condition:

> *If we confess our sins, he is faithful and just to forgive us our sins and to cleanse us from all unrighteousness. (1 John 1:9)*

Make no mistake—God does *not* forgive all. God's forgiveness is conditional. In Chapters 3–4 I will explain this and why it is eternally important that we each understand what we believe about whether or not forgiveness is conditional.

And forgiveness is not only conditional for God. It should be conditional in our relationships, too. For sure, we must have an attitude of grace or a willingness to forgive all people. We are commanded to love our enemies and to pray for those who persecute us (Matthew 5:43–48). But complete forgiveness can only take place when there is repentance. I will develop this point in Chapters 3–4.

Statement #5: Jesus said little about how people should resolve interpersonal conflict. FALSE.

Jesus said a great deal about conflict resolution and forgiveness. One whole chapter of the Gospels (Matthew 18) is about Jesus teaching the disciples when they were having a conflict. Chapters 6–10 of this book will be devoted to a study of that chapter. Be encouraged. Jesus had a lot to say about how we work through broken relationships.

Statement #6: A willingness to forgive is a test of whether or not a person will go to heaven when he or she dies. TRUE.

A willingness to forgive is closely connected to how we can be sure that we are going to heaven. Jesus was very clear about this. In the Sermon on the Mount, he said:

> *"For if you forgive others their trespasses, your heavenly Father will also forgive you, but if you do not forgive others their trespasses, neither will your Father forgive your trespasses." (Matthew 6:14–15)*

I will devote all of Chapter 10 to considering the relationship between a willingness to forgive and assurance of salvation. For now, notice two things in these verses. First, Jesus is talking about forgiveness. The word *forgive* appears four times in two verses. Second, Jesus is putting on the table the threat of eternal judgment or hell. If you have any questions about whether or not God has forgiven you, be sure to read Chapter 3 carefully.

Statement #7: Good people get to the bottom of all their disagreements. FALSE.

If you have been around families or the local church for any length of time, you probably got this one right. There are times when good people simply cannot reach agreement about what went wrong, why someone was offended, who was right and who was wrong.

What are Christians to do when they cannot agree or find closure? Chapter 15 addresses what Christians should do when they come to an impasse.

Statement #8: There are times when it is wrong to forgive. TRUE.

Some argue that it is *never* wrong to forgive. But this cannot be the case. As I will explain in Chapter 3, God does not forgive the unrepentant. It would be wrong for him to do so because it would go against his own justice and holiness.

Others counter that while there may be times when God does not forgive, people must always forgive. They insist that whenever a wrong is committed, regardless of whether or not the offender is repentant, Christians should automatically forgive the offender. But this teaching is too simplistic. It encourages forgiveness so broadly that it diminishes the justice of God and compromises the integrity of true forgiveness. This is what Dennis Prager pointed out in a *Wall Street Journal* article:

> The bodies of the three teen-age girls shot dead last December by a fellow student at Heath High School in West Paducah, Ky., were not yet cold before some of their schoolmates hung a sign announcing, "We forgive you, Mike!" They were referring to Michael Carneal, 14, the killer.
>
> This immediate and automatic forgiveness is not surprising. Over the past generation, many Christians have adopted the idea that they should forgive everyone who commits evil against anyone, no matter how great and cruel and whether or not the evildoer repents.
>
> The number of examples is almost as large as the number of heinous crimes. Last August, for instance, the preacher at a Martha's Vineyard church service attended by the vacationing President Clinton announced that the duty of all Christians was to forgive Timothy McVeigh, the Oklahoma City bomber who murdered 168 Americans. "Can each of you look at a picture of Timothy McVeigh and forgive him?" the Rev. John Miller asked. "I have, and I invite you to do the same."
>
> Though I am a Jew, I believe that a vibrant Christianity is essential if America's moral decline is to be reversed. And despite theological differences, Christianity and Judaism have served as the bedrock of American

civilization. And I am appalled and frightened by this feel-good doctrine of automatic forgiveness.[3]

This book will interact with Prager's legitimate concern. It will present the beauty of God's grace and the necessity of forgiveness. But it will also teach the reader that forgiveness must take place in a way that is consistent with justice. We must move beyond a "feel-good doctrine of automatic forgiveness." Christians must *always* have a willingness to forgive or an attitude of forgiveness. But this does not mean that forgiveness always takes place.

Chapters 11–12 will focus entirely on this area. If you have been deeply hurt, and the other person is not sorry about it, read these chapters. If you wonder how Christians should respond to the Holocaust, 9/11, Columbine, Oklahoma City, Virginia Tech, or Rwanda, then read chapters 11–12.

● ● ●

Although we live in different states now, I recently called up my friend Deb, the lady who went through the loss of a son and a divorce. I wanted her permission to share her story, and I wanted to hear how she is doing. Her story is such a blessing. Deb remarried, and she and her husband have two children. They have a happy, Christ-centered home. I don't mean that Deb does not have any scars. But she is through the worst of it. I wish I could communicate how much joy it gives my heart to hear how God has blessed Deb.

Even as I share Deb's joy, I am sure of this: there is no way Deb could have gotten through the trials she faced on her own. Only God and his Word can unpack forgiveness. The questions were too complex for her to untangle on her own. The wounds were too deep.

I am praying for more stories like Deb's. I pray that the Triune God will be pleased to use this book to help many others unpack forgiveness, not because I have some super-keen insight but because God is pleased to work in and through the clear teaching of his Word. I understand that people will read this book who have been hurt deeply, those whose problems are terribly complicated. But be confident. There is no wound too deep for God to heal; there is no question too complex for him to answer.

---

[3]Dennis Prager, "The Sin of Forgiveness," *The Wall Street Journal*, December 15, 1997.

chapter one

How to Begin Unpacking

"Come to me, all who labor and are heavy laden, and I will give you rest."

MATTHEW 11:28

Wherefore, if anyone is weary, if any is in prison, if anyone is in captivity, if anyone is in the wilderness, let him come to the blessed Jesus, who is as the shadow of a great rock in a weary land. Delay not, arise and come away.

JONATHAN EDWARDS[1]

I have never met Jennifer Thompson. She is from North Carolina; I grew up in Iowa. We do have this in common: in 1984 we were both working hard to graduate from college. So as contemporaries we must share some of the same memories. I assume college students in North Carolina listened to the same music we heard in Iowa: "Footloose" by Kenny Loggins, "Against All Odds" by Phil Collins, stuff like that. Styles were probably similar, though I suspect that we were a little behind in the Midwest. Fashion had a hard time finding us in the cornfields.

Then again, there's a lot that Jennifer Thompson and I didn't have in common. She maintained a 4.0 grade point average. My successes in college had more to do with an intramural basketball team called the Squids.

---

[1] Jonathan Edwards, *Altogether Lovely: Jonathan Edwards on the Glory and Excellency of Jesus Christ,* ed. Don Kistler (Morgan, PA: Soli Deo Gloria, 1997), 107.

Jennifer Thompson was Homecoming Queen. At our Homecoming, I was awarded the title of Grand Lemming. It's a long story and not as glamorous as if I had been Homecoming King, though they did play "Hail to the Chief" whenever I came into a room. Like I said, it would take a while to explain.

Still, Jennifer Thompson and I are contemporaries, and when I read her heartbreaking story, it makes me remember those days of working on resumés and trying to get job interviews or to be accepted into graduate programs. And my heart so goes out to her: to have so much ahead of you, and then to have someone do something so evil to you . . . I can't imagine.

It is hard to even write about this, but here it is. One night in 1984 a man broke into Jennifer Thompson's apartment, held a knife to her throat, and raped her.

It might have finished her. But Jennifer Thompson was a determined young lady. Even in the midst of her ordeal, she studied her assailant's face looking for tattoos or scars, anything she could use to identify him. She resolved, "When and if I survived the attack, I was going to make sure that he was put in prison and he was going to rot."[2]

Within a few days she identified her rapist from a series of police photos. She picked out the same man from a lineup. Courageously, Jennifer Thompson put her hand on a Bible and testified in court. Based on her testimony, Ronald Cotton was sentenced to prison for life.

Jennifer Thompson celebrated. Now she was rid of her luggage. Ready to go on with life. Or maybe not. Jennifer could not have anticipated the weight of the baggage that she would carry through years of her life because of what happened that horrible night in 1984.

Jesus' Invitation

How about you? Are you carrying baggage through life? Are questions and wounds weighing you down? Maybe your baggage contains abuse or divorce or unfaithfulness or mistakes you have made. If so, are you learning how to unpack the baggage that comes with those wounds and to deal with them so they do not continue to affect how you relate to people today?

If that is where you are, meditate with your heart and mind on the invitation of the Lord Jesus Christ: "Come to me, all who labor and are heavy laden, and I will give you rest" (Matthew 11:28).

Here is help for the hurting. Jesus extends a special invitation to those who are being crushed under a load of brokenness. In the original context,

---

[2]Jennifer Thompson-Canino, "I Was Certain, but I Was Wrong," *New York Times*, June 18, 2000; http://www.afterinnocence.com/jenstory.html (accessed July 17, 2007).

Jesus offered rest to people burdened by an intricate religious system. The Pharisees of the first century had developed a complex set of rules. The rules began with the goal of helping people to be more righteous, but in the end they focused on minutiae and neglected the more important matters of justice, mercy, and faithfulness (Matthew 23:23). Jesus said that the Pharisees were straining gnats from their beverages while guzzling down camels. And all the attention to religious trivia wore people out (Matthew 23:4, 24).

The baggage of broken relationships can be every bit as fatiguing as the religious system of the Pharisees. Are you haunted by your relationship with your father or mother? Do you feel constant guilt about a broken marriage? Are you filled with bitterness over abuse you endured? Or hopelessly disillusioned by your own failures? If so, Jesus invites you to come to him. He will give you rest. *Real* rest.

•   •   •

Unbelievably, two years after Ronald Cotton was sentenced to life in prison, he was granted another trial. Still determined that justice be done, Jennifer Thompson took the stand again. This time the defense brought in another suspect. She testified that she had never seen him. Again Ronald Cotton was convicted and sentenced to life in prison. And again Jennifer Thompson relished the justice.

Eleven years passed. Jennifer Thompson got married and had triplets. She was now well past the nightmare of 1984. But once more she was asked to assist the prosecution. This time they asked her to provide a blood sample for DNA. She agreed, confident that it would only solidify the case against Ronald Cotton.

And then the unthinkable happened.

A police detective and the district attorney knocked on Jennifer Thompson's front door. They told her that DNA testing had proven that Ronald Cotton was not her assailant. Bobby Poole (the man she testified she had never seen before in her life) was the man who had raped her.

Jennifer Thompson helped send the wrong man to prison. Her testimony had stolen eleven years of freedom from Ronald Cotton. She was devastated. "How do I give someone back eleven years?" she asked the district attorney.[3]

---

[3]Helen O'Neill, "Even the Perfect Witness Can Make a Mistake," *The Lansing State Journal*, September 24, 2000.

Now in addition to the nightmare of having been raped, Jennifer Thompson had to drag around the luggage of her own guilt. She would wrestle with that burden for years.

As I pointed out in the Introduction, forgiveness questions can get so complicated. How do you unpack luggage like Jennifer Thompson's? Maybe your problems seem just as complex and hopeless. It feels as though there are no answers. If that's where you are, I would say to you that there *are* answers. You don't have to be naive to believe that. A great ending can be written to your story.

You might answer, "Well, I'm not sure I can believe that." Here is what you can do. Fix your eyes on the majestic loveliness of the One who extends an invitation to those who are weary and heavy-burdened. Get this: this One is God himself. He is the "Wonderful Counselor" (Isaiah 9:6). The word translated "Wonderful" is used in Scripture to describe miracles (Exodus 3:20; 15:11). "Counselor" refers to a giver of the kind of wisdom that helps in guidance and planning (Proverbs 11:14; 24:6). Jesus, who offers you rest, is wonderfully wise, the Lord of awesome answers, the God of incredible insight and godly guidance. He will lead you perfectly through the minefields of your broken relationships if you will come to him.

Nothing gets me more fired up about the glory of Christ than witnessing him as he unties the tightest knots and heals the deepest wounds in human hearts. In a newspaper article with the title "Even the Perfect Witness Can Make a Mistake," Helen O'Neill told the story of how Jennifer Thompson moved forward in life.

> For two years after [learning that Cotton was innocent] Jennifer Thompson never stopped feeling ashamed.
>
> Over and over she wondered: How could she have made such a terrible mistake?
>
> And what of the man whose life she had ruined? All those years, locked away from his family. Now that he was free, did he hate her as much as she hated herself?
>
> Then one day she stopped crying. She knew exactly what to do.
>
> A few weeks later, she drove 50 miles to a church in the town where she was raped.
>
> She had prayed for the strength to face this moment. She had prayed for the strength to face Ronald Cotton.
>
> "I'm sorry," she said. "If I spent every day for the rest of my life telling you how sorry I am, it wouldn't come close to what I feel."
>
> Ronald Cotton was calm and quiet.

Finally he spoke.

"I'm not mad at you," he said softly. "I've never been mad at you. I just want you to have a good life."

For two hours they sat and talked while their families paced outside. They talked about the pitfalls of memory, the power of faith, the miracle of DNA. They talked about Bobby Poole.

"We were both his victims," Cotton said, and Thompson nodded in agreement.

As dusk fell, they made their way out of the church. In the parking lot, their families weeping, Jennifer Thompson and Ronald Cotton embraced.[4]

In the article, there is a picture of Ronald Cotton and Jennifer Thompson sitting on a park bench. They are both smiling in a way that could not be faked, the smiles of people at peace with one another and at peace with themselves, free from weighty burdens.

You might ask, how was Ronald Cotton able to forgive the woman who had wrongly accused him? That in itself is an amazing story. In prison, Ronald Cotton hated Bobby Poole, the man who actually had committed the crime. Cotton made a blade out of a piece of metal and planned to kill Poole. But his father pleaded with him not to do it. He told him that if he killed Bobby Poole, he would be like him. Instead his father encouraged him to turn to Christ. And Ronald Cotton did. He found that Jesus was the One who could and would unpack the burdens pressing down on him. Because Ronald Cotton had himself received the gracious forgiveness of his Heavenly Father, he was able to forgive Jennifer Thompson graciously. Worn-out and broken, carrying the burden of being convicted for a crime he had not committed, Ronald Cotton turned to Jesus and found a Savior who was more lovely and gracious and gentle than he could have ever imagined. And the brilliant light of Christ shone through his own life so that he could in turn demonstrate Christ's grace to Jennifer Thompson.

●　　●　　●

Along with his matchless wisdom as Wonderful Counselor, the Lord Jesus Christ is also "Mighty God" (Isaiah 9:6). Jesus rules with complete power. There is nothing he cannot accomplish. Think of what a tremendous combination his almighty power is with his wonderful wisdom. Not

---

[4]Ibid.

only does Jesus always know the right thing to do, he can always do it. Nothing in heaven or hell could ever thwart his purposes. If God be for us, who can be against us (Romans 8:31)? Jesus can do for you what he did for Ronald Cotton and Jennifer Thompson.

Think again of the invitation of Jesus. This time, read the following two verses as well.

> *"Come to me, all who labor and are heavy laden, and I will give you rest. Take my yoke upon you, and learn from me, for I am gentle and lowly in heart, and you will find rest for your souls. For my yoke is easy, and my burden is light." (Matthew 11:28–30)*

Just for a moment now, block out all your concerns about whatever fight you may face at home or at church or in the world. Consider Christ even more deeply. Even as I have reminded you that he is the Wonderful Counselor and Almighty God, notice that when Jesus invites you to come to him, he describes himself as "gentle and lowly in heart." Though he is supremely exalted, Christ is not a vindictive taskmaster who would rub your face in your mistakes and beat you down over your failures. Such a combination isn't possible in the Savior of the Bible! He stands ready to help. He is gentle and humble in heart. Why would you not accept his invitation to unload the weight of your burdens?

How to Accept Jesus' Invitation

But wait. Before you accept Jesus' offer to find rest, read the invitation closely. Jesus does not invite worn-out people to take a nap. Nor does he suggest that if we will chant a one-time prayer, refreshment will be granted automatically. No; Jesus says to assume his *yoke* and learn from him. Jesus invites those who need rest to come *work* with him.

Jesus' offer of discovering rest by means of a yoke is a paradox. A yoke is a harness used for labor. You might legitimately ask, how in taking on Jesus' equipment would I find rest? The answer is, as we follow Jesus and learn from him, the Holy Spirit graciously operates in our lives. This is how we who are weak can move forward—not in our strength, but in his. This is the kind of thing that Paul pointed to in Philippians 2:12–13 when he said, "Work out your own salvation with fear and trembling, for it is God who works in you, both to will and to work for his good plea-sure." The reason Paul told the Philippians to *work* out their salvation with fear and trembling is that when they do, God will graciously work in and through them. God works in and through us as we cooperate with his gracious work in our lives.

A sailing illustration might help make this point. Suppose you are in a boat and you have to travel an incredible distance. And to further complicate things, you don't even know there is such a thing as sailing.

What would you do? You would try and propel the boat in all kinds of futile ways. You might lie on your stomach and paddle over the side. If you were a little more creative, you might use a stick as an oar and row in circles. But soon you would be worn-out and frustrated.

But then imagine that someone stepped onto your boat and said, "I see that you are exhausted. How about I teach you how to get somewhere?" He would then show you how to raise a sail and catch the wind.

You get the picture. Sailing is still hard work. There is a reason that sailors like Popeye have big forearms. But it is not futile hard work. Hoist a sail into the breeze, and soon you are gliding forward in a strength that is beyond yourself.

This is the invitation that Jesus gives. Are you tired of trying to work your way through forgiveness with one oar? Are you worn-out from trying to paddle with your hands? Come and sail in the wind of his strength. Soon you will be gliding forward in the breeze of his grace.

Of course, that brings us to the question, how do I work in such a way that God gives me strength and grace? How specifically do I assume the yoke of Jesus and learn from him? How do I raise a sail into the breeze of God's strength? The answer to *how* is that God works in our lives through certain appointed means. Sometimes theologians call these "means of grace." Means of grace are how God pours out his grace into the life of a Christian. These means of grace include his Word, prayer, fellowship with other believers, and worship.[5] When you participate in any of these means of grace, you hoist your sail into the wind of God's love and favor. If you have been trying to work through forgiveness

---

[5] The idea of "means of grace" may be new to you. But I assure you it is not something I invented. Louis Berkhof writes, "Sanctification takes place partly in the subconscious life, and as such is an immediate operation of the Holy Spirit; but also partly in the conscious life, and then depends on the use of certain means, such as the constant exercise of faith, the study of God's Word, prayer and association with other believers." Louis Berkhof, *Systematic Theology*, fourth edition (Grand Rapids, MI: Eerdmans, 1976), 534.

Grudem adds, "The New Testament does not suggest any short-cuts by which we can grow in sanctification, but simply encourages us repeatedly to give ourselves to the old-fashioned, time-honored means for Bible reading and meditation (Ps. 1:3; Matt. 4:4, 17:17), prayer (Eph. 6:18; Phil. 4:6), worship (Eph. 5:18-20), witnessing (Matt 28:19-20), Christian fellowship (Heb. 10:24-25), and self-discipline or self-control (Gal. 5:23; Titus 1:8)." Wayne Grudem, *Systematic Theology: An Introduction to Biblical Doctrine* (Grand Rapids, MI: Zondervan, 1994), 755.

without consistent involvement in the means of grace, you are only pad-
dling with your hands.

The way to accept Christ's invitation to find rest is to be in his Word,
to listen to biblical preaching, to pray, and to be sharpened by other
Christians. While at first it may seem like you are moving only a bit,
before long you will be sailing forward, ridding yourself of the baggage
that weighs you down.

You may object at this point, "I have already tried the Christian way
of unpacking my burdens, and it didn't really work. I tried Jesus! He
didn't give me rest."

Did you really? Did you really assume Jesus' yoke, his instrument of
work, and learn from him?

• Have you been involved consistently in a local church where the Bible is
preached? Have you participated in Sunday school or small groups or whatever
Christian education opportunities your church offers?

• Do you pray consistently in a disciplined way? I'm not just talking about
praying in the car on the way to work. Have you really gotten down on your
knees and earnestly prayed?

• Are you involved in a Christian community or fellowship? Are you sharing your life with other Christians?

• Do you worship Christ on a regular basis? Do you take part in Christ-
centered worship and listen to Christ-centered preaching? Have you identified
with Christ in baptism? Do you faithfully participate in observing the Lord's
Supper at your church?

These means of grace are how we take Christ's yoke upon us and
learn from him. Christ's way of unpacking forgiveness is not three easy
steps. It is a way of life, following Jesus, learning from him, being involved
in his church, hearing his Word preached. Apart from consistent involvement in these disciplines, you are trying to paddle with a stick. And that
just won't work.[6]

Conclusion

The most important line in Jennifer Thompson's story is this one: "Then
one day [Jennifer] stopped crying. She knew exactly what to do." She took
action. Jennifer Thompson was able to unpack her baggage because she

---

[6]If you would like to learn more about this area, I *highly* recommend Jerry Bridges's award-winning
book *The Discipline of Grace*. In it, Bridges wrote, "Grace and the personal discipline required to pursue
holiness, however, are not opposed to one another. In fact, they go hand in hand. An understanding of
how grace and personal vigorous effort work together is essential for a life-long pursuit of holiness."
This is what Bridges will help you understand—how grace and vigorous effort work together. Jerry
Bridges, *The Discipline of Grace: God's Role and Our Role in the Pursuit of Holiness* (Colorado Springs:
NavPress, 1994), 13.

made a decision to deal with it. How about you? Are you ready to decide? Are you ready to accept the invitation that Jesus offers? Be assured that everything you want in a Savior is found in Jesus! Why not take action—take on his yoke and learn from the "Wonderful Counselor, Mighty God, Everlasting Father, Prince of Peace"? Why not determine to cooperate with his grace in your life. My goal in this book is to help you do just that. Together let's drench ourselves in the Word. Let's prayerfully learn from him so we can unpack the baggage that weighs us down.

The way you RSVP to Jesus' invitation is to send back a response that says, "I accept your invitation. I am determined to cooperate with your grace in my life. The first thing I am going to do is prayerfully understand all that your Word teaches about forgiveness."

Discussion Questions

What invitation from Jesus was discussed in this chapter?

How is the invitation Jesus offers accepted?

Define "means of grace."

Read Philippians 2:12–13. According to the apostle Paul, do we work out our salvation or does God? Explain.

Read Acts 2:37–47. Does this Scripture stress a point of decision, ongoing involvement with God's people, or both?

How would you talk with a person who says that he or she has tried to find rest in Christ but it didn't work?

chapter two

Motivation to Unpack

If you are wise, you are wise for yourself.
PROVERBS 9:12A

God is most glorified in us when we are most satisfied in
him.
JOHN PIPER[1]

This chapter aims to fortify your decision to unpack forgiveness
with the right motivation. Upon hearing Jesus' invitation to the weary and
burdened, many accept in a preliminary way but do not continue on in
the decision. This chapter should further motivate you to continue finding
rest in Christ and in him alone (Psalm 62:1).

Being properly motivated is essential. There is a long list of reasons
why someone would read twenty or thirty pages of this book and go no
further. Unpacking forgiveness requires much effort. Many would rather
go on dragging their luggage around. My goal in this chapter is to change
that. By God's grace, I want to persuade you to be *driven* to understand
forgiveness and to live out that understanding in your relationships.
Without a burning passion to back it up, your decision to accept Jesus'
invitation to unpack forgiveness will not stand. You will likely shelf this
book twenty pages in or a phone call away from doing what needs to be
done.

There are two main reasons why unpacking forgiveness requires so

---

[1]John Piper, *Desiring God: Meditations of a Christian Hedonist* (Sisters, OR: Multnomah, 1996), 50.

much determination. First, forgiveness is an emotionally charged topic. As a pastor, I have witnessed this aspect of it time and again. Inevitably if I explain to a group of people that I am going to preach or teach on forgiveness, eyes begin to glisten with tears.

I remember talking with a young mother who was scared to unpack forgiveness. She had grown up with a stepfather who repeatedly abused her. He had never owned up to what he had done, never apologized or tried to make amends. She dealt with baggage from her stepfather's abuse every day. Now her pastor was telling the congregation that he was going to challenge them with forgiveness. She was afraid of what that would mean. Concern for her own children gripped her heart. If she were to forgive her stepfather, would there be consequences? Would it mean she should allow her own children to stay with her mom and stepfather? What if her stepfather were ever to molest her own daughter? Could she face the thought of exposing her own children to what she had been subjected to as a child? If she were to refuse to allow her daughter to stay there, would that mean she was dishonoring her mother or being unforgiving toward her stepfather? The thought of it all made her sick to her stomach.

Forgiveness is so emotionally charged. Field this question: should infidelity be confessed, even if it was an undiscovered, isolated instance many years ago? What will happen if that confession does happen? Could it end the marriage? What might the confession do to the spouse? Is it more selfish to confess than it would be to conceal? On the other hand, if the unfaithful person does not confess, will the sin always be a source of torment for him or her? Even beginning to contemplate such questions surfaces a huge range of emotions. Without the right motivation to move forward, the person may prefer to avoid dealing with it.

The second reason that we must be extremely motivated to unpack forgiveness is that it is so intellectually demanding. Forgiveness is a practical area of living. But how we live forgiveness out must rest on what we believe theologically. Start with the doctrine of salvation (soteriology). How we believe God forgives us shapes how we forgive others. Or there is the doctrine of the church (ecclesiology). For Christians, forgiveness happens in the local church. Our understanding of the doctrine of the church is key to understanding some of the most important Bible passages on forgiveness such as Matthew 18 or Colossians 3. It may not be immediately obvious, but the doctrine of the future work of Christ and the end times (eschatology) is also critical in how we view forgiveness. What happens to people who are not forgiven? To people who won't forgive?

If you cannot quite trace those connections just yet, don't worry. I will explain how our beliefs in these areas form our view of forgiveness in later chapters. For now, understand that unpacking forgiveness requires a mental workout. If we are not motivated, then we will not follow through.

So why do it? Here is the short answer. You should be motivated to unpack forgiveness so you can know maximum happiness. When your alarm clock screeches at you to get out of bed at some desolate hour so you can get up to study the Bible and pray, you should listen to it because you want to be happy. When you contemplate calling up someone to ask forgiveness or to offer grace, perhaps someone to whom you never wanted to talk again, you should challenge yourself to do so because you want to be happy. When you are deciding whether or not to watch television or to learn prayerfully about forgiveness, tell yourself, I am going to do this because I believe it will maximize my happiness.

Of course, there is more to it than a flippant idea of happiness-hunting. Let me explain.

How John Piper Helped

For years I struggled to understand the relationship between God's glory and my happiness. To begin with, as a child and young person, I had the sneaking suspicion that a person really committed to God would serve him out of some sense of duty. And I also assumed that dutifully serving would be a miserable task. Songs we sang at church—for example, "So Send I You"—didn't help. Think about these words:

> So send I you to labor unrewarded,
> To serve unpaid, unloved, unsought, unknown,
> To bear rebuke, to suffer scorn and scoffing,
> So send I you to toil for me alone.

Kind of makes you want to sign up for missions, doesn't it? Wow, did I respect missionaries, especially missionary doctors! They could have made a great living, but instead they sailed off to Kookamonga to be miserable (but dutiful!) servants of God.

I respected them, but I didn't want to get on the boat with them. So I tried to live the Christian life on my own terms. That route, I found, was the truly miserable one.

Finally, as a graduate student, I began to really grow for Christ. To my surprise, I found far more joy in following Christ than I had known living on my own terms. And after a few years my wife and I were leaving my first career and going off to seminary.

Yet even then, I did not really understand the relationship between all that the Bible says about God's glory and my own desire to be happy. It was about this time that I came across John Piper and the central thesis of his life, ministry, and writings.

Piper says it this way: "God is most glorified in us when we are most satisfied in him." Reading his books, I finally realized there is no competition between God's passion for his glory and our desire for true, lasting joy or happiness. It is not one or the other. It is both. Glory for God and real joy for us are not mutually exclusive possibilities.

The goal of this chapter, then, is to apply this thesis—that God is most glorified in us when we are most satisfied in him—to the area of forgiveness. We should seek to glorify God in how we work through broken relationships, knowing that even as we glorify God, we will maximize our joy. Or to use my words, we ought to unpack forgiveness because it is both right (it glorifies God) and best (it maximizes my happiness).

You cannot "get" this truth just by reading it once. Think about it more deeply. "*God is most glorified in us when we are most satisfied in him.*" As Piper points out, this statement brings together two truths.[2]

The first truth is that *God's central passion is for his glory.* Everything should be done for the glory of God. We are called to be mirrors that reflect the glory and the brilliance of Christ. "So, whether you eat or drink, or whatever you do, do all to the glory of God" (1 Corinthians 10:31). We are blessed so we can praise his glory (Ephesians 1:6, 12, 14).

The second truth is that *all people pursue joy or happiness.* This is true of all people in all places. The great thinker Blaise Pascal said:

All men seek happiness, this is without exception. Whatever different means they employ, they all tend to this end. The cause of some going to war, and of others avoiding it, is the same desire in both, attended with different views. The will never takes the least step but to this object. This is the motive of every action of every man, even of those who hang themselves.[3]

People, by nature, go after happiness. They pursue it wherever they believe they will find it. Piper emphasizes that this striving after happi-

---

[2]John Piper, "God's Passion for His Supremacy, Part I" (audio), Desiring God Ministries, 2007; http:// www.oneplace.com/ministries/Desiring_God/archives.asp?bcd=3/16/2007 (accessed April 9, 2008).
[3]Quoted in Piper, *Desiring God*, 16.

ness "is a law of the human heart as gravity is a law of nature."[4] Think carefully about this point, or as Piper calls it, this "law." You *will* pursue your own happiness.

Now here is the magnificent bringing together of these truths. We do not have to choose between one of the two, God's glory or our happiness. In fact, we cannot truly have one without the other. Where forgiveness is concerned, if I do what is right (what glorifies God and is most Christlike), then I will also do what is best (that which maximizes my own joy and happiness).

This is how we can understand what the Bible teaches about forgiveness and act (with determination) upon that understanding. Not because unpacking forgiveness is a bitter pill you must swallow, but because you desire more than a grudge or long-term baggage from the past. You can be motivated to forgive because you long for God's glory and because you long for a better country, a sweeter place.

This book is about broken relationships and how they can be healed. When it comes to looking to Christ for answers to broken relationships, there may be no better example than the story of Rahab. Hebrews 11 gives this one-verse summary of that woman:

> By faith Rahab the prostitute did not perish with those who were disobedient, because she had given a friendly welcome to the spies. (v. 31)

Rahab's life was full of pain. She lived in a city that was so evil, God cursed it. It was so wicked that God destroyed it completely—every man, woman, and child (Joshua 6:21). Further, he commanded that Jericho was never to be rebuilt again (Joshua 6:26). This was Rahab's background.

Not only was Rahab a citizen of that evil empire, she was on the bottom rung of the ladder—a prostitute. We do not know how Rahab became a prostitute. Was she an addict? Did she encounter difficult financial circumstances? Was she abused? Whatever the reason, we know that her life was a mess. Talk about baggage! Rahab had a lot to unpack.

Rahab's city was doomed. Even before Israel crossed the Jordan River into the Promised Land, they began to plan how they would attack and defeat Jericho. Joshua sent two spies into Jericho to look for weaknesses in the city (Joshua 2:1). A bordello would have offered a perfect place for spies to stay incognito. As Aquinas noted, prostitutes received guests indiscriminately, especially at nighttime.[5]

---

[4]Ibid.
[5]Aquinas's comment is included in Philip Edgcumbe Hughes, *A Commentary on the Epistle to the Hebrews* (Grand Rapids, MI: Eerdmans, 1977), 503, n. 85.

It was when Rahab met the spies from Israel that she turned in faith to the God of Israel (Joshua 2:8–14). She chose to hide the Hebrew men even after the king of Jericho learned that they were spies (Joshua 2:2). She did so because she knew that God was most glorious.

You think you are nervous about following Christ. Can you imagine how scary this was for Rahab? Jericho was a heavily fortified city. Their soldiers were described as "mighty men of valor" (Joshua 6:2). If the leaders in Jericho had discovered that she hid spies, she and her entire family would have almost certainly been tortured and killed. There was no human reason to believe that Israel could defeat Jericho. But Rahab feared God anyway and believed that he rewards those who earnestly seek him. She acted on her faith.

Was Rahab rewarded for seeking the God of Israel? Yes. Beyond what she could have ever asked or imagined! First, she and her family were spared. When God gave Jericho into Israel's hands, Joshua gave orders that Rahab's family should not be harmed. In addition, Rahab was allowed to become a part of Israel. She married into one of the most prominent families in Israel, and God gave her a son. And it gets even better—way better! Rahab, a ruined prostitute, ultimately became a part of the line of her future Savior! In the accounts of Jesus' genealogy, Rahab is one of four Old Testament women mentioned. It boggles the mind.

Whatever your situation, you can be rewarded like Rahab. Determine to understand biblical teaching on forgiveness. Know that if you seek the face of Christ in this matter, and every other, you will not regret it. First, delight yourself in the Lord. Make it your goal to glorify him. As you live for his glory, "he will give you the desires of your heart" (Psalm 37:3–4). God is real. If you seek him where forgiveness is concerned, he will reward you (Hebrews 11:6).

You Will Not Learn in an Instant That Following Christ Is Both Right and Best

If this concept that God is most glorified in us when we are most satisfied in him is new to you, it will take you time to really absorb it. Personally, I have been working on really absorbing it for over ten years, and I still have far to go.

But it is critical. You must believe that following Christ in the area of forgiveness and broken relationships is both right and best. The very first thing you must do is pray that the Holy Spirit will grow in your heart the conviction that you are commanded to find joy and happiness and maximum pleasure in glorifying Christ. This chapter does not suggest a proposition to be understood—it is about a life to be lived, a life of glorifying Christ by enjoying him totally. This will not be immediate. You have to begin pursuing it every morning. It does not happen all at once. The way of the righteous is like the first gleam of dawn (Proverbs 4:18). You won't even be sure at first if it is getting lighter. But keep walking. Soon the full light of day will blaze, and your life will be full of the joy of Christ. You will be so thankful that you unpacked forgiveness.[6]

Conclusion

We have been given a sweet, sweet gospel. In the gospel, not only are our sins forgiven through the shed blood of our Lord, but we are called to infinite and unbounded joy. Understanding what the Bible teaches about forgiveness—both how we can be forgiven by God and how we should and can love and forgive one another—should not be unpacked with a sense of dread. Rather, there should be a confident certainty that those who unpack forgiveness and put it into action will reflect and show the brilliant beauty of Christ, finding their maximum joy and happiness in him.

Take Jesus' yoke upon you, and learn from him. Following Christ is the right thing to do. And it is the best thing. There is nothing better.

Discussion Questions

According to this chapter, why are many people afraid to understand what the Bible teaches about forgiveness?

What is the relationship between God's glory and human happiness?

Read Hebrews 11. Why were the individuals in this chapter motivated to make the right decisions?

According to Hebrews 11:24–26, what motivated Moses to identify with God's people rather than Egyptian royalty? Do you know any recent examples of people who have made decisions similar to the one Moses made?

What should be said to a person who is afraid to study forgiveness

---

[6]For help in learning how to fight for joy, see John Piper, *When I Don't Desire God: How to Fight for Joy* (Wheaton, IL: Crossway Books, 2004). Desiring God Ministries (www.desiringgod.org) offers a wealth of material on their website. If you are looking for a place to begin, start by listening to John Piper's sermon, "God's Passion for His Supremacy, Part I"; http://www.oneplace.com/ministries/Desiring_God/archives.asp?bcd=3/16/2007.

for fear he or she might find something in the Bible he or she doesn't like or doesn't want to do?

This chapter quoted lyrics from the hymn "So Send I You."

So send I you to labor unrewarded,
To serve unpaid, unloved, unsought, unknown,
To bear rebuke, to suffer scorn and scoffing,
So send I you to toil for me alone.

In what sense is the message of this hymn accurate for those who choose to make sacrifices in following Christ? In what sense is it misleading?

chapter three

Defining Forgiveness:
The Divine Pattern

If you, O LORD, should mark iniquities, O Lord, who could
stand? But with you there is forgiveness, that you may be
feared.

PSALM 130:3–4

The crux of the matter is, of course, the question of forgiveness.

SIMON WIESENTHAL[1]

If we are going to unpack forgiveness, then we need to know
what forgiveness is. The goal of this chapter and the next is to define
forgiveness. That goal is not as straightforward as you might think. Go
looking for a definition of forgiveness and you will find a wide range of
opinions. Three friends counseling you to "forgive" may mean three different things. "Experts" differ profoundly. Theologian and writer Scot
McKnight observed that "the debate over [the meaning of forgiveness]
is bedeviled by clumsy definitions, confusing categories, and contextual
dislocations."[2] And whatever a "contextual dislocation" is, it can't be
good.

Getting one's mind around forgiveness is especially difficult when it is

---

[1]Simon Wiesenthal, *The Sunflower: On the Possibilities and Limits of Forgiveness* (New York:
Schocken, 1998), 97.
[2]Scot McKnight, "Slowing Down the Runaway Forgiveness Truck: Is There Such a Thing as Too Much
Mercy?" *Books and Culture*, July 1, 2004.

in the context of having been deeply wounded. Billy Graham's daughter Ruth Graham wrote about the pain of trying to define forgiveness after her husband confessed infidelity. Friends and family counseled her to forgive him. But she wondered, "What did forgiveness really mean? What did it look like? . . . What was forgiveness? I did not know. Everyone seemed to have a definition."[3]

This will not do. If we are going to unpack forgiveness, we must first understand precisely and objectively what it is. What does it mean for a wife to forgive a husband who has been unfaithful? What does that involve? What does it look like?

The Key Principle

The goal, of course, is to make sure that a definition of forgiveness squares with biblical teaching. But how, specifically, do we ensure that a definition is biblical? Do we just begin reading in Genesis and try to put together all the teaching about forgiveness? That would be an overwhelming task. Fortunately, it is easier than that. Here is a truth that shows us where to begin our search for a definition of forgiveness:

God expects believers to forgive others in the way that he forgave them.

That is, we should define forgiveness between ourselves and other people the way God defined it in forgiving us.

God's forgiveness for Christians is the model he expects Christians to live out. We find this principle stated more than once in the Scriptures. Jesus included this point in the Lord's Prayer. The key word is "as."

And forgive us our debts, as we also have forgiven our debtors. (Matthew 6:12b)

Paul stressed this in both Ephesians and Colossians.

Be kind to one another, tenderhearted, forgiving one another, as God in Christ forgave you. (Ephesians 4:32)

. . . bearing with one another and, if one has a complaint against another, forgiving each other; as the Lord has forgiven you, so you also must forgive. (Colossians 3:13)

---

[3]Ruth Graham and Stacy Mattingly, *In Every Pew Sits a Broken Heart: Hope for the Hurting* (Grand Rapids, MI: Zondervan, 2004), 50.

The first thing to do in developing an understanding of how we should forgive one another is to understand how God forgives us. This simplifies defining forgiveness because the Bible says far more about how God forgives people than it does about how people should forgive people.

So let's review the key points of how God forgives sinners.

How God Forgives

We all have needed God's forgiveness because everyone has offended God. The Bible tells us that God placed our ancestors, Adam and Eve, in a perfect creation. Adam and Eve were God's special representatives, and they were given responsibility over what God had created.

Sadly, Adam and Eve rebelled against God and ate of the tree of knowledge of good and evil. When they did, they destroyed their relationship with God, both for themselves and for all of humanity. Now all *are born* sinners. And all *choose* to sin.

It gets worse. The Bible teaches that there is a penalty for sin and that the penalty must be paid. The penalty for sin is the wrath of God— everlasting hell. It sounds so blunt to say it that way. But this is the truth of the Word of God.

Most of us tend to compare ourselves to other people. Comparing by that standard, we may not seem so bad. But we are not accountable to measure up to other people. We answer to a perfectly holy and just God. And we have all offended his standard in a way that we can never hope to repair through our own goodness.

So how God forgives becomes the most important truth that any human being ever considers. Here is a summary of what God's forgiveness is like:

God's forgiveness is gracious but not free.

I have talked with many different people about how God forgives. Often I ask them whether they believe they have been forgiven by God, or I might ask whether they think they will go to heaven when they die. But occasionally I ask someone to evaluate *me* instead. I say to them, "Well, what do you think? You don't know me that well, but do you think if I got hit by a truck in the parking lot this evening, I would go to heaven?"

To date, no one has ever said that I would not make it. Often they say, "Oh, by all means. You're in. No question about it."

Then I follow up that question by asking them, "Why? My wife and children would tell you that I am a sinner. I am far from perfect. Why do you think that God will forgive me?"

On any number of occasions, the person has responded confidently, "Well, you're a pastor. I mean if *you're* not going to heaven, then we're *all* in trouble."

If a person answers like that, I know that he or she misunderstands the basis for biblical forgiveness. The Bible teaches that we are forgiven and saved only by grace. By "only by grace," I mean that salvation rests entirely on the unmerited favor of God. Forgiveness is a gift that God *graciously* offers us.

> For by grace you have been saved through faith. And this is not your own doing; it is the gift of God, not a result of works, so that no one may boast. (Ephesians 2:8–9)

I could pastor for a million years, and it would get me no closer to being forgiven by God. I am forgiven only by grace. God's forgiveness to me is a gift.

Did God offer me this gift because he saw that I had a small seed of goodness or potential? Not at all. Forgiveness is a gift motivated by the love of the one true God. You have to grasp this verse:

> But God, being rich in mercy, because of the great love with which he loved us . . . (Ephesians 2:4)

So, motivated by love, God graciously offers the gift of forgiveness.

Understand that although salvation is offered to us as a gift, God bought that gift at an infinitely high price. Our salvation was purchased at the expense of the shed blood of the Lord Jesus Christ.

> In this is love, not that we have loved God but that he loved us and sent his Son to be the propitiation for our sins. (1 John 4:10)

The word "propitiation" here means "the turning away of wrath by an offering."[4] The only way anyone can be forgiven is for Christ to pay the penalty. Forgiveness is not free. Christ suffered in our place.

We can put this all together with a definition for grace that I got

---

[4]Leon Morris, "Propitiation," in *The Evangelical Dictionary of Theology*, ed. Walter A. Elwell (Grand Rapids, MI: Baker, 1990), 888.

from D. James Kennedy. If you can remember how to spell *grace*, you can remember this definition. Grace is:

God's
Riches
At
Christ's
Expense

Motivated by love, God offers forgiveness graciously. God wraps the present of forgiveness and gives it to anyone who will accept the gift. This gift was purchased by the shed blood of the Lord Jesus Christ.

God's forgiveness is conditional. Only those who repent and believe are saved.

So God offers the present of forgiveness to all people. Does this mean that all people are forgiven?

The answer to that question is emphatically no. Like any present, the gift of forgiveness must be opened. We receive the gift of forgiveness by turning in faith to Christ. There are two aspects of this turning to Christ. First, we turn away from trusting in ourselves and away from the idea that our own goodness could ever be the basis for salvation. We need to turn away from our sin. The Bible calls this turning away *repentance*.

The second aspect of turning to Christ is that we turn to Christ and trust in him alone for salvation. The Bible calls this *faith* or in other places *believing*.

Repentance. Faith. These two terms are emphasized many places in Scripture. In Acts 20:21 Paul summarized his ministry in this way.

"I have declared to both Jews and Greeks that they must turn to God in repentance and have faith in our Lord Jesus." (NIV)

In this verse Paul used both terms. We must turn to God in repentance, and we must have faith in our Lord Jesus. God's forgiveness is a package that he wraps up and offers. But the package of forgiveness must be opened. The Bible teaches that the way that the package is opened is through repentance and faith.

God's forgiveness is a commitment.

Keep the previous points in mind. First, God forgives us graciously. Motivated by love, he offers forgiveness as a gift. It is an expensive present, for it was purchased at the price of the shed blood of God himself.

Second, not everyone is forgiven. Only those who turn away from trusting in themselves or anything else (repentance) and turn to Christ (faith) are saved.

The next thing we need to see about God's forgiveness is that it is a commitment by God to those he forgives. This commitment is the essence of God's forgiveness.

The most common word for forgiveness in the Bible is the Greek Word ἀφίημι/aphíēmi. This word means, "To release from legal or moral obligation or consequence."[5] When God forgives, he commits or promises that he will no longer hold the sin against the person being forgiven.[6]

If we put our faith and trust in Christ, then we are "justified" (Romans 3:28; 5:1), declared to be righteous. God makes a legal declaration that we are no longer condemned for our sin. The reason we can be justified is that Jesus paid the penalty for sin and Jesus' righteousness was credited to us. As the old gospel hymn "To God Be the Glory" says, "The vilest offender who truly believes, that moment from Jesus a pardon receives."[7]

Forgiveness lays the groundwork for and begins the process of reconciliation.

God's forgiveness does not mean simply the elimination of guilt. When God forgives us, not only are we declared righteous, but we also begin a new relationship with him.

L. Gregory Jones writes:

> People are mistaken if they think of Christian forgiveness primarily as absolution from guilt; the purpose of forgiveness is the restoration of communion, the reconciliation of brokenness.[8]

God's forgiveness is inextricably linked to reconciliation. No one is forgiven by God without being reconciled to God. We see this in the thought of the apostle Paul. At some points he refers to the gospel as "the forgiveness of sins" (Colossians 1:14; cf. Ephesians 1:7). But at other points he points to the gospel with the word "reconciliation." For example:

---

[5]William F. Arndt, F. Wilbur Gingrich, and others, *A Greek-English Lexicon of the New Testament and Other Early Christian Literature (Electronic Version)*, third edition (Chicago: University of Chicago Press, 2000).
[6]Jay Adams, *From Forgiven to Forgiving: Learning to Forgive One Another God's Way* (Amityville, NY: Calvary Press, 1994), 12.
[7]Fanny Crosby, "To God Be the Glory," 1875.
[8]L. Gregory Jones, *Embodying Forgiveness: A Theological Analysis* (Grand Rapids, MI: Eerdmans, 1995), 5.

Therefore, if anyone is in Christ, he is a new creation. The old has passed away; behold, the new has come. All this is from God, who through Christ reconciled us to himself and gave us the ministry of reconciliation; that is, in Christ God was reconciling the world to himself, not counting their trespasses against them, and entrusting to us the message of reconciliation. Therefore, we are ambassadors for Christ, God making his appeal through us. We implore you on behalf of Christ, be reconciled to God. For our sake he made him to be sin who knew no sin, so that in him we might become the righteousness of God. (2 Corinthians 5:17–21)

Salvation and new birth are inextricably connected to reconciliation. You cannot be forgiven by God without being reconciled to him.

Forgiveness does not mean the elimination of all consequences.

If you believe in the Lord Jesus Christ, then you are saved (Acts 16:31). As far as east is from the west, so far does God remove the transgressions of his children from them (Psalm 103:11–12). There is *no* condemnation for those who are in Christ (Romans 8:1). Nevertheless, these truths do not teach that those forgiven by God face no consequences for sin. On the contrary! This side of heaven, we will continue to work through the consequences of our rebellion against God. One of the most famous examples of this involves the consequences that David faced for his adultery with Bathsheba and his subsequent attempts to cover up the sin through deceit and murder.

When God used the prophet Nathan to confront David (2 Samuel 12:7–12), the king realized the magnitude of his sin and was truly repentant, and Nathan told David that God would forgive him for his sin (2 Samuel 12:13). However, there were still consequences, and severe ones at that. Nathan told David that there would be violence among his family (2 Samuel 12:10) and that the baby that Bathsheba and he had conceived would die (2 Samuel 12:14). Even after the death of the baby, David faced horrible consequences of ongoing violence in his family. One son, Amnon, raped David's daughter Tamar (2 Samuel 13:1–22). Another son, Absalom, then killed Amnon (2 Samuel 13:23–33). Later Absalom attempted to take over David's kingdom (2 Samuel 15–18).

The reality of consequences raises a question: if God truly forgives, if he no longer holds the sin against the forgiven, then why are there still consequences? The answer is that God disciplines his own not for the purpose of punishing them but for his glory and for their joy in the future. These consequences are not punishment. Rather, they are how God trains and teaches.

The author of Hebrews stressed this point in Hebrews 12:5–12 when he wrote that God disciplines his children as a father disciplines the son in whom he delights. Two words are used to refer to the idea of disciplining. The first one means "to train."[9] This word was used in relation to raising children. Believers can expect to be trained by God. The second word we see is a harsher one. It means to scourge or punish. The ESV translates it "chastises." This word, in the original Greek, appears seven times in the New Testament, and every other time it literally refers to flogging. Hebrews 12:6 says we can expect discipline and direction from God, and at times it will be painful.

The reason God disciplines his children is given in Hebrews 12:10–11.

> *Our fathers disciplined us for a little while as they thought best; but God disciplines us for our good, that we may share in his holiness. No discipline seems pleasant at the time, but painful. Later on, however, it produces a harvest of righteousness and peace for those who have been trained by it. (NIV)*

God allows us to face the consequences of sin for our own ultimate good, that we may eventually share more fully in his holiness and reap an abundant harvest of righteousness and peace.

Once when our son Christopher was only two, he made an unauthorized trip to our neighbors' house. He snuck out our front door and crossed the street before my wife, Jamie, even missed him. He trotted up to our neighbors' front door, knocked, and asked if he could play with their sons. Now obviously we could not allow a toddler to leave our home without permission and cross a street *again*. So we did our best as parents to make that a painful memory for Christopher. We lovingly sought to associate pain with his memory of disobedience.

Why did we do that? It certainly wasn't because we wanted to get him back for going out on the street. Jamie and I weren't thinking, *Okay, buddy, now you're gonna pay.* Rather, we were seeking to train and instruct him for the future.

If you choose to disobey, expect consequences. God loves his children too much to allow you to "play in the road." But don't confuse discipline and penalty. Discipline is the loving correction of a parent. Penalty is the price required for the offense. If you are a believer, the purpose of God's

---

[9]Arndt, Gingrich, and others, *A Greek-English Lexicon of the New Testament and Other Early Christian Literature.*

discipline is not to inflict upon you the punishment you deserve. If that were the case, then God would send you to hell. God disciplines his children so they will understand the seriousness of sin and will be increasingly conformed to the image of his Son.[10]

A Definition for Forgiveness

With each of these aspects of God's forgiveness in mind, forgiveness can be defined in the following way.

> God's forgiveness: *A commitment by the one true God to pardon graciously those who repent and believe so that they are reconciled to him, although this commitment does not eliminate all consequences.*

God's forgiveness is *gracious.* He offers forgiveness freely. This is not because forgiveness is free in terms of cost. It is a very expensive gift that can be offered freely because, motivated by love, God sent his one and only Son to pay the price for it.

God's forgiveness is a *commitment.* When God forgives us, he makes a commitment that we are pardoned from our sin and that it is no longer counted against us.

God's forgiveness is *conditional.* Only those who repent and have saving faith are forgiven.

God's forgiveness lays the groundwork for and begins the process of *reconciliation.* When God forgives us, our relationship with him is restored.

Not all *consequences* are immediately eliminated. God disciplines his children as a father disciplines his children (Proverbs 3:12).

Are You Forgiven?

It may be that you are reading this book because you are deciding whether or how to forgive someone. Or perhaps you are wondering whether it will ever be possible to be forgiven by another person. Such questions about interpersonal forgiveness are important. But what is infinitely more important is to first consider whether or not you have been forgiven by God. Here is the most important question anyone will ever ask you: have you received the gift of God's forgiveness by turning *from* your sin in

---

[10]Piper writes, "But the aim of God-sent consequences of forgiveness of sin are: (1) To demonstrate the exceeding evil of sin, (2) to show that God does not take sin lightly even when He lays aside His punishment, and (3) to humble and sanctify the sinner." John Piper, "How Do I Understand the Ongoing Consequences of Forgiven Sins?," *The Journal of Biblical Counseling*, 16, No. 3 (1998): 54–55.

repentance *to* Christ in faith? If you have any questions about whether or not God has truly forgiven you, I encourage you to read carefully the first question in Appendix 1 on page 195, "How can I be sure that God has forgiven me?"

Conclusion

If we are to understand how we should forgive one another, we must begin with this key principle: God expects Christians to forgive one another in the same way that he forgave them. The Bible teaches us that God's forgiveness is a commitment by the one true God to pardon graciously those who repent and believe so that they are reconciled to him and will one day be glorified. This serves as the blueprint for how all forgiveness should take place.

Remember, the most important forgiveness question any of us will ever ask is, has God forgiven *me*?

Has he?

Discussion Questions

What key principle is the foundation of understanding how Christians should forgive?

Give one or more definitions of *grace*.

How can God's forgiveness of people be defined?

What is the relationship between faith and repentance?

Read Ephesians 2:8, Romans 10:9–10, John 3:16, Acts 20:21. How is forgiveness or salvation received?

What is the most important forgiveness question? What is your answer to that question?

chapter four

Defining Forgiveness for Christians

Be kind to one another, tenderhearted, forgiving one another, as God in Christ forgave you.

EPHESIANS 4:32

The quality of mercy is not strained,/It droppeth as the
gentle rain from heaven,/Upon the place beneath: it is
twice blessed;/It blesseth him that gives and him that
takes.

SHAKESPEARE, *THE MERCHANT OF VENICE*, IV, 1

My Christmas list might have looked similar to Chris Carrier's
in December 1974.[1] Chris was ten then; I was eleven. I wanted things
like a train set, a rock polisher, and a woodburning kit. My parents, who
otherwise had good judgment, gave me the woodburning kit.

I have no idea when Christmas break began thirty years ago in my
hometown of Keosauqua, Iowa. The Carrier family of Coral Gables,
Florida, will never forget. Chris Carrier's school let out for Christmas
break on December 20, 1974. His school bus dropped him at the corner.
Halfway up the block to his house, he was approached by a man. The
man introduced himself as "Chuck" and said he was friends with Chris's

---

[1] Sources for the material about Chris Carrier include Chris Carrier, "I Faced My Killer Again: After
22 Years, I Found the Man Who'd Left Me for Dead," *Today's Christian*, 1998, http://www.christiani-
tytoday.com/tc/8r1/8r1031.html (accessed July 9, 2006); Leonard Pitts, "God Is in the Rain, Not the
Thunder," *Miami Herald*, September 29, 1996, http://guweb2.gonzaga.edu/~dewolf/pitts.htm.

father. In fact, Chuck said Chris looked like his father. Chris beamed. The man asked Chris if he would like to help him get a special party ready for his dad. Chris was glad to help.

Chris rode with Chuck to his nearby motor home, in which the two of them rode to an unknown destination. Chuck was cordial enough, but Chris began to worry when he did not recognize where they were. In spite of his uneasiness, there was nothing he could do about it by this time, nothing but wait.

Finally Chuck pulled the motor home over in a remote area. Without a word of explanation, he went to the back of the motor home while Chris waited up front. Chuck came back with an ice pick and a lit cigarette. He pinned Chris to the floor and began stabbing and burning him. Chris tried to hold him off, but the ten-year-old boy didn't have a chance against a grown man.

Chris had been a regular church attender. In the midst of being stabbed and burned, he cried out, "Father, forgive him because he doesn't know what he's doing!"

Chuck finally stopped with the ice pick and told Chris he was going to leave him in the Florida Everglades. He got behind the wheel of the motor home and drove still further. Eventually they pulled over, and Chuck forced Chris away from his vehicle. Then he took out a gun, shot Chris in the head, and left him to die under some bushes.

All over southern Florida, people searched for Chris. Desperate, his parents offered a $10,000 reward for information leading to his safe return.

How Should Christians Forgive Interpersonally?

Like so many forgiveness examples, the details of what happened to Chris Carrier are almost too much to hear. How could the Carrier family possibly process their son's abduction? But a story like Chris Carrier's is needed in order to give context to this chapter's main question: how should Christians forgive others?

The previous chapter established that the key to understanding how people should forgive one another is to begin with this principle: God expects Christians to forgive in the same way that he forgives them. From there, a definition of God's forgiveness was developed. *God's forgiveness is a commitment by the one true God to pardon graciously those who repent and believe so that they are reconciled to him, although not all consequences are eliminated.*

Now, picturing ten-year-old Chris Carrier, we can adapt the above definition of God's forgiveness to a general definition for human forgiveness:

Forgiveness: A commitment by the offended to pardon graciously the repentant from moral liability and to be reconciled to that person, although not all consequences are necessarily eliminated.

This definition retains the central elements of how God forgives. First, Christians should forgive *graciously*. Biblical forgiveness is a freely offered gift motivated by love. In biblical forgiveness, the forgiving person pays the price of forgiveness.

We find this emphasis on gracious forgiveness in Paul's language. Recall these verses.

Be kind to one another, tenderhearted, forgiving one another, as God in Christ forgave you. (Ephesians 4:32)

. . . bearing with one another and, if one has a complaint against another, forgiving each other; as the Lord has forgiven you, so you also must forgive. (Colossians 3:13)

In these verses, Paul chose a less common word for "forgive." This word translated "forgive" is based on the same word as the word normally translated "grace." Ephesians 4:32 could be translated, "Be kind to one another, tenderhearted, being *gracious* to one another, as God in Christ was *gracious* to you."

The gracious *offer* of forgiveness is unconditional. Christians should always have a disposition of grace toward those who offend them. This is what Jesus modeled on the cross when he prayed, "Father, forgive them, for they know not what they do" (Luke 23:34). Even while he was dying an excruciating death, and before there was any repentance on the part of those who crucified him, he offered grace. We are to follow his example.

●　　●　　●

Chris Carrier did follow the example of Jesus.

Chris lay unconscious for six days in the Florida Everglades. He regained consciousness the day after Christmas. He didn't remember being shot, and he had no idea that so much time had passed. Confused, he kept thinking his father would be arriving soon to celebrate Christmas with him.

A hunter found Chris sitting on a rock with two black eyes and a bloody shirt. He took Chris to local law enforcement, and Chris called his father.

By this time, Chris's parents had been receiving prank phone calls. They weren't sure if they could believe that it was Chris. They asked him to tell them the name of their family dog and the number of their boat.

After his ordeal, Chris was physically scarred. The bullet passed behind his eyes and exited his right temple. Miraculously, he suffered no brain damage, but he lost vision in his left eye.

The emotional scars were worse than the physical. Nightmares terrorized Chris for years. He imagined an intruder breaking in the back door. Many nights, he slept at the foot of his parents' bed.

Chris's assailant was a man named David McAllister. He had worked for Chris's elderly uncle but was fired for drinking. He wanted to get back at the Carrier family for firing him.

The police suspected David McAllister. They brought him in for questioning and a lineup. But Chris was unable to identify him. Lacking any other evidence, McAllister was never charged.

Even though Chris was scarred emotionally and physically, and despite his attacker going unpunished, Chris's attitude was gracious from the beginning—from his first desperate prayer that God would forgive David McAllister to the attitude he maintained ever after. When people asked Chris what he would do if he had the opportunity to speak personally with his kidnapper, he said he would jump at the chance.

Of course, it would be one thing for Chris to claim that he would meet with the man who blinded him in one eye. But Chris would never truly know unless he was given the opportunity. As it turned out, Chris did have the chance to talk personally with David McAllister.

• • •

Keep the definition of forgiveness in mind. Forgiveness is *a commitment by the offended to pardon graciously the repentant from moral liability and to be reconciled to that person, although not all consequences are necessarily eliminated.*

Not only is forgiveness gracious, it is also a *commitment*. Forgiveness is a promise to pardon another. Ken Sande summarizes four promises that Christians make when they forgive another:

> "I will not dwell on this incident."
> "I will not bring up this incident again and use it against you."
> "I will not talk to others about this incident."
> "I will not let this incident stand between us or hinder our personal relationship."[2]

Sande writes:

> By making and keeping these promises, you can tear down the walls that stand between you and your offender. You promise not to dwell on or brood over the problem or to punish by holding the person at a distance. You clear the way for your relationship to develop unhindered by memories of past wrongs. This is exactly what God does for us, and it is what he calls us to do for others.[3]

You might respond at this point, "Well, this is all fairly obvious." But recall the example of Chris Carrier. In his case, forgiveness would mean that, should he forgive his attacker, the matter would in no way stand between the two of them or hinder their personal relationship.

Christian forgiveness is a commitment to the *repentant*. It is *not* automatic. Christians are to forgive others as God forgave them. God's forgiveness is conditional. To be sure, God offers grace to all people, but he forgives only those who repent and believe. Likewise, Jesus said that Christians should forgive *if* the other party repents.

> *"Pay attention to yourselves! If your brother sins, rebuke him, and if he repents, forgive him, and if he sins against you seven times in the day, and turns to you seven times, saying, 'I repent,' you must forgive him."* (Luke 17:3–4)

Biblically, to repent means to change behavior as a result of a complete change of thinking and attitude.[4] People in our culture sometimes limit *repentance* to an emotion, and certainly emotions should be included. But at its center to *repent* means to turn around in actions and attitude. Christians must always forgive the repentant.

---

[2] Ken Sande, *The Peacemaker* (Grand Rapids, MI: Baker, 2004), 209.
[3] Ibid.
[4] J. P. Louw and Eugene Albert Nida, *Greek-English Lexicon of the New Testament: Based on Semantic Domains*, second edition, 2 vols., Vol. 1 (New York: United Bible Societies, 1989).

Think of it this way. Christians are called to offer a present to those who have hurt them. That package should be wrapped and tied with ribbon, with a tag addressed, "To you, regardless of what you've done." Forgiveness is what is found inside if the offender chooses to open the package. (I will return to the conditional nature of forgiveness in the next chapter and especially in Chapter 12).

Forgiveness is inextricably linked to *reconciliation*. When God forgives, he not only pardons sinners from guilt. He also begins a new relationship with them. The Bible never speaks of God's forgiveness apart from reconciliation.

The assumption today seems to be that you can forgive someone but not be reconciled to them. This would be like leaving the gift on their doorstep, ringing the bell, and driving away, never to return. But remember our foundational principle: we are to forgive others as God forgave us. And God never forgives anyone without being reconciled to them.

Play the tape in your mind. In the case of Chris Carrier, if he was willing to forgive David McAllister, he also should be willing to be reconciled with him. What would that look like?

Finally, forgiveness does not mean the elimination of all *consequences*. When Christians forgive, they promise that the matter will no longer stand between them and the repentant party. This, however, does not mean there are no consequences.

This is another fact that can cause people to flinch. One of our pastoral staff members once shared in a meeting that forgiveness does not mean the elimination of consequences. A number of people immediately reacted, saying, "That isn't forgiving."

I stepped in at that point and said, "If as your senior pastor I disqualified myself from ministry, you would forgive me, right? Say, if I robbed a bank but was later repentant, you would all forgive me, right?"

They all agreed that they would. But they also agreed that if I did rob a bank, I would need to forfeit my job as their senior pastor.

Consequences are important for the sake of justice. A willingness to accept consequences for sinful behavior is actually good evidence that the offender truly is repentant.

•   •   •

Chris Carrier lived out Christian forgiveness.

Over twenty years after Chris was kidnapped, he received a call from one of the police officers who had worked on the original investigation. Chris was told that David McAllister was dying in a nursing home and that he had admitted to Chris's abduction. The police officer asked if Chris would like to meet with McAllister.

Chris went. Now blind from glaucoma, McAllister had at first denied that he'd kidnapped Chris. But he eventually confessed. Chris held his hand and told him that he had forgiven him. As he left, he told McAllister to have a good night's rest. McAllister responded, "I will now."

That was not the end for Chris's relationship with David McAllister. Reconciliation followed. He continued to visit McAllister in the nursing home. He even took his young daughters to meet him. He shared the gospel, and David McAllister professed faith in Christ. McAllister told a CNN reporter that Chris Carrier was the best friend he had ever had.

Here is the stunningly beautiful, full-orbed picture of Christlike forgiveness. Not only did Chris Carrier make a commitment to what David McAllister had done to him not standing between the two of them, he was also reconciled to him. They became friends. Is that not incredible? And is it not gloriously wonderful that Chris Carrier forgave David McAllister as Christ had forgiven him? Review the highlights of this story:

- Chris had an attitude of grace from the beginning. Even while McAllister was stabbing him, he prayed that God would forgive him. When asked if he would meet with McAllister, given the opportunity, he said that he'd jump at the chance.
- Chris Carrier did meet with David McAllister, held his hand, and told him that he had forgiven him.
- Chris Carrier's forgiveness did not stop with a mere pardon. He began a relationship with David McAllister. At one point he visited McAllister five times in six days. McAllister said that Chris was the best friend he ever had.

I will never meet David McAllister in this life. He died shortly after professing faith in Christ. Nor do I suppose I will shake hands with Chris Carrier. We live a long way apart, and life goes by quickly. But I plan to look up both of them in heaven. I imagine that when I meet them, they will be together, completely reconciled to one another and glorified in Christ.

A Word on Reconciliation and Consequences

At this point you might have questions about the emphasis on reconciliation. Maybe you object, reconciliation worked for Chris Carrier, but does everyone need to pursue reconciliation with the people they forgive? Take, for instance, the case of a woman who has been raped? Does she need to be reconciled to the rapist if he is repentant?

Let me answer that question in three parts. First, as I have stressed, forgiveness does not mean the elimination of all consequences. Certainly in a case like a violent sex crime, part of the consequences would be that the rapist would have limited access to the victim. There may even be rare occasions in a marriage when the consequences include divorce. (See "Must a person always stay married to a spouse who says he or she is repentant?," page 202).

Second, a Christian victim must be willing to forgive a repentant rapist graciously. I flinch even in writing that. I have no idea what it would be like to suffer in that way. Yet Christians are called to forgive others the way God forgives them. In a case like this, the victim might communicate to a repentant rapist through a letter or through a supervised meeting. If you are a Christian, always remember this: whatever someone has done to offend you pales in comparison to what you have done to offend a holy God. If you are unable or unwilling to forgive someone, be sure and read Chapter 10.

Third, if the rapist were to become a Christian, or if both parties are Christians, there is the hope of heaven. And in heaven all relationships with God's people will be completely and totally restored. In fact, one of the things that Chris Carrier told David McAllister when he shared the good news about Jesus, when he told McAllister that he could be forgiven by God, was that he wanted to have a relationship with him beyond this life.

Whether or not you have been through something as horrible as rape or torture, you see the incredible standard that God has preordained for his people. He expects us to forgive one another even as he forgave us. Christian forgiveness is not simply about the removal of guilt. It is about the restoration of relationships.

Conclusion

Perhaps nothing is more glorifying to Christ than Christians forgiving others as God forgave them. Chris Carrier's forgiveness of David McAllister did not go unnoticed. Columnist Leonard Pitts wrote:

> The man is serious about God. I don't say that because he has a master's degree in divinity and until recently was the director of youth ministries at his church. Nor because by the time you read this, he will have

moved to Texas, where he and his wife and two daughters plan to open a Christian bookstore.

I say it because he bowed alongside a man who tried to kill him.

I know I couldn't do it. . . . [Yet Chris] tried against all logic to redeem one weak and dirty little scrap of man.[5]

The last line Pitts wrote is the one that really captures Christian forgiveness. Chris Carrier *"tried against all logic to redeem one weak and dirty little scrap of man."* Which is exactly what Christ did. Though all our righteousness was as filthy rags, Christ gave himself, against all logic, for those who turn in faith to him.

Here it is: Christians are to forgive others as God forgave them. Graciously, willingly, and freely, they should offer a costly present to any who offend them. Those who do repent and unwrap the offered package will find forgiveness and reconciliation inside.

Discussion Questions

Must a Christian always offer forgiveness to offenders? Why or why not?

How did this chapter define Christian forgiveness?

Does forgiveness mean the elimination of consequences?

What is the relationship between Christian forgiveness and reconciliation?

Read Jesus' Sermon on the Mount, Matthew 5–7. From these chapters, identify at least five principles for relating to someone who has offended you.

According to Ken Sande, what four promises does a Christian make when he or she forgives? Is there someone to whom you need to make these four promises? Perhaps you should write a personal note to that person and express these four promises in your own words.

---

[5]Pitts, "God Is in the Rain, Not the Thunder."

chapter five

More Than a Feeling

He has delivered us from the domain of darkness and transferred us to the kingdom of his beloved Son, in whom we have redemption, the forgiveness of sins.

COLOSSIANS 1:13–14

Cheap grace is the preaching of forgiveness without requiring repentance.

DIETRICH BONHOEFFER[1]

Let's review the logical progression so far:

• Chapter 1 explained that Christians accept Jesus' invitation to find rest by actively taking his yoke upon themselves and learning from him. If you are burdened with the baggage of broken relationships, then know this: rest will be found when, in an ongoing process, you immerse yourself in the Word, involve yourself in a local church, pray, and worship. Forgiveness is unpacked by following Jesus.

• Chapter 2 described the basic motivation for unpacking forgiveness. We should be determined to unpack forgiveness because it will glorify our God and maximize our joy. Don't approach living out Christian forgiveness with a sense of dread. God will be most glorified in you when you are most satisfied in him. Be excited to live for Christ. There is nothing better.

• Chapter 3 established that the foundational principle for understanding forgiveness is that Christians are called to forgive others as God forgave them. God's forgiveness is *a commitment by the one true God to pardon graciously*

---

[1]Dietrich Bonhoeffer, *The Cost of Discipleship*, trans. R. H. Fuller and Irmgard Booth (New York: Macmillan, 1963), 47.

those who repent and believe so that they are reconciled to him, although not all consequences are eliminated.

• From there, Chapter 4 argued that Christian forgiveness is *a commitment by the offended to pardon graciously the repentant from moral liability and to be reconciled to that person, although not all consequences are necessarily eliminated.* Christian forgiveness must be gracious, but it is not automatic. Christian forgiveness values reconciliation, but it does not negate the reality of consequences. Any Christian who is offended should graciously wrap a present of forgiveness and offer it to all who offend him or her. If the offenders choose to open the package, they will find forgiveness and reconciliation inside.

I believe that these points rest on the clear teaching of Scripture. But not everyone agrees with me. Let's consider now in more detail where some of the controversy about Christian forgiveness is rooted.

Biblical Forgiveness versus Therapeutic Forgiveness

In 1984, a man named Lewis Smedes published a book titled *Forgive and Forget: Healing the Hurts We Don't Deserve.* This book sold hundreds of thousands of copies. It is both representative of, and responsible for on some level, a great deal of wrong Christian thinking about forgiveness.

Smedes essentially defined forgiveness as ceasing to feel resentment or anger over an offense or perceived offense. The way he views it, forgiveness is a private strategy for defeating bitterness and hate. L. Gregory Jones summarized:

> [According to Smedes], forgiveness becomes a means of being "healed"
> of your "hate," of which Smedes argues people have a *right* to be healed.
> Smedes internalizes and privatizes forgiveness by making it primarily an
> activity that goes on within individual persons' hearts and minds.[2]

A side-by-side comparison of Smedes's understanding of forgiveness and the one advanced here demonstrates that the two are very different. For the purposes of the discussion, I will refer to Smedes's definition of forgiveness as "therapeutic forgiveness."[3] And I will refer to the definition I have argued for as biblical forgiveness. Of course, the labels themselves are a not-so-subtle way of arguing for the definition I propose.

---

[2]L. Gregory Jones, *Embodying Forgiveness: A Theological Analysis* (Grand Rapids, MI: Eerdmans, 1995), 49.
[3]The label "therapeutic forgiveness" is from Jones, *Embodying Forgiveness*, 35–69.

Fig. 5.1 Therapeutic vs. Biblical Forgiveness

Therapeutic Forgiveness	Biblical Forgiveness
Forgiveness is a *feeling*. It is ceasing to feel resentment or bitterness.	Forgiveness is a *commitment* to pardon the offender.
Forgiveness is private or individual. It is "primarily an activity that goes on within individual persons' hearts and minds."[4]	Forgiveness is something that happens between two parties.
Forgiveness is unconditional. Forgiveness should be granted regardless of whether or not the offender is repentant.	Biblical forgiveness is conditioned upon repentance.
Forgiveness is motivated primarily by self-interest. You should forgive others for your own sake. According to Smedes, "Every soul has a right to be free from hate, and we claim our rightful inheritance when we forgive people who hurt us unfairly, even if their intentions were pure."[5]	Biblical forgiveness is motivated by love for neighbor and love for God. It is for God's glory and our joy.
A standard of justice is not critical—it is about how the person "feels." According to this definition, you can legitimately choose to forgive someone who has not done anything wrong.	Justice is the basis for forgiveness. You cannot legitimately forgive someone if he or she has not done anything wrong according to God's standards.
Forgiveness can happen apart from reconciliation.	Biblical forgiveness is inextricably connected to reconciliation.

Is the Difference Really That Important?[6]

The logic of Smedes's "therapeutic forgiveness" is initially compelling. There is a reason that his books have sold so many copies. Smedes argued:

- Feeling anger and bitterness is very damaging to a person.
- Therefore, we should all forgive the wrongs done to us. That is how we cease to feel anger and resentment.

It sounds good, right? It is never healthy to be bitter.

The problem with what Smedes advocates is that he redefines forgiveness. According to Smedes, forgiveness becomes an emotion rather than a transaction or commitment between two parties. Specifically, forgiveness becomes the universal antidote for bitterness.

I have discussed this with many who defend Smedes's position. Sure

---

[4]Ibid., 49.
[5]Lewis Smedes, *Forgive and Forget: Healing the Hurts We Don't Deserve* (HarperCollins, 1984), 30.
[6]For a thorough critique of therapeutic forgiveness, see Jones, *Embodying Forgiveness*, 35–69.

enough, their first objection is to say, "Well, if we do not automatically forgive all people, we will be bitter."

I then explain, "No, because Christians must graciously *offer* forgiveness to all people, just as God offers forgiveness to all. A Christian who loves and offers grace is not bitter."

Eventually the person with whom I am talking will say something like, "Actually, we agree. We are just using the word *forgiveness* in different ways. I say that everyone should be forgiven. You say everyone should be offered forgiveness. It is just a matter of how we are using words. Is it really that important?"

My answer to that question is an emphatic yes! As I have said, a therapeutic approach to forgiveness is fundamentally wrong because it redefines the biblical term of forgiveness. Therapeutic forgiveness is also precarious because of where it takes us. When we define forgiveness therapeutically, we risk making several errors. The following list is incomplete, but it gives you some idea why it is important to define forgiveness biblically.

Therapeutic forgiveness distorts people's understanding of true forgiveness.

If we say that we must forgive everyone unconditionally, then we cheapen what happens when forgiveness truly does take place. Suppose two people stole money from you. Later, when they were caught, one was repentant and did his best to pay you back. On the other hand, the other person never expressed any regret over what he had done. In fact, you found out that he would often brag to others about doing it.

Now, in both cases it would be the responsibility of the Christian to offer grace. Christians must always stand willing to forgive. However, only the repentant offender would "open the package" and be forgiven. To say that both are forgiven diminishes what happened with the person who was repentant and with whom the relationship was restored.

You might respond, "You are confusing forgiveness with reconciliation." But as I explained in Chapter 4, forgiveness should include reconciliation, though it does not necessarily mean the elimination of consequences.

Therapeutic forgiveness attempts to redefine how people understand God's forgiveness.

Unfortunately, some who say that forgiveness happens privately within a person will in turn use that understanding to redefine how God forgives people. They insist that when God forgives, it does not *necessarily* mean that the relationship is restored. One pastor recently wrote, "Hell is full of forgiven people God loves, whom Jesus died for."[7]

Do you see how this view has attempted to redefine forgiveness on its own terms? Forgiveness is no longer about the pardoning of moral responsibility. According to this definition, you can be forgiven by God and still go to hell.

That statement cannot go unchallenged. If a person can be forgiven and yet still go to hell, then forgiveness does not mean what the Bible says—that when God forgives us, he makes a commitment that he will no longer hold our sin against us and that he will pardon us from the wages of sin.

Therapeutic forgiveness suggests that some people may even need to forgive God.

There are times in life when people succumb to the temptation to be angry at God for pain and suffering they face in life. When forgiveness is defined as automatically ceasing to feel resentment or bitterness, it is inevitable that some will believe it is legitimate to resolve this anger by "forgiving" God. After all, it cannot be a positive thing to be angry at God.

Again quoting Smedes,

> Would it bother God too much if we found our peace by forgiving him for the wrongs we suffer? What if we found a way of forgiving him without blaming him? A special sort of forgiving for a special sort of relationship? Would he mind?[8]

The answer to that question is, yes, God would mind. God is perfect and holy. He does not need to be pardoned of any wrongdoing. And when people say they forgive God, there is a clear implication of blame, regardless of whether we claim to do it without blame.

Smedes also shared the following:

> There is an old, old story about a tailor who leaves his prayers and, on the way out of the synagogue, meets a rabbi.
>
> "Well, what have you been doing in the synagogue, Lev Ashram?" the rabbi asks.

---

[7]Rob Bell, *Velvet Elvis: Repainting the Christian Faith* (Grand Rapids, MI: Zondervan, 2005), 146. Smedes also implies that God forgives everyone of everything. See Smedes, *Forgive and Forget*, 118–119.

[8]Smedes, *Forgive and Forget*, 112. Later Smedes adds, "I think we may need to forgive God after all. Now and then, but not often. Not for his sake. For ours!," 119.

"I was saying prayers, rabbi."

"Fine, and did you confess your sins?"

"Yes, rabbi, I confessed my little sins."

"Your little sins?"

"Yes, I confessed that I sometimes cut my cloth on the short side, that I cheat on a yard of wool by a couple of inches."

"You said that to God, Lev Ashram?"

"Yes, rabbi, and more. I said, 'Lord, I cheat on pieces of cloth; you let babies die. But I am going to make you a deal. You forgive me my little sins and I'll forgive you your big ones.'"

The Jewish tailor grabbed hold of God and held him to account.[9]

Smedes holds this out as something of a model to follow. But this is *disastrous* and blasphemous thinking. While it is true that it is difficult to understand suffering, the reason that we suffer is because humanity has rebelled against God. Although God is sovereign and in control of all things, he is not morally at fault for evil. To suggest that it is in any way appropriate to forgive God is terribly wrong. But this is where a therapeutic understanding of forgiveness leads.[10]

To be sure, there are times when we are tempted to be angry with God for the pain and suffering we face. This was Job's struggle. But ultimately, to the extent that Job blamed God for his suffering, he repented. He did not "forgive" God.[11]

To "forgive" God when we feel angry with him is to put an emotional bandage on a deep wound. Instead we must accept that we cannot understand why events happen as they do. But we can be confident that God loves us and shared in our suffering on the cross. We can trust that ultimately he is always doing the right and best thing for his greatest glory and his people's greatest good. Soon Christ will return, and there will be no more death, mourning, crying, or pain (Revelation 21:3–5). Those who suffer and long for reprieve must learn to say with Habakkuk,

> *I hear, and my body trembles; my lips quiver at the sound; rottenness enters into my bones; my legs tremble beneath me. Yet I will quietly wait for the day of trouble to come upon people who invade us. Though the fig tree should not blossom, nor fruit be on the vines, the produce of the*

---

[9]Ibid., 111.

[10]It is beyond the scope of this book to develop a theodicy—a defense of why there is evil in the world when God is both sovereign and good. For those interested in doing more reading in this area, I would point them to the excellent book by Os Guinness, *Unspeakable: Facing up to Evil in an Age of Genocide and Terror* (San Francisco: HarperCollins, 2005).

[11]David Powlison, "Anger Part 2: Three Lies About Anger and the Transforming Truth," *The Journal of Biblical Counseling*, 14, No. 2 (1996): 14.

olive fail and the fields yield no food, the flock be cut off from the fold and there be no herd in the stalls, yet I will rejoice in the LORD; I will take joy in the God of my salvation. (Habakkuk 3:16–18)

Therapeutic forgiveness results in "cheap grace" and a reluctance to identify and name evil.

As we have seen, when it is assumed that Christians ought to forgive automatically, it is not long before people begin to assume that God ought to forgive automatically. Many today suppose they are Christians even though they have not genuinely repented and believed. This undermining of the gospel is what Dietrich Bonhoeffer called "cheap grace."

The tragedies of "cheap grace" are multiple. First, there is a large group of people who think they are Christians when they are not. A second negative consequence of "cheap grace" is that the believers fail to think discerningly about what is right and wrong. When evil is not identified and named, it soon flourishes.

Bonhoeffer argued that it was because of "cheap grace" that Christians in Germany did so little to stand up to Nazism. L. Gregory Jones summarizes:

> Cheap grace denies any real need for deliverance from sin since it justifies the sin instead of the sinner. As such, cheap grace offers consolation without any change of life, without any sense of either dying or rising in Christ. . . . Bonhoeffer concluded that . . . the Lutheran church in Germany had been unable to resist Hitler because cheap grace had triumphed. . . . Repentance and confession must be practiced in specific and concrete ways, as part of the larger craft of forgiveness, if they are to result in that truthfulness that empowers people for faithful discipleship to Jesus Christ. That is why Bonhoeffer stressed the importance of church discipline and why he insisted that forgiveness cannot be unconditional.[12]

Listen to Bonhoeffer's own words. Keep in mind that Bonhoeffer speaks as a German, and this is his explanation for why the church was so ineffective in standing up against the Nazis:

> But do we also realize that this cheap grace has turned back on us like a boomerang? The price we are having to pay today in the shape of the collapse of the organized church is only the inevitable consequence of our policy of making grace available to all at too low a cost. We gave

---

[12]Jones, *Embodying Forgiveness*, 13, 19.

away the word and sacraments wholesale, we baptized, confirmed, and absolved a whole nation unasked and without condition. Our humanitarian sentiment made us give that which was holy to the scornful and the unbelieving. We poured forth unending streams of grace. But the call to follow Jesus in the narrow way was rarely ever heard.[13]

We must see this warning as relevant for today. Just as it was in Germany in the late 1920s and 1930s, evil is on the rise in the twenty-first century. The church ought to identify and name evil, not declare that all must be unconditionally forgiven.

Therapeutic forgiveness discourages healing in Christian community.

When forgiveness is viewed primarily as something that happens privately and individually, the importance of reconciliation is undermined. Therapeutic forgiveness makes it too easy for people to distance themselves from those who have offended them rather than going through the difficult work of reconciliation.

I speak from firsthand experience. Like most pastors, I have gone through painful trials with the people in my churches. In fact, my ministry in one church came to a disappointing and premature end. It was terribly painful, both personally and for my wife and young children. But soon enough we had other opportunities for ministry, and we moved on.

It was tempting to try to forget the other experience altogether. The easiest thing for our family would have been to close that chapter of our lives and never think again about the conflict. And if I viewed forgiveness strictly as something that happens privately apart from any conditions, forgetting it all is exactly what I would have done. As I worked through the material for this book, however, I found I could not in good conscience do that.

In particular, as I thought about our disappointing time at my previous ministry, I was convicted of an area where I had made a bad decision. This matter continued to come to mind over time. Finally I realized that it was something I needed to address. So I made a phone call, set up a meeting, and did my best to share what was on my heart.

You say, "That must have been a blessed, joyful time."

No, it wasn't. To be honest, it was awful. My confession was not what the other party was looking for, and the meeting did not go well. Later we had more communication, and that went much better. But initially,

---

[13]Dietrich Bonhoeffer, *A Testament to Freedom*, ed. Geffrey B. Kelly and F. Burton Nelson (San Francisco: HarperSanFrancisco, 1995), 310.

pursuing reconciliation was painful, risky business. Our differences were not completely resolved, although we did take a big step forward.

That is what the Lord wants. God did not intend that we would forget about relationships and move on. Members of the Body of Christ ought to be distinguished by our self-sacrificing love for one another (John 13:34–35), not by our ability to start over with a clean slate and a different set of people.

Therapeutic forgiveness may make individuals feel licensed to avoid dealing with their own sin.

With therapeutic forgiveness, feelings rather than truth become the standard. If a person *feels* bitterness or resentment, the legitimate response is to forgive. This approach fails to recognize that on many occasions people are wrong in how they feel. Proverbs 16:2 says, "All the ways of a man are pure in his own eyes, but the LORD weighs the spirit."

There are times when we deceive even ourselves. We persuade our consciences that our motives are pure. In reality, only God knows us in the depths of our being.

Working through forgiveness biblically will force us to wrestle with the truth rather than only with feelings. We may have to talk to someone else about how we feel. And perhaps we will find that we were wrong for being offended in the first place.

Therapeutic forgiveness does not prepare us as Christians for the persecution and evil that we may face.

Before I share this next illustration, let me warn you. It is a *terrible* incident. It is as brutal as anything you will read, and if such things bother you, you may want to skip the next few paragraphs. I want to assure you, however, that I include this example after careful thought. There is evil in the world that seems beyond comprehension. Yet, it is real, and if forgiveness is really to be unpacked, then our understanding of it must interact with examples such as this one.

A couple of years ago I was preparing to preach a sermon series on pain and suffering. As a part of my preparation, I was reading Os Guinness's arresting book, *Unspeakable: Facing up to Evil in an Age of Genocide and Terror*. In it, he shared this account of the Bosnian war, as told by Eleonore Stump:

> A young Muslim mother was repeatedly raped in front of her husband and father, with her baby screaming on the floor beside her. When her tormentors seemed finally tired of her, she begged permission to nurse

the child. In response, one of the rapists swiftly decapitated the baby and threw the head in the mother's lap.[14]

It is hard to fathom that there is such unthinkable evil in the world. Somehow we would expect that in a modern age this would be no more. But the reality is quite the opposite. What a murderous one hundred years was the twentieth century! Pol Pot slaughtered two million people in Cambodia; Stalin, thirty million in Russia; Mao, sixty-five million in China.[15] In Rwanda, the Hutus slaughtered at least eight hundred thousand Tutsis in just a hundred days. Some argue that the number was much higher.[16] How should Christians respond to such evil? How does justice fit with Christian forgiveness?

A therapeutic understanding of forgiveness would tell us that the Bosnian woman who was raped and saw her baby decapitated should be told to stop feeling anger and resentment against these men because otherwise she will become bitter and continue feeling bad. A therapeutic understanding of forgiveness would encourage this woman to forgive automatically.

What do you suppose this woman would say to you if you suggested to her that the men who raped her and decapitated her baby should be automatically forgiven? Is that what we should counsel her to do? Or should we point her to Christ and the prayers of the saints in Revelation 6?

> They cried out with a loud voice, "O Sovereign Lord, holy and true, how long before you will judge and avenge our blood on those who dwell on the earth?" (Revelation 6:10)

In Chapters 11–12 I will summarize how I believe Christians should respond to such evil. For now it is enough to say that therapeutic forgiveness does not prepare us for the possibility of the evil we may face in life, whether in Bosnia, Iraq, or rural Illinois.

Conclusion

This book has argued that forgiveness should be defined as *a commitment by the offended to pardon graciously the repentant from moral liability and to be reconciled to that person, although not all consequences are necessarily eliminated.*

---

[14]Guinness, *Unspeakable*, 35–36.
[15]Ibid., 43.
[16]James Waller, *Becoming Evil: How Ordinary People Commit Genocide and Mass Killing*, second edition (Oxford: Oxford University Press, 2007), 16.

In contrast to this definition, forgiveness would be alternatively defined according to the therapeutic approach. In the therapeutic line of thinking, forgiveness is a private matter that means shutting down anger, bitterness, and resentment. In other words, Christians should always forgive automatically. Because therapeutic forgiveness is based on feelings, it posits that people may even find it necessary to forgive God.

Ultimately, the question for the reader must be this: which definition do you think is more biblical? This is not a theoretical question that can be avoided. Life is relationships. In a fallen world, relationships get damaged and broken. What we believe about forgiveness will determine whether or not we can move forward for God's glory and our own joy.

Discussion Questions

What is the relationship between forgiveness and feelings?

What are some of the results of the position that forgiveness is fundamentally a feeling?

Do you believe someone can be forgiven by God and still go to hell? Why or why not?

Do you believe it is legitimate for people to forgive God? Why or why not?

Read Deuteronomy 29:29 and Romans 11:33–36. (You could also read Job 38:1–42:6.) How might these verses be used to respond to the story about the tailor who said that he forgave God?

The great American pastor and theologian Jonathan Edwards died when he was only fifty-four years old. Shortly after her husband's death, Sarah Edwards wrote to her daughter:

> What shall I say? A holy and good God has covered us with a dark cloud. O that we may kiss the rod, and lay our hands on our mouths! The Lord has done it. He has made me adore his goodness, that we had him so long. But my God lives; and he has my heart. O what a legacy my husband and your father has left us! We are all given to God; and there I am, and love to be.

How is Sarah Edwards's response to her husband's death a contrast with the idea of someone forgiving God for a tragedy? Has there been a time when you have accepted a difficult circumstance even though you didn't understand why it happened?

chapter six

The Way Up Is Down

"But this is the one to whom I will look: he who is humble and contrite in spirit and trembles at my word."

ISAIAH 66:2B

No subject of contemplation will tend more to humble the mind, than thoughts of God.

CHARLES SPURGEON[1]

Forgiveness is about the resolution of conflicts. And certainly it is unwise to live with conflict. Would you not agree? Proverbs says it so vividly:

It is better to live in a desert land than with a quarrelsome and fretful woman. (Proverbs 21:19)

Better is a dry morsel with quiet than a house full of feasting with strife. (Proverbs 17:1)

Paraphrased, these verses are saying, "Better to thirst in the Gobi Desert than to sip ice-cold bottled water where people bicker! Better to eat macaroni and cheese for Thanksgiving dinner (which my children might prefer anyway) than to live with constant conflict!"

Granted, there are a few who like to chase quarrels rather than escape

---

[1]Charles Spurgeon, *The Immutability of God* (1855); http://www.spurgeon.org/sermons/0001.htm (accessed September 10, 2007).

them (Proverbs 17:19). But most long for harmony at home, uncompli-
cated friendships in the neighborhood, and unity at church. Only fools
are quick to quibble (Proverbs 20:3).

And yet, despite our longing for harmony, it eludes us. We don't like
conflict, and yet we have so much of it. Looking back over a number of
years in ministry, I grieve to consider how much time I have spent working on conflict resolution. I am not alone in the amount of time I spend
on broken relationships. Whether it is marriage counseling or differences
within the church, unsuccessful conflict resolution clogs the calendars of
too many pastors.

Jesus on Conflict

Too much unresolved conflict is why we need to know Matthew 18 well.
This chapter offers the most concentrated teaching on conflict resolution
and forgiveness anywhere in Scripture.

The context of the chapter is that the disciples had been arguing about
who was the greatest.

> And they came to Capernaum. And when he was in the house he asked
> them, "What were you discussing on the way?" But they kept silent, for
> on the way they had argued with one another about who was the great-
> est. (Mark 9:33–34)

Jesus had just told the disciples that he was going to die. In no time
they began to argue about who would be the greatest in the coming kingdom. Needless to say, it was not their finest hour. Jesus responds to the
disciples' bickering with Matthew 18. I marvel at his patience. He knew
these were the leaders who would begin his church. And they were already
fighting about status. In his place, many would have gone looking for a
different set of leaders. But Jesus gently brought them along.

Of course, this chapter was given not only for the disciples' benefit
but for ours. Many of us posture ourselves to be in first place. Indeed,
Bonhoeffer said there is no Christian community if there is always a
struggle as to who will be the greatest.[2]

But that does not mean there is nothing we can do to reduce the number of conflicts. And that is where Matthew 18:1–4 can be such a blessing.
Imagine saying to Jesus, "There is just way too much conflict in my life.

---

[2]Dietrich Bonhoeffer, *Life Together*, trans. John W. Doberstein (New York: Harper & Brothers, 1954),
90–91.

How can I get rid of some of the quarreling or at least solve differences in the right way?" Jesus answers that question in Matthew 18. If we really *get* his words, we will have fewer conflicts in the first place. And when we do have differences, we will resolve them far more effectively.

Be Humble

Jesus begins his discourse on relationships with a surprising object lesson. You may have heard this story many times. Try and see it with fresh eyes.

> *At that time the disciples came to Jesus, saying, "Who is the greatest in the kingdom of heaven?" And calling to him a child, he put him in the midst of them and said, "Truly, I say to you, unless you turn and become like children, you will never enter the kingdom of heaven. Whoever humbles himself like this child is the greatest in the kingdom of heaven." (Matthew 18:1–4)*

Picture the scene: Jesus called over a small child. The little one was probably three or four, old enough to understand simple commands, small enough to be held. Since small children are shy around people they don't know, we might assume Jesus knew this little one well. Perhaps it was Peter's son or daughter.[3] The toddler came running into his arms.[4] And Jesus said in essence, "This is what you should be like if you want to enter the kingdom of heaven."

Do not give children more credit than they deserve. Jesus' point is not that children are pure. No honest parent would argue that children are as innocent as they look when they're asleep. I have learned this firsthand as a parent. When my oldest daughter was about three years old, she kept playing with a tube of toothpaste. She knew the toothpaste was off-limits, but she persisted in disobeying. I didn't want her to make a mess, so I said to her, "If you pick up the toothpaste tube again, you will be spanked."

My stern warning didn't faze her. She looked me directly in the eye, raised the toothpaste about a millimeter off the dresser, and said, "I picked it up."

I was amazed. It was as if a three-year-old female version of Clint

---

[3]D. A. Carson, "Matthew," in *The Expositor's Bible Commentary*, ed. Frank E. Gaebelein (Grand Rapids, MI: Zondervan, 1984), 396.

[4]The text says, "And calling to him a child, he put him in the midst of them and said . . ." (Matthew 18:2). So I speculate that the child actually ran into his arms. But I think it is reasonable speculation given that he called the child and then "put" the child in the midst of them.

Eastwood with dark curly hair had looked me dead in the eye and said, "Go ahead, make my day, punk."

My daughter found that this "punk" was a man of his word.

Many of you could tell similar stories. There is a reason that James Dobson's book on *The Strong-Willed Child* sold hundreds of thousands of copies. Children in Jesus' day were not perfect either. Innocence was not the attribute Jesus had in mind when he told us to be childlike. Rather, Jesus was pointing out two qualities of children that we should all strive to emulate. First, in the ancient Near East children understood that they were to be "*unseen* and not heard." A child's job in any formal gathering was to be invisible. That may overstate it a smidge. But children were expected to sit on the silent fringe, not stand in the vocal center. They did not pursue status.

Second, children depend on their parents. Even strong-willed children rely completely on their parents. If they skin their knees, they cry for their moms. When families travel, the children sleep in their car seats, confident their parents know where they are going (however misguided they may be). Often they don't even wake up when their fathers extract them from a car seat and carry them up to bed.

Jesus' first point in instructing about forgiveness and conflict resolution was to tell his disciples to be humble. Dependent children, who accept a modest place in society, picture a biblical definition of humility. Biblical humility is seeing self in proper relationship to our Heavenly Father—completely dependent on him. The biblically humble do not chase status.

The Way Up Is Down

At the same time, Jesus did not tell the disciples to abandon the pursuit of greatness. Think about it. The whole dispute between the disciples happened because they set their sights on greatness. Jesus could have told them that they were sinful to aspire on any level. Instead Jesus redefined greatness and told them how to pursue it. This takes us back to Chapter 2 and the idea that it is not wrong to want happiness or rewards. Jesus does not forbid the pursuit of greatness or honor. Instead he teaches what true greatness is like and how we can go about achieving it.

Consider Mark 10:43–45:

> "But it shall not be so among you. But whoever would be great among you must be your servant, and whoever would be first among you must

be slave of all. For even the Son of Man came not to be served but to serve, and to give his life as a ransom for many."

In these verses, Jesus encouraged the disciples to pursue greatness, and the way he taught them to pursue it was by serving one another, by being truly humble.

True humility as the legitimate path to greatness is also taught elsewhere in the Bible. Proverbs repeatedly describes how honor can be found legitimately:

The fear of the LORD is instruction in wisdom, and humility comes before honor. (15:33)

Before destruction a man's heart is haughty, but humility comes before honor. (18:12)

The reward for humility and fear of the LORD is riches and honor and life. (22:4)

One's pride will bring him low, but he who is lowly in spirit will obtain honor. (29:23)

If you want to get honor, here is how you go about it: rather than thrusting yourself into a place of prominence, be like a child. Assume nothing. Recognize your complete and utter dependence on God. "Serve others for the glory of God!"[5] Wait for honor to come from and through him. The way up is down.

How Humility Helps

Now remember, Jesus delivers this lesson on humility in the context of teaching on conflict resolution and forgiveness. We see quickly how relevant humility is to those situations. First, true humility nips conflict in the bud. In one way or another, selfish pride causes all quarrels and fights (James 4:1–10; Matthew 7:1–5). Second, if we are truly humble, then when we do have conflicts, they will be resolved far more quickly.

It is so instructive to analyze a conflict in your own life in terms of Jesus' teaching on humility. Even in a pastor's family, there are occasional conflicts. I know you are stunned to learn this (yeah, right), but it is true. A few days ago I was taking my children home from church, and there

---

[5]C. J. Mahaney, *Humility: True Greatness* (Sisters, OR: Multnomah, 2005), 44.

was a disagreement about what I'll call "shotgun policy." For one reason or another, my children prefer to ride up front. To avoid conflict about whose turn it is to ride shotgun, we (my wife actually) implemented an elaborate policy about who rides up front and when. I don't understand all the intricacies of the policy, which is probably why things broke down when I was in charge of getting them home. For the record, it is less than two miles from our church to home. We live in rural America, so it takes somewhere between three and four minutes to make our sojourn from church to our residence.

Nevertheless, my children like to ride up front, and they were arguing about whose turn it was, clearly evidencing qualities they inherited from their mother's side of the family. I was on my cell phone, discussing a highly important church matter, I'm sure, and I could see that a seating dispute was unfolding. So with an angry face and a series of pointing, jerking, waving, threatening motions, I made it clear that everybody better find a seat or they would face the anger of their father—"righteous" anger, you understand, because, after all, I am a pastor—all this while retaining a properly pastoral tone in my cell phone conversation with a church deacon. Woe to the child who argues about seating while his or her pastoral father is on the phone with a deacon. So my children piled into the car and avoided any further conflict (until a few minutes later when they had to decide who would check his or her e-mail first).

Now, let's suppose that everyone in my family had been acting out biblical humility. How would that have affected the whole situation? Well, in the first place we would not have had the conflict because my children would not have been seeking for themselves the privilege of sitting up front. But suppose that for one reason or another, through the purest of intentions, there was *confusion* about seating. Again, childlike humility would have ensured that the problem was quickly resolved.

But the most convicting thing about that incident is to analyze my own conduct, not the children's. Why did I seek to resolve the situation with angry gestures and motions? Was it because I was humbly seeking to teach my children and raise them in the nurture and admonition of the Lord? No. I was frustrated with them because I allowed my own pride to get in the way. My angry reaction was about *me*, not them. And I succeeded only in elevating the conflict to the next level, because I did not exhibit an attitude of childlike humility.

How about you? How would you have unpacked forgiveness differently in your most recent conflict if you had responded with biblical humility? What caused the conflict in the first place? How would true humility have helped you to resolve it?

You Can't Be Humble Through Sheer Determination

So, that is it. Be humble. Pretty simple, right? True, it is an easy point to understand conceptually. But it is a difficult one to live out. People laughed in the 1970s when Mac Davis sang, "Oh Lord, it's hard to be humble when you're perfect in every way. I can't wait to look in the mirror 'cause I get better lookin' each day." The song was so blatantly arrogant that it was funny. But the reality is, true humility can be very elusive. Granted, most do not sing with Mac Davis that they get better looking each day. More commonly, people *complain* about their looks. And while it may *sound* more humble than bragging about their looks, complaining about them is every bit as self-centered.

Therein lies an important point. Pride is not limited to arrogance or cockiness; it is not just an inflated opinion of oneself. Pride is any way of putting self into the central focus. This distinction is critical because if we understand it, we can identify more subtle, more insidious kinds of pride. In addition to arrogance or conceit, pride might express itself in any of the following ways:

• Are you overly critical? Discernment is a good thing (Philippians 1:9–11; Romans 12:1–2). But discerning people sometimes go a step too far in feeling the need to critique everything. Pride is the root problem.

• Are you insecure? Insecurity often betrays a person too narrowly focused on self.

• Are you shy? For instance, are you unwilling to pray in front of others? Why is that? Is it because your central concern is how you will appear in front of others?

• Are you overly sensitive? People who are too sensitive sometimes imagine criticisms when they have not even been given because they center too much on themselves.

• Do you tend to presume upon others? Are you slow to meet with others or to follow through? Do you do poorly at returning phone calls? Any of those may reflect a tendency to elevate self.

• Are you impatient with the shortcomings of others? Do you ever get frustrated and use the phrase, "I don't have time for this"? Who does not have time?

• Do you find yourself easily embarrassed by friends or family? This may indicate that you are too concerned with how others make you appear.

• Are you given to worry? Worry may betray self-reliance (or at least relying on someone other than God).

If you couldn't find yourself in this list, you are not off the hook. We all struggle in some way with centering too much on ourselves. C. S. Lewis said, "If you think you are not conceited, then you are very conceited indeed."[6] He also said that "there is no fault which we are more unconscious of than in ourselves."[7] The question is not *if* you struggle with pride but how.

If you are really going to unpack forgiveness, one of the first things to do is to see how self-centeredness or pride shows up in your life. Remember, pride is often why conflicts happen in the first place. And pride often prevents forgiveness and resolution from happening.

Once we have identified where pride shows up in our lives, we can determine to put off that sinful behavior, to be made new in the attitude of our minds, and to put on the right behavior (Ephesians 4:22–24).

But understand, you will never become more humble through sheer force of will. If all you do is tell yourself over and over again, "Be more humble," it will not work. That approach is ineffective because the reason we struggle with pride in the first place is because we are all wrapped up in ourselves. If our only remedial strategy is to look inward, we will just reinforce the problem.

The only way to grow in humility truly is to take our eyes off ourselves and meditate on the beauty and glory of the Lord Jesus Christ. Humility is a matter of perspective, of seeing ourselves in right relationship to God. When Isaiah looked at the holiness of God (Isaiah 6:3–5), he did not go in with a goal of becoming more humble. But that was certainly the outcome.

If you want to be humble, grow in your understanding of the majesty and greatness of God. Read a section of Scripture such as Isaiah 40 aloud. Read through it more than once. Reflect deeply on the vastness of our Lord. Savor these questions about the Person and work of God:

Who has measured the waters in the hollow of his hand and marked off the heavens with a span, enclosed the dust of the earth in a measure and weighed the mountains in scales and the hills in a balance? Who has measured the Spirit of the LORD, or what man shows him his counsel? Whom did he consult, and who made him understand? Who taught him the path of justice, and taught him knowledge, and showed him the way of understanding? Behold, the nations are like a drop from a bucket,

---

[6] C. S. Lewis, *Mere Christianity* (San Francisco: Harper, 2001), 128.
[7] Ibid., 121.

*and are accounted as the dust on the scales; behold, he takes up the
coastlands like fine dust. (Isaiah 40:12–15)*

If we begin to get a glimpse of the vast glory of God, we will realize
that many of our conflicts are like two ants arguing about which is taller
while standing in front of Mount Everest. We quibble over some infinitesi-
mal difference of opinion while the vastness of Almighty God soars into
the heavens. We need to stop looking at one another relative to ourselves
or, better yet, stop looking in the mirror. And we need to turn our eyes to
the loveliness of Christ in his Word.

Conclusion

The first truth that Jesus stresses in his discourse on relationships in
Matthew 18 is that the way up is down. Jesus does not necessarily tell his
disciples to abandon the pursuit of greatness. Rather, he redefines greatness and teaches them that humility is the proper way to pursue it. True
humility is not self-deprecation. Biblical humility is increasingly seeing
ourselves as completely dependent on God. It is serving others for God's
glory. We achieve humility only by seeing and savoring Christ. The more
we see Christ, the more we will be truly humble, the more conflicts we will
avoid, and the more easily the ones we do encounter will be resolved.

Discussion Questions

Define humility.

How does humility help us where conflicts and forgiveness are concerned?

What is the only way to pursue true humility? Why do all other
approaches fail?

Read Isaiah 40. This chapter was written at a time of great stress and
anxiety for Israel. How does Isaiah go about offering comfort? How does
humility make it possible to wait on the Lord (Isaiah 40:28–31)?

Can you think of a recent time when a lack of humility on your part
caused a conflict or at least some tension in a relationship? (Be careful. If
you can't think of a time when you have struggled with pride, it may say
something about your lack of humility.)

chapter seven

Unpack with Great Urgency

"But whoever causes one of these little ones who believe in me to sin, it would be better for him to have a great millstone fastened around his neck and to be drowned in the depth of the sea."

MATTHEW 18:6

Tell me, how are we going to face the Day of Judgment? The sun is witness that it has gone down on our anger not one day, but many a long year.

ST. JEROME, IN A LETTER WRITTEN TO HIS ESTRANGED AUNT[1]

What Should Bev Do?

I am going to share a warning from Jesus and an illustration from Spider-Man 3. But first let me give a fictional example. It is not authoritative like Jesus' warning or as exciting as a superhero movie, but it is the kind of situation that often occurs. Read this and decide what you would do in Bev's place:

> Bev and Sue had been close, close friends for years. They lived two blocks apart, and for the last twenty years they had attended the same church. They co-led a mothers' Bible study for four years. Their husbands fished together; their daughters were born a few days apart. They talked on the phone several times a week.

---

[1]Quoted in Grace Ketterman and David Hazard, *When You Can't Say I Forgive You: Breaking the Bonds of Anger and Hurt* (Colorado Springs: NavPress, 2000), 3.

Recently, however, their friendship broke. Bev suspected that Sue had been talking about her to other women in the church. In Bev's mind, Sue had always been a bit of a talker, but she now wondered if Sue had been talking about things in Bev's life that Bev had shared in confidence.

Bev thought about it over and over again.

After tears, prayer, and a lot of mental turmoil, Bev approached Sue. She hated to do it. But she felt that it was necessary to confront Sue about her gossip. Bev was optimistic. She had little doubt in her mind that Sue would own up to her mistakes.

Bev could not have been more wrong. When they sat down to talk over coffee, Sue blew up. With a red face and raised voice, she told Bev that she was being too sensitive and that others had mentioned to her that Bev was overly sensitive. When Bev asked who, Sue refused to tell her. When Bev suggested that Sue should have talked to her directly, Sue said that it was not worth it.

Bev was upset. After a couple of sleepless nights, she and her husband met with an elder in the church. She knew that in Matthew 18:15–17 Jesus said that Christians should first privately confront those who sin against them. Then if the person will not listen, the one offended should take one or two others along the next time. So Bev and her husband asked the elder to go with them to talk to Sue. The elder listened patiently to Bev's concerns. He asked Bev for permission to pray about it.

A few days later the elder called Bev and suggested she "drop the matter." He told her, "love covers a multitude of sins" (1 Peter 4:8) and that in this case he believed Bev need not take it to the next step. The elder also warned that a number of young Christians in the church would be hurt if this disagreement were to be pressed further. He reminded Bev that she and Sue had significant influence and told them if they continued to have an unresolved difference, many people could be hurt.

Bev and her husband decided not to push it. But the damage was done, and Bev's wounds were deep. Bev and Sue did their best to avoid seeing one another. When they were forced to be in contact at all, they barely spoke.

Stop!

Before you read further, answer this question: do you think Bev is handling this correctly? Should Bev:

a. Go to Sue's home at once and hug her.
b. Write a loving note, but at the same time give Sue some space.
c. Keep her distance and not communicate at all.
d. Other.

Continue reading after answering the above question.

Then tragedy struck. A mutual friend called Bev with the news that Sue's only daughter, Rachel, had been killed in a car accident. When she got the call, Bev's knees literally buckled. She sat down in a chair and sobbed. She loved Rachel. She remembered holding her in the hospital. She had rocked her and watched her grow up. Bev could not imagine how Sue would deal with this. And she wondered what she should do, given all that had happened and the tragedy in Sue's life.

Now answer the same question. Should Bev . . .

a. Go to Sue's home at once and hug her.
b. Send a card so that she shows concern but at the same time gives Sue space.
c. Keep her distance and not communicate at all.
d. Other.

Hear a Warning from Jesus

Keeping that situation in mind, read Jesus' words in Matthew 18. Remember, the context of this chapter is that the disciples had been arguing about who would be greatest in the Kingdom of Heaven. Again, remember that in this chapter Jesus taught about how his followers should relate to one another and work through differences.

> *"Whoever receives one such child in my name receives me, but whoever causes one of these little ones who believe in me to sin, it would be better for him to have a great millstone fastened around his neck and to be drowned in the depth of the sea. Woe to the world for temptations to sin! For it is necessary that temptations come, but woe to the one by whom the temptation comes! And if your hand or your foot causes you to sin, cut it off and throw it away. It is better for you to enter life crippled or lame than with two hands or two feet to be thrown into the eternal fire. And if your eye causes you to sin, tear it out and throw it away. It is better for you to enter life with one eye than with two eyes to be thrown into the hell of fire. See that you do not despise one of these little ones. For I tell you that in heaven their angels always see the face of my Father who is in heaven." (Matthew 18:5–10)*

With a series of violent word pictures, Jesus urgently cautioned the disciples against causing others to stumble. He stressed this point several ways. He warned, "Woe to the world for temptations to sin! For it is necessary that temptations come, but woe to the one by whom the temptation comes!" (v. 7). The word translated "temptation" is a Greek word from which we get the English word *scandal*. It means "an action or circumstance that leads one to act contrary to a proper course of action or set of beliefs." So Jesus warns against anything that might cause another person to walk away from the faith.[2]

To this warning Jesus added, don't "despise" one of these little ones (v. 10). The verb here translated "despise" means "to think less of or to consider unworthy of concern."[3] The implication is that when we participate in scandals that cause others to sin, we despise them. Few would ever admit that they think very little of some people in their local church. But the reality is that they are quite willing to participate in conflicts that might cause some to walk away. Is that not the case? Can you think of a time when conflict in a church or family has caused some to stumble?

The urgency with which Jesus warns his disciples to avoid causing others to stumble is graphic.

• "It would be better for him to have a great millstone fastened around his neck and to be drowned in the depth of the sea" than to be part of a scandal that causes others to stumble (v. 6b).

• Jesus warns, "Woe to the world" (v. 7). "Woe" means "a state of intense hardship or distress." It is disastrous to cause another to sin.

• Jesus talks about tearing out one's eye in order to avoid this kind of mistake. Is that a gross picture or what?

• Jesus encourages the disciples to cut off a hand to avoid causing another to leave the faith. Play that tape in your mind. Picture yourself lopping off your hand at the wrist. Of course, Jesus did not intend that we literally maim ourselves. But he did mean that we should take radical and decisive action rather than cause another to stumble.

The Lord was not being a sensationalist or gross. Rather, he attached to his warning as much gravity as possible. Jesus warned the disciples that if they were willing to participate in conflicts that caused others to stumble, they should consider the possibility that hell awaits them. Of course, the Lord is not saying that the resolution of conflicts is what saves a person. But he is saying that if a person is truly a believer, he or she will not cause this kind of damage in the Body of Christ. Be urgent about this *now*. Don't wait for a catastrophe.

---

[2]Craig L. Blomberg, *Matthew*, ed. David S. Dockery, The New American Commentary, Vol. 22 (Nashville: Broadman, 1992), 274.
[3]William F. Arndt, F. Wilbur Gingrich, and others, *A Greek-English Lexicon of the New Testament and Other Early Christian Literature (Electronic Version)*, third edition (Chicago: University of Chicago Press, 2000).

Time for a superhero illustration. In *Spider-Man 3*, Peter Parker, a.k.a. Spider-Man, struggles with relationships. In just this one movie, our favorite arachnid action hero clashes with his best friend, his girlfriend, a competitor at work, his boss at work, the guy who shot his uncle, his landlord, his landlord's daughter, and an alien symbiote that represents bitterness. It is a bad day on the spider web. Even Batman (who was by no means a stable personality) had a better interpersonal *batting* average (get it?).

Here is what is instructive. Spider-Man and his friends begin to patch things up fast when they spot Spidey's girlfriend, M.J., dangling from a web in a taxicab. Nothing raises the stakes like seeing the vile villain Venom go after your girl, although it's not a problem most of us routinely face. Because the situation is so desperate, Spider-Man and his friend, Harry, realize they need to move beyond their differences and focus on thumping some villains. Not since Underdog saved Polly Purebred has there been such a rescue. And that is the point. Once Spider-Man recognizes the right and appropriate level of urgency, he quickly resolves interpersonal differences. Jesus taught that we ought to have that level of urgency all the time.

If we don't work through conflicts immediately, there is a possibility we may cause others to stumble, and that is a responsibility we do not want to shoulder: better to gouge out our eyes, cut off our hands, or tie an anchor to our ankles and pitch it over the side of the boat than to do that.

Consider Jesus' admonition from a different passage:

> *"Therefore, if you are offering your gift at the altar and there remember that your brother has something against you, leave your gift there in front of the altar. First go and be reconciled to your brother; then come and offer your gift. Settle matters quickly with your adversary who is taking you to court. Do it while you are still with him on the way, or he may hand you over to the judge, and the judge may hand you over to the officer, and you may be thrown into prison." (Matthew 5:23–25, NIV)*

Apply Jesus' Point to Bev's Decision

Now, with Jesus' grave warning in mind, let's go back to the opening example of this chapter. What did you say that Bev should do? I have offered this scenario to a number of people. The first time it was posed was before Sue's daughter was killed. The second time I asked the question was after her daughter's death.

Relative to the second question, after Sue's daughter is killed, almost without exception, people say the same thing: "Bev should go to her friend in her time of grief." One person responded: "She needs to go to Sue's home and hug her and tell her how much she loves her. Bev needs to be by her side the whole time."

The reason people rightly say that Bev should go to Sue is because the tragedy put things in a different perspective. When someone loses a daughter, concerns about gossip are not nearly so important. Another responded, "Go to Sue and hug her and ask if there is anything she can do to help Sue or the family. This is not a time for pettiness."

The point from Matthew 18 is that Bev should have had that same level of urgency *before* the tragedy with Sue's daughter. She should have gone to Sue and hugged her in the first place. Christians should urgently pursue conflict resolution all the time.

Here's the thing—nearly everyone would reach out to an estranged friend who suffered the loss of a child. The reason is that such a tragedy gives scale to petty quarrels. Amid a tragedy, we realize that some concern about a slight or a harsh word cannot stand in the way of love.

In this passage, Jesus calls on us to compare the importance of whatever scandal we are involved in to the possibility of God's judgment. Okay, someone was rude to you. It hurts. But how big of a deal is it when you consider that creating a scandal over it might result in God's judgment? Better to have a millstone tied around your neck and be thrown into the heart of the sea than to be a stumbling block for others over something that wasn't that big a deal in the first place.

You might raise several objections to Bev being required to go to Sue even before Sue lost her daughter. First, there is the possibility that Sue will reject her hug. And that is true. She might. I have faced that myself. But all Bev can do is try. The last time she talked with Sue, she did so accusing her of gossip. Why not try once with just love and a hug?

You might also respond, "Well, yes, but Sue is unrepentant. And she did gossip." That may be true. However, there are times when the Bible says that our wisdom should give us patience (Proverbs 19:11) and that love covers a multitude of sins (1 Peter 4:8). I'll give you more insight on how to know when to confront and when not to confront in Chapter 10. But in this case, there is strong evidence that Bev should have dropped this matter. Remember, when Bev involved an elder from her church, he encouraged her that this was a time when love should cover the matter. The elder essentially said to Bev, "You are being too sensitive."

And yet Bev continued to hold onto the matter. The example read, "Bev and Sue did their best to avoid seeing one another. They barely spoke when they were forced to have contact." Clearly, love was not covering the matter, nor were they overlooking it. Bev held on, even when an elder advised her not to pursue it.

Further, remember these words from the example: "The elder also warned that a number of young Christians in the church would be hurt if this disagreement went further." This is not surprising. Bev and Sue had led a Bible study together for four years. Their disagreement could easily trip young believers.

Now, if Bev really had in mind Jesus' warning in Matthew 18:5–9, those words would have made her tremble. The possibility of causing "little ones" or other people in the church to stumble should have motivated her to resolve her conflict with Sue long before the tragedy with Sue's daughter. By not speaking to Sue, Bev was potentially creating a scandal for many. This is a responsibility she did not want. It would be better for her to gouge out her eye or cut off her hand or tie herself to an anchor and throw it over the side of the boat.

Take Action

How about you? Is there something in your life that could cause someone to stumble? Maybe there is a conflict in your marriage. Perhaps you are angry with your spouse because of something that he or she did. You want to hold onto it and get back a little revenge before working things out.

But don't you realize that continuing the conflict one more day may cause your children or friends or family to stumble? Is that a responsibility you want to have? Take radical action as soon as possible to work things out.

How about at your church? Is there a conflict there that you are holding on to? Maybe you are right, but is holding on to this conflict going to cause people to stumble? To you, Jesus says, "Don't do it. Take decisive and drastic action to avoid that responsibility. Better to have a massive rock tied around your neck and be thrown into the heart of the sea than to be responsible for causing someone to walk away from the faith."

Jesus continued to encourage the disciples to be urgent in the next three verses.

"What do you think? If a man has a hundred sheep, and one of them has gone astray, does he not leave the ninety-nine on the mountains and go in

search of the one that went astray? And if he finds it, truly, I say to you,
he rejoices over it more than over the ninety-nine that never went astray.
So it is not the will of my Father who is in heaven that one of these little
ones should perish." (Matthew 18:12–14)

Would you like to be the cause of a celebration in heaven? Then urgently pursue one who has wandered away. It may be because of a broken relationship. Or it might be that he or she was distracted. Whatever the case, urgently pursue those who have drifted way.

When I was growing up, one of my favorite stories was about a fifteen-year-old girl named Kate Shelley. It is a true story that took place near Boone, Iowa, when the primary mode of transportation was the railroad. In July 1881, there was a terrible thunderstorm. The water in the Des Moines River rose so rapidly that the Honey Creek bridge washed out. The only way to stop a passenger train that was coming was for Kate Shelley to walk in a thunderstorm across a different bridge that the train would reach before coming to the destroyed bridge. Of course, if she did not get all the way across before the train arrived, she would die.

Her trip across the bridge was harrowing. Partway across the river, her lantern went out. This meant that she was left to go the rest of the way on her hands and knees. But finally she made it and the train was stopped. Kate Shelley's sense of urgency saved many lives.

I love that story because it shows what people will do when they have the right sense of urgency. Even though she was only fifteen, Kate Shelley realized that she had to do whatever was necessary to stop that oncoming passenger train from attempting to cross the washed-out bridge. Every time I heard that story when I was growing up, I wondered if I would have been able to be a hero like Kate Shelley. Would I have crawled across a trestle bridge in a thunderstorm to save a train? Of course, most of us will not be called upon to demonstrate heroism in that way. But we will have the opportunity to take extraordinary chances to stop scandals in the Christian community.

I have prayed a lot about this book. I picture how it might be used in the lives of people who read it and envision someday hearing a story about how someone was encouraged. I have prayed the following prayer many times.

Our Father in Heaven, I understand that when relationships are broken and forgiveness is needed, things are often so very complicated. But, God, I am asking, based on the truth of your Word, that someone would be warned that he or she cannot delay another second before seeking reconciliation. Lord, I pray that someday I will meet a person who put down this book, got in his car, and drove over to hug someone—not that they resolved every detail of their differences in an instant by that hug, but rather that they realized life is too short and urgent to hold onto an issue.

Lord, I pray in Jesus' name that you would use this book to spare a church from dissension that is beginning to brew. I pray that you would use this book to protect some grandparent from another day of not seeing a grandchild.

Lord, I pray that you will use the encouragement of this chapter to help someone avoid the responsibility of causing a single "little one" to stumble. Amen.

Conclusion

In Matthew 18:4–14 Jesus taught that we must work out differences with the greatest sense of urgency. Christians should take drastic measures to avoid causing another brother or sister to walk away from the faith. We should love one another with the same level of risk-taking urgency that we would demonstrate in the face of some great crisis. There will probably be a time when you are called to resolve a situation even though you don't feel you can handle it perfectly. Do it. Be urgent. Those who are willing to continue conflicts even at the expense of a negative impact on others should fear for their souls.

To this whole chapter, you might object, but aren't there some things that we cannot let go?

The answer is, absolutely. The next chapter will help determine which matters can be dropped and which cannot.

Discussion Questions

What did Jesus warn against in Matthew 18:6–10?

What graphic pictures did Jesus use in giving this warning?

Why do people often put off the resolution of conflicts even though they intend to eventually be reconciled to the other person?

This chapter opened with the illustration of a conflict between two fictitious characters named Bev and Sue. In this illustration what evidence was there that Bev should have made a decision to move beyond her conflict with Sue?

Read the book of Philemon. (It is only twenty-five verses long.) This letter demonstrates how committed the early church was to resolving conflict. Onesimus was an escaped slave whom Paul led to Christ. When Paul found out that Onesimus' former owner was Philemon, whom Paul had also led to Christ, Paul sent Onesimus back to be reconciled to him. Onesimus carried the letter that is now the book of Philemon with him. How did Paul motivate Philemon to forgive and be reconciled to Onesimus?

Can you identify a situation in your own life where you need to unpack forgiveness with greater urgency?

chapter eight
Should I Just Get Over It?

Good sense makes one slow to anger, and it is his glory
to overlook an offense.

PROVERBS 19:11

It is noteworthy that all these [Old Testament] episodes of
forgiveness turn on matters of life and death . . . It seems
that writers of the stories that make up the Bible felt no
need to attend to the smaller crises of life.

DAVID J. REIMER[1]

Let's review. Matthew 18 is Jesus' most extended teaching on how
believers should work through differences. Jesus gave this discourse at a
time when his disciples were arguing about who would be the greatest.

• Jesus first stressed humility (Matthew 18:1–4). We saw in Chapter 6 that
biblical humility is seeing self in proper relationship to our Heavenly Father—
completely dependent on him. Biblical humility stops conflict where it begins by
dealing with our own selfish desires. The only way to truly grow in humility is
to know God more.

• Chapter 7 covered Matthew 18:5–14. Jesus taught that Christians should
be urgent in resolving differences. Believers should fear creating or prolong-
ing any scandal that would cause others to sin. Conflicts should be resolved as
though lives depend on it.

Having laid this groundwork, Jesus next taught in Matthew 18:15–21

---

[1]David J. Reimer, "Stories of Forgiveness: Narrative Ethics and the Old Testament," in *Reflection
and Refraction: Studies in Biblical Historiography in Honour of A. Graeme Auld*, ed. Robert Rezetko,
Timothy H. Lim, and W. Brian Aucker (Leiden: Brill, 2007), 376.

how a believer should go about approaching someone who has offended him. In the following chapter we will see that in these verses Jesus laid out very specific steps to take when working through forgiveness.

Before considering how we should approach someone who has caused offense, however, we should first ask, should everything be confronted? In this chapter we will consider how to discern whether a matter should be dropped. A true story about a bar tab in Virginia is a good place to begin. See if you don't agree that this is a sad and ridiculous story.

A Sad, Ridiculous Story

It started out simply, as complicated things often do. On a night long ago, Denis O'Brien walked into a restaurant called the Mousetrap. [He] was looking for friends, and when he found them, he turned to walk out.

A cashier stopped him. Apparently O'Brien had misplaced a red tab that the restaurant issued to its customers to keep track of their food and drinks. The Mousetrap required a $5 fee for lost tabs, O'Brien was told.

It could have ended there, but it didn't. O'Brien could have paid the fee, but he wouldn't. The restaurant could have let him go, but it wouldn't. Instead, the dispute escalated over a decade into a series of suits and two countersuits in two states and two countries.

The restaurant has gone out of business, but the $5 red tab has grown to more than $165,000.

On that night, Feb 29, 1980, O'Brien, who was then a University of Virginia graduate student in pharmacology, screamed that paying anything would violate his rights because he had eaten nothing and drunk nothing. At the Mousetrap's request, he was taken by police to the Charlottesville jail. There, a magistrate refused to issue an arrest warrant. O'Brien was released.

O'Brien could have let the matter end there, his indignation justified by the magistrate, but he demanded a printed apology from the restaurant and threatened to sue. . . . O'Brien's lawsuits eventually were dismissed for various reasons, writing another possible ending to the incident. But the Mousetrap sued O'Brien after he had moved. . . . [O'Brien failed to show up for the trial and] . . . without O'Brien in the courtroom, the jury awarded $60,000 in damages to the restaurant.

[The prosecutor] said O'Brien is to blame for his problems. "All he had to do all these years was come and tell the judge the story. He knew the suit was coming. Had he come to the judge, the judge would have reopened it. He didn't tell anybody he was in town. He just decided he was going to be clever, I guess."

O'Brien did not pay the judgment and [the prosecutor] pursued him in Massachusetts courts. O'Brien said that the matter still was not decided when he left the country for New Zealand in 1984.

For nearly seven years, O'Brien found peace from the Mousetrap suit.

But the search for O'Brien had not ended. . . . On a cool New Zealand evening last October, an officer of the court appeared on O'Brien's doorstep. He carried papers saying O'Brien, who is now a 42-year-old lecturer in pharmacology at the Central Institute of Technology in Trentham, still owed the $60,000 judgment plus interest.

[As of the time of the writing of this article], the matter is under consideration in a New Zealand courtroom.[2]

Can you believe it? A hotheaded college student set out to make a point about a five-dollar bar tab. And because he insisted on proving that he was right, he ended up fleeing to the other side of the world with a $165,000 debt hanging over his head. Ironically, O'Brien later discovered that he had the tab in his pocket the entire time. Just reading it, I wish that I could have been there to say, "Here, I'll pay the $5!"

Of course, O'Brien wouldn't have accepted because he was so committed to proving that he was right.

But even as we shake our heads, most of us need to admit there has been a time when we insisted on pursuing a matter because "it was the principle of the thing." Looking back on it, we would have to admit that it was foolish to pursue it. It was never that important in the first place.

Stop for a moment. Can you think of a time in your marriage or friendships that you blew something up when you should have let it go?

This brings us to an important truth: we do not need to formally resolve every conflict that takes place. Some offenses need to be dropped. There are times when we should go to another party and say, "You have offended me," and we will talk about those occasions in the next chapter. But there are other times when we just need to get over the matter. Proverbs 17:14 warns, "The beginning of strife is like letting out water, so quit before the quarrel breaks out."

In *The Message*, Eugene Peterson paraphrases this, "The start of a quarrel is like the leak in a dam, so stop it before it bursts."[3]

Starting a quarrel is like playing with explosives at the base of Hoover Dam. If you are not careful, you will end up blowing up the dam, and

---

[2]DeNeen L. Brown, "U-Va. Student's $5 Bar Tab Now a $165,000 Hangover," *Washington Post*, April 29, 1991.
[3]Eugene Peterson, *The Message: Proverbs* (Colorado Springs: NavPress, 1995), 58.

all the king's horses and all the king's men won't be able to put the thing together again. Starting a quarrel is like flinging a glass of water across a room. Once you have done it, you can never reverse the process.

Other verses make a similar point.

- "Good sense makes one slow to anger, and it is his glory to overlook an offense" (Proverbs 19:11).
- "The vexation of a fool is known at once, but the prudent ignores an insult" (Proverbs 12:16).
- "It is an honor for a man to keep aloof from strife, but every fool will be quarreling" (Proverbs 20:3).
- "Above all, keep loving one another earnestly, since love covers a multitude of sins" (1 Peter 4:8).

To Drop or Not To Drop?

Now at this point, you may find yourself getting frustrated. I have already stressed that forgiveness is something that takes place between two parties and that it should not be automatic. The next chapter will outline steps to take when resolving a conflict. You might legitimately say, how do I know when to confront something and when to overlook it?

The short answer is that it is a matter of wisdom or discernment. Each time you are offended, you need to wisely decide whether or not you need to bring it up. Only you can make the decision, but several diagnostic questions can help you work through it.

1. Before confronting, ask, "Have I examined myself yet?"

One of the most well-known verses in the Bible is Matthew 7:1—"Judge not, that you be not judged." Even people who are not Christians quote this verse. Unfortunately, most people believe this verse means that people should never make discerning evaluations about the spiritual condition of another. Clearly, this was not Jesus' intent. Five verses later, he warned, "Do not give dogs what is holy, and do not throw your pearls before pigs, lest they trample them underfoot and turn to attack you" (Matthew 7:6). Obeying this verse requires us to make the judgment that some fit the figurative description of "dogs" and "pigs."

Jesus was not warning categorically against making judgments or evaluations. Rather, his point in Matthew 7:1–5 was that before we make such an evaluation about someone else, we should first examine our own lives. The Lord knew that we are inclined to point out minor problems in the lives of others while we overlook major flaws in ourselves. Or, in his words,

"Why do you see the speck that is in your brother's eye, but do not notice the log that is in your own eye? Or how can you say to your brother, 'Let me take the speck out of your eye,' when there is the log in your own eye? You hypocrite, first take the log out of your own eye, and then you will see clearly to take the speck out of your brother's eye." (Matthew 7:3–5)

The first thing you should do when you are offended is prayerfully evaluate yourself. This will take work and careful thought. Do not assume that you know your own motives. Proverbs 16:2 says, "All the ways of a man are clean in his own sight, but the LORD weighs the motives" (NASB).

According to this proverb, there are times when we fool ourselves. We believe that our ways are clean. But God knows the reality. It is only as we see ourselves in the mirror of God's Word, only as we are sharpened and strengthened in the community of God's people, that we begin to understand ourselves more truly.

So if you are offended, the first thing you should do is prayerfully examine your own life. If you do this, many times you will decide to drop the matter.

2. Before confronting, ask, "How sure am I that I am right?"

Almost always, a conflict between two parties is complicated. Even if you were genuinely offended, right and wrong might not be immediately clear. You may be hurt that someone was rather curt about you being late for an appointment. And maybe the other party was too direct. On the other hand, perhaps it was inconsiderate for you to be late.

In those instances where right and wrong are not clear, it is usually best to drop the matter. "Love covers a multitude of sins" (1 Peter 4:8). A person's wisdom gives him patience.

Two other observations are in order. First, if there truly is sin in the life of the other person and it is someone with whom you interact on an ongoing basis, then it will probably come up again. You can talk about it at that time. Second, if you always—or *almost* always—think you are right, you have a *pride problem*.[4]

3. Before confronting, ask, "How important is this?"

You may or may not be aware that a large variety of substances are used for Communion bread in churches. The choices range from small Styrofoam-like squares to oyster crackers to broken-up saltines to com-

---

[4]Credit for this material goes to James Jeffery's unpublished lecture on "When to Confront."

plete loaves where pieces are torn off as Communion is served. I despise the Styrofoam variety. I don't have anything against Styrofoam per se. However, I see it as a substance better suited for making coffee cups or insulation than for dicing into little squares to be served at Communion. And I personally believe that the American Medical Association should do a study on the long-term health effects of eating Styrofoam for Communion.

Having said that, there are people—even Christians!—who *like* the Styrofoam-like Communion wafers. I suspect part of the reason is that they are more convenient to prepare. And since I usually (okay, never) prepare Communion, I prefer taste over convenience.

Honestly, this is true: I have actually been in a deacons' meeting where we did a taste test to decide what kind of Communion wafers to use. The decision was not driven by any theological truths. There were simply conflicting preferences about what should be served for Communion. Fortunately, there was a good spirit in the room, and we ended up deferring to the majority consensus. I think we chose "Styrofoam," and I humbly lived with the choice (although I am now complaining about it in a published book).

But you know where this is going. While I have a preference about what we should use for Communion, it is not an important issue. It doesn't matter. No matter how strongly I might feel about our church forcing people to digest Styro-wafers, it would be totally out of place for me to make a big deal about it. If the source of your conflict is not that important in the long run or the big scope, then drop the matter. Don't start a quarrel over it.

I made the point above that if you always think you are right, you have a pride problem. Similarly, if you think that everything is important, you have a *sensitivity problem*.[5] We all know someone who thinks every offense is a big deal. We each need to evaluate ourselves and see if we are too sensitive.

4. Before confronting, ask, "Does this person show a pattern of this kind of behavior?"

If you have read The Chronicles of Narnia, you know that there is a point early in *The Lion, the Witch and the Wardrobe* where the children have a conflict. (If you have not read the Chronicles, you should put this book down and read them at once.) Lucy tells Peter and Susan that she and Edmund have been to Narnia and that it is a real place. Edmund,

---
[5]Ibid.

who was in Narnia with Lucy, treats her horribly. He tries to get Peter and Susan to believe that Lucy is losing her mind, refusing to give up her childhood "pretend" games.

Ultimately Susan and Peter decide to approach the elderly professor with whom they have been staying and ask his advice. He asks them, "Does your experience lead you to regard your brother or your sister as the more reliable? I mean, which is the more truthful?"[6]

Both Susan and Peter agree that Lucy is more reliable. But Susan is still mystified about whether or not they should confront Lucy further. The professor tells Susan and Peter to drop it.

There is real wisdom in the professor's counsel. If someone to whom you are close has offended you, one of the first questions that you ought to ask is, is this typical from this person? If it seems totally out of character for the person, then perhaps you should let the matter go. You may have wrongly interpreted the offense itself or you may have mistaken the offender's intentions. On the other hand, if the person is developing a pattern of this kind of thing, maybe you should talk to him or her about it.

Consider the example of conflicts that happen because someone is not on time. If someone is ten minutes late on one occasion, it is probably not a matter worth confronting. If the person is perpetually late, then you may want to point out that he is cultivating a selfish habit. Or we could come at it from the opposite angle. If someone is irritated one time because everyone else is not as punctual as he or she, you may not choose to say anything. But if you notice that this person is becoming a "time Nazi" who loses it each time someone shows up a few minutes late, you may want to address it as a potential problem.

5. Before confronting, ask, "What do wise people counsel me to do?"

If it is appropriate to do so, seek wise counsel. Be careful in this. Don't use the "wise counsel" excuse to gossip to someone else. But suppose there is someone who is already aware of the situation. If that is the case, ask whether he or she thinks you should pursue resolution or if you should let the matter go. We could go back to the example from *The Lion, the Witch and the Wardrobe*. Peter and Susan sought the professor's counsel on whether or not they should confront Lucy. He encouraged them to let the matter go, and they did well to listen to him.

Jesus taught that the second time we confront someone we should take one or two others along. I believe one reason he taught this is that

---

[6]C. S. Lewis, *The Lion, the Witch and the Wardrobe* (New York: Collier Books, 1970), 44.

those one or two others might encourage us to drop the matter. In which case, we should let love cover the matter.

6. Before confronting, ask, "What else is going on in the other person's world?"

Before you confront someone who has offended you, think about the circumstances that have been going on in the other person's life. If the person has been under a great deal of pressure for one reason or other, maybe you should choose to drop it.

Likewise, if you have been under a great deal of pressure yourself, or if you are very fatigued, then you should take into account the possibility that you are being more sensitive than normal. Remember, "Good sense makes one slow to anger, and it is his glory to overlook an offense" (Proverbs 19:11).

Of course, this is a matter you will need to work through with each situation. Pressure does not exempt us from striving for godly reactions in our relationships. If the other person has a habit of responding negatively, in various ways, when under pressure, it may be appropriate to say, "You know, it seems as if you tend to respond in a negative way whenever you're under pressure." In this way, you can help the person learn to deal with pressure in a more productive and positive manner.

But certainly there should be times when you choose to let love cover a matter because of the circumstances surrounding the offense.

What "Dropping It" Doesn't Mean

"Dropping it" does not mean talking to everyone else about it. If you decide to drop the matter, then do not say another word about it. And if someone comes to you complaining about how he or she has been treated, encourage him or her to go directly to the other person. Avoid a person who talks too much (Proverbs 20:19). If the person responds that it is not that big of a deal, then remind him or her either to approach the other person or let go of it. Where there is no gossip, a quarrel will soon fizzle (Proverbs 26:20). If a person comes to confide in you and insists that the other party will not listen, offer to go with him or her on the second visit (Matthew 18:15–17).

Conclusion

This chapter began with the story of a man who made a mountain out of a bar tab. Denis O'Brien insisted on trying to prove a point, and he ended up altering his entire life over a five-dollar dispute. It should have been immediately dropped. Any one of the diagnostic questions in this chapter would have saved Denis O'Brien.

• If Denis O'Brien had prayerfully examined his own life, he would have seen that this was not a matter worth pursuing.

• He should not have been so sure he was right. As it turned out, he had the bar tab in his pocket the entire time.

• It was not that important. O'Brien could have put the whole thing behind him for five dollars.

• As for wise counsel, any wise person would have told him to drop the matter and be done with it.

• In context, O'Brien should have known that the bar had to deal in some fashion with students who tried to take advantage of them.

• There did not need to be a pattern. O'Brien could have stayed away from the Mousetrap the rest of his life.

We can shake our heads at Denis O'Brien, but the reality is that most of us are not above turning a minor disagreement into a major dispute. How about you? Is there some situation in which you are insisting on pursuing justice when you should just overlook the matter? "Good sense makes one slow to anger, and it is his glory to overlook an offense" (Proverbs 19:11).

Discussion Questions

What is the point of Proverbs 17:14?

What six questions should you ask yourself when considering whether or not to drop an offense committed against you?

What should a person who is always sure that he or she is right consider?

What should a person who thinks *every* offense is important enough to confront consider?

What does the chapter say that "dropping it" *doesn't* mean?

Read the story of David, Nabal, and Abigail in 1 Samuel 25. How do Abigail's actions relate to Proverbs 17:14? What, specifically, does Abigail warn David against (vv. 30–31)?

Are you more inclined to be too confrontational or not confrontational enough?

chapter nine

How Should I Go about It?

"So if you are offering your gift at the altar and there remember that your brother has something against you,
leave your gift there before the altar and go. First be reconciled to your brother, and then come and offer your gift."
MATTHEW 5:23–24

She knew what was required of her. Not simply a letter,
but a new draft, an atonement, and she was ready to
begin.[1]

In the last chapter we saw that not every offense should be confronted. There are times when the best thing to do is drop the matter and
let love cover it.

Having said that, not every offense can be overlooked. In those
instances, we need an approach or course of action to follow in seeking
forgiveness and reconciliation when there has been a conflict. That is what
this chapter will address. It will consider the action plan Jesus gave for
people who have been offended. Here is what Jesus said:

> "If your brother sins against you, go and tell him his fault, between you
> and him alone. If he listens to you, you have gained your brother. But
> if he does not listen, take one or two others along with you, that every
> charge may be established by the evidence of two or three witnesses.
> If he refuses to listen to them, tell it to the church. And if he refuses to

---

[1]Ian McEwan, *Atonement* (New York: Anchor Books, 2001), 330.

listen even to the church, let him be to you as a Gentile and a tax col-
lector. Truly, I say to you, whatever you bind on earth shall be bound
in heaven, and whatever you loose on earth shall be loosed in heaven.
Again I say to you, if two of you agree on earth about anything they
ask, it will be done for them by my Father in heaven. For where two
or three are gathered in my name, there am I among them." (Matthew
18:15–20)

You will notice in these verses that Jesus included steps that a church
should take. In that sense, the immediate application of these verses takes
place within the local church. Jesus laid out the process of church discipline, how local churches should correct and admonish Christians who
are struggling. However, it is a mistake to think of these verses as applying
only to church discipline.[2] The principles of these verses can be applied
to other relationships as well.

So, what specifically should an individual do if he has been offended?
What course of action did Jesus say to take?

First, Go

Jesus does not make it complicated. He says, "go." Do not fret. Do
not stew. Once you have decided that it is not a matter that should be
dropped, and certainly after you have examined your own life carefully
(Matthew 7:1–5), go and take care of the matter.

Jesus does not prescribe the particulars in how the offended should
approach the other party. There is flexibility here. Each situation should
be evaluated individually. If it is not a serious matter, then only a phone
call may be necessary. On the other hand, you may need to schedule a time
formally to sit down and talk in person.

The point is that if you have been offended, and if it is not a matter
that can be dropped, you ought to connect with the offender as soon as
possible.

The exhortation to "go" is actually for the offender as well! In a
complementary passage, Matthew 5, Jesus teaches that if you realize you
have offended someone, you should be the one to approach him or her to
make things right. Jesus says:

---

[2]David L. Turner writes, "The common view of Matthew 18 as a church discipline passage is rather
superficial and simplistic. . . . A more accurate understanding approaches Jesus' fourth discourse as a
sermon on the values of the kingdom and how these guide the community in handling interpersonal relationships. Jesus continues here what he began in earnest in Matt. 13:54—the preparation of his disciples
to function as community in his absence." David L. Turner, *Matthew*, Baker Exegetical Commentary on
the New Testament (Grand Rapids, MI: Baker, 2007), 431.

"So if you are offering your gift at the altar and there remember that your brother has something against you, leave your gift there before the altar and go. First be reconciled to your brother, and then come and offer your gift." (vv. 23–24)

Let me insert a parenthesis here to say that our responsibility to admonish is not limited to when we have personally been offended. In Luke 17:3–4 Jesus said:

"Pay attention to yourselves! If your brother sins, rebuke him, and if he repents, forgive him, and if he sins against you seven times in the day, and turns to you seven times, saying, 'I repent,' you must forgive him."

Jesus taught that if we see another believer sinning, even if we are not the one offended, we have a responsibility to lovingly confront that person.

The thought of confronting someone about his or her sin runs against the culturally conditioned sensibilities of our culture. Radical individualism teaches that what someone else does is not any of our business unless we are directly offended. But this is not what Jesus taught.

Similarly, Proverbs 27:5–6 states:

Better is open rebuke than hidden love. Faithful are the wounds of a friend; profuse are the kisses of an enemy.

Now back to the case where one party has been directly offended by another. This is a good place for me to reiterate that forgiveness is not fundamentally a feeling. If forgiveness were something that happened only within a person, then Matthew 18:15–20 would not be necessary.[3] Believers could work through forgiveness privately. But Jesus taught that forgiveness is something that happens between two parties. Forgiveness is a figurative handshake. You cannot shake hands alone. For forgiveness to happen, you need to seek out the offending party (or the *offended* party if you are the offender), extend your hand, and pray that the other party will offer his or hers to you.

Unfortunately, few people follow Jesus' directives in these verses. Many deal with conflict in one of two dysfunctional ways. The first is to blow up completely and have a shouting match with the offender. Invariably an explosion like this causes additional damage beyond what-

---

[3] We know based on Peter's follow-up question in verse 21 that this is about forgiveness.

ever caused the conflict in the first place. Both parties say things they later regret.

The second dysfunctional way in which people respond to conflict is to avoid it entirely. An evasion like this often follows an initial blowup. Once the lines have been drawn, the two parties simply keep their distance. At the same time they're avoiding one another, they may be talking and involving all kinds of other people unnecessarily.

Extended families often bury conflict in this way. In most cases the initial conflict blew over and is forgotten, but it was never dealt with biblically or satisfactorily. There was no ownership of nor true repentance for mistakes made. There was no true forgiveness.

Not working through forgiveness biblically often results in tragic stories like this one that I came across:

> I myself was banned from seeing family members as a child by my father. When I was 5 years of age my parents divorced and my father believed I should not see my mother. It was made clear to me that if I attempted to see her, he would never speak to me again and that I should go and live with her. I was even made to write a letter to her (at 6 years of age) saying that I wanted no contact with her at all.
>
> I didn't see her for twenty years. I was also never allowed to meet or contact my father's brothers and sisters (my aunts and uncles) and still don't know who they are. When my grandmother and grandfather died I was not allowed to attend the funeral and so never met that side of my family. There was never any real explanation as to why I wasn't allowed to see them. All I know is that through some kind of family feud or fall out [sic], I became separated from them without choice.
>
> I did see my mother after twenty years (after my father died) but our relationship had obviously suffered through time. If I had been able to contact her through something like familiesreunited.net I'm sure it would have been easier to get to know her better before I went to see her. I am still looking for other family members but was never allowed to know their names.[4]

You probably respond, "That is so terrible. I would never take anything that far." But do you blow up or cover up things in less extreme ways? When there are conflicts in your extended family do you truly resolve them? Or after an initial blowup do you just bury the conflict?

---

[4]John Tobias Cotton, "Our Story"; http://www.familiesreunited.net/ourstory.asp (accessed August 14, 2007).

You might counter, "Well, I am willing to go and talk with the one who offended me, but I don't know what I should say."

No two situations are the same, so it would be foolish to try to provide a script. But keeping several guidelines in mind will help.

Keep the circle small.

As I have already said, when we have been offended there is a tremendous temptation to talk to others. This is understandable. We might legitimately desire prayer. Or we may feel the need to get some perspective to help us discern whether or not we are being too sensitive. We might be tempted to ask someone else, "Am I the only person who has been hurt in this way?" Human beings are also hard-wired with a sense of justice (Romans 2:14–15); so when we believe we have been treated unjustly, we naturally seek to defend ourselves.

But we must make every effort to avoid unnecessarily involving others. Jesus was clear: "If your brother sins against you, go and tell him his fault, *between you and him alone*" (Matthew 18:15a).

Failure to follow Jesus' instruction in this area often causes terrible damage. Unnecessarily involving others can ruin friendships and divide churches. Consider the following proverbs and their implications:

"A dishonest man spreads strife, and a whisperer separates close friends" (Proverbs 16:28). If you insist on talking to others, it is possible that you will ruin a friendship.

"For lack of wood the fire goes out, and where there is no whisperer, quarreling ceases" (Proverbs 26:20). A failure to keep conflicts private often provides the fuel that keeps a quarrel going. This is a responsibility that you do not want to have.

"The words of a whisperer are like delicious morsels; they go down into the inner parts of the body" (Proverbs 18:8).[5] Listening to gossip is like eating candy. It tastes good. It is nice to be in the loop, and it feels affirming to have someone listen to us. But gossip also goes down to our spiritual waistlines and changes who we are.

Finally, "Argue your case with your neighbor himself, and do not reveal another's secret, lest he who hears you bring shame upon you, and your ill repute have no end" (Proverbs 25:9–10).

Jesus' emphasis on keeping the circle small should also be kept in mind when listening to others. If someone comes to you and complains about how he or she has been treated, the first thing you should ask is

---

[5]So important is this proverb that it is repeated verbatim later in Proverbs 26:22.

whether he or she has first gone to the offending party. Often you will receive one of several stock excuses.

- "She won't listen to me."
- "It won't do any good."
- "It's not that big of a deal."

Do not accept those excuses. If it is important enough to talk to you about, then it is important enough to the person involved. Jesus does not tell us to go only when we think it will help. We are to go regardless.

Be gracious.

A second guideline for approaching another person about an offense is to be gracious. Being gracious means you are willing to grant forgiveness as a gift and you will not demand that the other person first pay a price.

Do not expect someone to earn forgiveness from you. Remember, the Word of God says, "Be kind to one another, tenderhearted, forgiving one another, as God in Christ forgave you" (Ephesians 4:32). Christians are expected to absorb personally the cost of the offense. If you are a Christian, then remember, whatever someone has done to offend you pales in comparison to what you have done to offend God. If the person says, "I am sorry," hold out your hand and say, "I forgive you."

No revenge, not even a little.

Most of us know that revenge is wrong. And few of us would admit to consciously settling scores like Michael Corleone in *The Godfather*— "Leave the gun, take the cannoli!" But the reality is that nearly all of us want those who have injured us to pay in some manner. Resist the temptation to hurt the person who has hurt you, even if it is "only" through a harsh word or a hard attitude.

I'll have more to say about revenge in Chapter 11. For now it is enough to say that when you go to someone who has offended you, do not take revenge in any form (Romans 12:17–21).

Listen first, and be prepared to ask forgiveness yourself.

Forgiveness is seldom one-sided or simple. In a typical conflict, complex circumstances are involved. If you go to another person who has offended you, a good way to begin may be to say, "I have been so troubled by our interaction recently. It has really been on my heart. Have I done something to hurt you?" Then listen! Be humble. Don't react. Keep your cool. And if necessary, ask forgiveness in an unqualified way.

Again, don't be surprised. Going into a confrontational meeting, you should expect to learn about some mistakes that you yourself have made. Be prepared to own up to those.

Take the other person at his word.

Do not try to determine the motives of another person's heart. If someone says to you, "I am sorry," take him at his word. "Love bears all things, believes all things, hopes all things, endures all things" (1 Corinthians 13:7).

Choose the time and place carefully.

Proverbs seems to chide with a smile when it says, "Whoever blesses his neighbor with a loud voice, rising early in the morning, will be counted as cursing" (27:14). Most of us don't want to receive phone calls at 5:00 A.M. telling us that we are great people. Even the timing of *positive* communication is important. How much more so a *rebuke*! Choose carefully a time and place to share your concern with the other person. Hopefully, both parties will be relaxed and well-rested.

Choose your words carefully.

When you talk to someone about how he or she has hurt or offended you, your choice of words will make all the difference. It would be a good idea to write out what you plan to say, whether you plan to read it or not. Include each of the following elements:

- Affirm why you are thankful for the other person.
- Explain how you have been hurt.
- Avoid using inflammatory words such as *always* and *never*.
- Avoid conveying harshness or melodrama.

It is, perhaps, even more important that you choose your words carefully when asking someone to forgive you:

- Carefully describe how you have hurt the other person.
- Assure the other party that you are truly repentant. Not only do you regret what you have done, but you are determined to do better in the future.
- Avoid the excuse words *if*, *but*, and *maybe*.[6] "If I have done something to offend you . . ." Nor is something like, "I am sorry for saying that, but you were being such a jerk, I couldn't help myself" helpful.
- Be specific rather than vague. Don't say, "Please forgive me for whatever I may have done to offend you." If you are truly repentant, you know what you did. So say it. Instead of saying, "I am sorry for what I may have done," say, "I am sorry that I knocked out the windows of your car with a ball-peen hammer."

Be patient and have modest expectations.

If you are the one who feels hurt, you may have been thinking about the offense for days, weeks, or even months. Keep in mind that the person

---

[6]See Ken Sande, *The Peacemaker* (Grand Rapids, MI: Baker, 2004), 127–128. If I could recommend only one resource on working through conflicts, it would probably be Ken Sande's *The Peacemaker*. It contains a wealth of practical information on how to work through conflict resolution. Sande and the organization he founded, Peacemaker Ministries, have decades of experience in working through conflict resolution, and this book is a gold mine of practical advice. See also www.hispeace.org.

you approach may not have given the incident another thought. He may not even be aware that you were offended. Be willing to give the person the opportunity to process prayerfully your concerns and to talk with you again.

Further, prepare yourself for the scenario that the person may not be willing to admit blame for what you bring to his attention. If that happens, it is not necessarily an indicator that your meeting was a failure. You have obeyed Christ. Jesus did not promise that the other party would always be repentant.

If the other party says to you something like, "I think you are being too sensitive," then respond, "That is certainly possible. But I am trying to go about fixing this the right way. I would ask you to think and pray about this some more, and I will do the same." Then give it some time before going to the next step.

Second, If Necessary, Take One or Two Others Along

Most of the time, the two parties immediately involved should be able to resolve their differences privately. But Jesus understood that this would not always be the case. So he continued:

"But if he does not listen, take one or two others along with you, that every charge may be established by the evidence of two or three witnesses." (Matthew 18:16)

If you cannot resolve your differences with someone, Jesus said to involve one or two others. Identify wise people who can think clearly about the offense. If the conflict is between two parties within a local church, then a third party should probably include someone from the church's leadership. After you have decided whom to ask, explain as fairly as you can what began the disagreement and what has transpired since. Decide to submit to the more objective counsel of this third person, and ask him to go with you to talk to the offender.

Let me stress the obvious. "One or two others" means "one or two others." Jesus was explicit. He didn't say, "Take along all the elders," or "take along three or four other people." Involving more people than necessary will prematurely escalate the conflict.

The first task of the one or two others involved is to determine whether the matter ought to be pursued further. If you are the one asking others to be involved, be prepared to heed their input. After listening to your situation, those you involve may tell you to drop the matter. If they do, then listen. Don't pout. "Put on love, which binds everything together in perfect harmony" (Colossians 3:14). "Love covers a multitude of sins" (1 Peter 4:8; cf. Proverbs 19:11).

But if the one or two others whom you involve agree that the person ought to be confronted, be wise and gentle. "A soft answer turns away wrath, but a harsh word stirs up anger" (Proverbs 15:1).

Read again what Jesus said in Matthew 18:1–4. If you go to show someone his fault, then go *humbly*. Before you talk with the offender, get on your hands and knees and pray for true humility. Recognize your complete and utter dependence on God. Remember, comparing yourself with another person spiritually is like an ant being proud of being taller than another ant while they are both standing in front of Mount Everest. Only God is great.

Go *urgently*. Tremble when you read Jesus' warnings in Matthew 18:5–14. You do not want this situation to create a scandal that causes another Christian to stumble. Pray that you will be able to resolve the matter soon.

Listen first. The one or two others who are now involved would do well to meditate on Proverbs 18:17: "The one who states his case first seems right, until the other comes and examines him."

Do not assume that you know all the facts about a situation until you have heard input from the other party. It is amazing how listening to another's perspective can shed new light on a situation. I remember once when my brother was young and single. He mentioned to me in a semi-hurt way that our oldest sister didn't seem that friendly or excited to hear from him the last time he called. Later my sister said to me, "Do you know Danny called me the other night at *midnight*?" My brother failed to disclose that my sister's unfriendliness had occurred at midnight. You can see how listening to my sister's perspective helped me understand why she might not have been completely cordial when she received a non-urgent phone call in the middle of the night (Proverbs 27:14).

Beyond this, review each of the guidelines given under Step 1. They still apply:

• Keep the circle small. Talk to as few people as possible.

• Be gracious. "Let your speech always be gracious, seasoned with salt, so that you may know how you ought to answer each person" (Colossians 4:6).

• Take no revenge, not even a little.

- Listen first and be prepared to ask forgiveness yourself. Even if you are the "one or two others" being taken along, you might be surprised. There may be something that you need to own up to.
   - Take the other party at his or her word. Don't try to evaluate motives.
   - Choose the time and place carefully (Proverbs 27:14).
   - Choose your words carefully. Proverbs 25:11 says, "A word fitly spoken is like apples of gold in a setting of silver." Pray that God would give you the grace and discernment to say the right thing in the right way.
   - Be patient and have modest expectations.

Third, If Appropriate, Pursue Church Discipline

But what happens if the offender is still unrepentant, even after you involve one or two others? If the person is not a part of the same church, then you will probably need to accept that the conflict may never be resolved.[7] In that case I would refer you to the next section because it discusses how to deal with people who are unrepentant.

If, however, the person is a part of your church, then formal church discipline may become the right thing to pursue. Jesus said:

> "If he refuses to listen to them, tell it to the church. And if he refuses to listen even to the church, let him be to you as a Gentile [unbeliever] and a tax collector. Truly, I say to you, whatever you bind on earth shall be bound in heaven, and whatever you loose on earth shall be loosed in heaven. Again I say to you, if two of you agree on earth about anything they ask, it will be done for them by my Father in heaven. For where two or three are gathered in my name, there am I among them." (Matthew 18:17–21)

Churches implement Jesus' teaching on church discipline in different ways. However it is done, it should include the church leaders asking the church family to pray that the person in question would repent. In a meeting involving only the church family, the pastor might say something along these lines:

> We would encourage you to pray for Ron. He has been dishonest in his business dealings. Ron was approached privately. And then two of our elders got involved. We confirmed that Ron is being dishonest, but he still refuses to change his behavior. We would ask that you pray for him on a regular basis.

---

[7] If both parties are Christians, it may be an option to pursue Christian arbitration. See Jay Adams, *The Handbook of Church Discipline*, The Jay Adams Library (Grand Rapids, MI: Zondervan, 1986), 99–110.

If after a period of time the offender is still unwilling to repent, then he should be treated as a "Gentile and a tax collector." That is, his church membership would be revoked, and he would no longer be part of the church family. This does not mean that the church family would no longer reach out to that person. This does not mean that the church family should shun him or refuse any contact. On the contrary, the church family should pray for the person to repent, and they should be willing and ready to welcome him back into the church.

Of course, Jesus knew that removing someone from membership would be a painful and difficult action for any local church. So he follows up by encouraging us: "Truly, I say to you, whatever you bind on earth shall be bound in heaven, and whatever you loose on earth shall be loosed in heaven" (v. 18).

This promise is an amazing display of how God is willing to use the local church. Jesus' point is that decisions made by local churches are bound or ratified in heaven. God gives the authority to local churches to make decisions about who will be kept in membership and who will be removed. When a local church solemnly determines that one must be removed from membership, that decision carries with it the approval and endorsement of God.

The Lord follows up this point by saying, "Again I say to you, if two of you agree on earth about anything they ask, it will be done for them by my Father in heaven. For where two or three are gathered in my name, there am I among them" (vv. 19–20).

Jesus' promise that "where two or three are gathered in my name, there am I among them" is among the most misunderstood in all the Bible. Often we hear people cite it as a theology to justify worshiping in small groups. While it is true that the Spirit is always present with his people, Jesus' point in this context is that the Spirit will work in and through his ordained process of church discipline in a special way.[8]

When encouraged to follow Matthew 18, some object, "It will never work." They argue that church discipline is harsh or that it does not mesh with our culture. Or they may argue on an individual level—"She'll never listen." This objection is wrong on two levels. First, we ought to follow Jesus' teaching regardless of whether or not we think it will work. But the objection "it won't work" is also wrong because church discipline,

---

[8]D. A. Carson, "Matthew," in *The Expositor's Bible Commentary*, ed. Frank E. Gaebelein (Grand Rapids, MI: Zondervan, 1984), 403 summarizes, "The promise, then, is that if two individuals in the church come to agreement concerning any claim they are pursuing . . . 'it will be allowed, ratified . . . on the part of the heavenly Father.'"

done in the right way, *does* work. This is the process that God often uses to restore his people to fellowship with him and with one another. His grace works in and through this process. Implementing church discipline is not what is cruel. What is cruel is a willingness to allow people to make terrible choices without confronting them. Dietrich Bonhoeffer rightly remarked:

> Nothing can be more cruel than the tenderness that consigns another to his sin. Nothing can be more compassionate than the severe rebuke that calls a brother back from the path of sin.[9]

One of my most meaningful moments in pastoral ministry happened when a lady in our church publicly shared with our congregation how thankful she was that our church had followed God's Word in working through church discipline with her. She recently told me that she considers it one of the most significant spiritual events of her life.[10]

An Illustration

Not long ago, I asked several of our church people to explain or promote their particular areas of ministry. On behalf of each ministry, a representative was scheduled to speak for a few minutes during a Sunday morning service. The idea was to update our congregation about various aspects of the behind-the-scenes work that goes on in the church, so they would be encouraged to participate and to pray. The effort went well, except that I neglected to include a representative from one particular ministry among the speakers on the list.

Granted, my oversight was unintentional. I just did not think of that ministry or that person. But that is the problem. It is kind of like when you space out and forget your spouse's birthday. It certainly does not help to explain, "I forgot about you."

One of the ushers noticed that a couple of leaders from that ministry were obviously hurt by the omission, and this usher brought it to my attention.

Soon I had the opportunity to talk to one of the leaders involved. I said, "I would like to talk to you." He responded, "Well, I've wanted to talk to you as well." At that point, notice, we both honored God. I was

---

[9]Dietrich Bonhoeffer, *Life Together*, trans. John W. Doberstein (New York: Harper & Brothers, 1954), 107.
[10]For more on church discipline, see Adams, *The Handbook of Church Discipline* and also Mark Dever, *Nine Marks of a Healthy Church* (Wheaton, IL: Crossway Books, 2004). The Nine Marks website also has information available: www.9marks.org.

doing the right thing according to Matthew 5:23–24. The other party was doing the right thing according to Matthew 18:15.

I chose my words carefully and asked forgiveness. The offended parties wanted to confirm that the omission was not deliberate, that I did support this particular ministry. I assured them I did. The ministry leaders forgave me. The matter ended there. To their credit, I have never heard another word about it.

That is how Jesus said it should work.

I shudder to think what might have happened had we not worked through Jesus' formula for pursuing forgiveness. The ministry that I failed to include involves some of the most faithful prayer warriors in our church. They pray regularly for sick people, for struggling marriages, for my preaching. Moments before writing this, I was in our church sanctuary praying about an urgent need in the life of our church. I know these people have been praying, too. If we had not reconciled, the cost and consequences would have been dire.

Conclusion

We are now in a position to give an overall summary of how Christians should approach conflict resolution:

• Be humble. Biblical humility is seeing ourselves as completely dependent on God. The only way we can truly grow in humility is to be increasingly absorbed in the greatness of the Triune God.

• Be urgent in avoiding and resolving any conflicts. The thought of causing others to stumble and walk away from the faith because of a conflict should terrify us all.

• Know when to drop the matter (Proverbs 19:11). Be sure first to remove the log from your own eye (Matthew 7:1–5).

• Follow the action plan that Jesus gave:

   • First, if possible, settle matters privately. Both the one offended and the offender are exhorted to approach the other party. When you do:

   • Keep the circle small. Talk to as few people as possible.

   • Be gracious. "Let your speech always be gracious, seasoned with salt, so that you may know how you ought to answer each person" (Colossians 4:6).

   • Take no revenge, not even a little.

   • Listen first and be prepared to ask forgiveness yourself. Even if you are the "one or two others" (Matthew 18:16) being taken along, you might be surprised. There may be something that you need to own up to.

   • Take the other party at his or her word. Don't try and evaluate motives.

   • Choose the time and place carefully (Proverbs 27:14).

- Choose your words carefully. Proverbs 25:11 says, "A word fitly spoken is like apples of gold in a setting of silver." Pray that God would give you the grace and discernment to say the right thing in the right way.
  - Be patient and have modest expectations.
  - Second, if necessary, take one or two others along.
  - Third, if appropriate, follow formal church discipline. God graciously works in and through church discipline.

I have taught and preached on this material enough to anticipate some of the questions that you may now be thinking. I'll address those in the ensuing chapters.

Discussion Questions

What three steps does Jesus outline in Matthew 18:15–17?

What guidelines were given in this chapter for confrontation? Are there any others you would add to the list?

What is the meaning of Matthew 18:18? Have you ever heard this verse taken out of context?

According to Matthew 5:23–24 and Matthew 18:15, is the offended person responsible for initiating contact? Or is it the responsibility of the person who did the offending?

Read 2 Thessalonians 3:6–15. What sin was in view in this passage? How did Paul instruct the Thessalonians to deal with it?

Can you describe a situation where the principles of this chapter were properly implemented?

chapter ten

What If I Won't Forgive?

" . . . and forgive us our debts, as we also have forgiven
our debtors. . . . For if you forgive others their trespasses,
your heavenly Father will also forgive you, but if you do
not forgive others their trespasses, neither will your Father
forgive your trespasses."

MATTHEW 6:12, 14–15

Formerly you never forgave anyone. You judged people
without mercy. And you praised people with equal lack
of moderation. And now an understanding mildness has
become the basis of your uncategorical judgments.

ALEKSANDR SOLZHENITSYN[1]

Consider two related questions.

- What should be said to the person who says, "I just cannot forgive"?
- What should be said to the person who says, "I will not forgive"?

On the one hand, these two questions are quite different. If you *won't*
forgive, that is a matter of the will. If you *can't* forgive, that is a matter
of ability. But both questions are alike in that they probe how far forgiveness should go. The implication of the first question is that there are times
when forgiveness can be limited by the seriousness of the offense. *Am I
really expected to forgive that kind of thing?*

The second question also probes the boundaries of forgiveness. The

---

[1]Quoted in David Aikman, "One Word of Truth: A Portrait of Aleksandr Solzhenitsyn," in *Unriddling
Our Times: Reflections on the Gathering Cultural Crisis*, ed. Os Guinness (Grand Rapids, MI: Baker,
1999), 89–90.

person who says, "I will not forgive" is arguing that some offenses are so serious that they do not deserve to be forgiven. Whether it is because of the seriousness of the offense or the number of times it has been committed, the person is unwilling to forgive.

The point of this chapter is to show, based on Jesus' teaching, that people who are unable or unwilling to forgive should be warned in the most serious way possible. Indeed, Jesus taught that if we are either unable or unwilling to offer forgiveness, we should question the reality of our salvation.

Jesus on the Limits of Forgiveness

Jesus speaks to the limits of forgiveness in Matthew 18:21–35. Like us, the disciples had questions about just how far forgiveness should go. And as was so often the case, Peter spoke up:

> *Then Peter came up and said to him, "Lord, how often will my brother sin against me, and I forgive him? As many as seven times?" (v. 21)*

Peter accepted that if someone sins against us and then later asks forgiveness, we should grant the request willingly. But Peter also reasoned that there must be some reasonable limit to how many times we are expected to forgive. Peter must have suspected that Jesus would probably be expecting a particularly generous amount of mercy from his disciples, so he guessed high. But if Peter thought he was being generous in asking whether we should forgive even as many as seven times, he surely must have been startled by Jesus' response: "Jesus said to him, 'I do not say to you seven times, but seventy times seven'" (Matthew 18:22).

The point is *not* that we ought to forgive someone up to 490 times. Jesus is obviously using hyperbole. So, if you are keeping a tally of how many times you have forgiven your spouse, stop. Jesus' point is that we ought to forgive an unlimited number of times.

You can imagine that if you were to tell your children they ought to be willing to forgive an unlimited number of times, they would no doubt respond, "But what about in cases where the offense is *really bad*?" Jesus anticipated this objection and shared a parable to answer it.

The Parable of the Unforgiving Servant

> *"Therefore the kingdom of heaven may be compared to a king who wished to settle accounts with his servants. When he began to settle, one was brought to him who owed him ten thousand talents. And since*

he could not pay, his master ordered him to be sold, with his wife and children and all that he had, and payment to be made. So the servant fell on his knees, imploring him, 'Have patience with me, and I will pay you everything.' And out of pity for him, the master of that servant released him and forgave him the debt. But when that same servant went out, he found one of his fellow servants who owed him a hundred denarii, and seizing him, he began to choke him, saying, 'Pay what you owe.' So his fellow servant fell down and pleaded with him, 'Have patience with me, and I will pay you.' He refused and went and put him in prison until he should pay the debt. When his fellow servants saw what had taken place, they were greatly distressed, and they went and reported to their master all that had taken place. Then his master summoned him and said to him, 'You wicked servant! I forgave you all that debt because you pleaded with me. And should not you have had mercy on your fellow servant, as I had mercy on you?' And in anger his master delivered him to the jailers, until he should pay all his debt. So also my heavenly Father will do to every one of you, if you do not forgive your brother from your heart." (Matthew 18:23–35)

You have to really get into the story if it is going to influence you. Picture in your mind who might have played the parts. In this parable we have to cast only three roles. First, we need a rich king. This is someone who has a lot of assets. He writes off a major loan, so he has to be loaded in order to afford to do that. He is kind at points (he initially writes off the debt), but he is also just and stern (he comes down hard on the first servant in the end). Who would play such a part?

Second, we need the guy who ends up being the loser in the story. He is the example *not* to be followed. This guy was not afraid to shamelessly beg, and yet he turned in an instant and was mean. Picture a weasely schemer.

The third character is an ordinary, hard-working guy who has had some bad breaks. By definition, this would not be played by anyone famous. Put an average person in the role.

So, in the parable the weasel owes the wealthy king a huge amount of money. It is an exorbitantly large amount. One commentator estimates that it would have been the equivalent of 193,000 years' wages.[2] It is such a grandiose amount that no one could pay it back. Not ever. This character certainly can't.

So the king summons this guy who owes him money. The debtor

---

[2]David L. Turner, *Matthew*, Baker Exegetical Commentary on the New Testament (Grand Rapids, MI: Baker, 2008), 450.

is begging from the get-go. He falls down on his knees and begs for an extension—just a little more time—and he promises to take care of the debt. Can't you just picture the scene? The king is a little put out by the whole business, kind of half-disgusted by the melodrama of someone falling at his shoes. He probably shakes him and says, "Get ahold of yourself; act like a man." But in the end he has pity on him, saying, "Hey, what's another billion! I'll write this debt off."

So the weasely schemer dusts himself off and flies away, happy as a lark. He has been forgiven his debt! It's gone! On the way home, though, he meets up with, of all people, an average guy who owes him a few months' wages.[3] Of course, the debt is nothing in comparison to the astronomical amount he himself had owed a mere ten minutes ago. But he spots him and wants what's coming to him, and he wants it now. The second servant doesn't have it, and there's no way he'll ever be able to get it if he's packed him off to debtors' prison. So he falls at the other man's feet and begs for another chance. And this guy who has just been forgiven a billion-dollar debt will not even consider giving him a few more days to cough up the cash. He certainly has no intentions of forgiving him the thousand dollars. In fact, he calls the authorities and has him arrested.

In due time, however, the guy to whom money was originally owed finds out about all this, and he cannot believe his ears. He has forgiven a huge sum. But now he hears that this weasel who has been forgiven a billion cannot find it within himself to forgive a paltry amount. So he reneges. He reams out the guy who originally owed him money, reinstates the once-forgiven debt, and throws his sorry carcass in prison. No mercy. He's stuck there until he can repay the amount, which of course, he will never be able to do.

Once you "see" the story, Jesus' point is clear. Turner summarizes:

> The point is the monstrous inconsistency between being forgiven "zillions" and refusing to forgive "peanuts." . . . The unforgiving servant does not do for the other what he would like the other to do for him (7:12), let alone do for the other what the king has already done for him. He hypocritically accepts mercy but is not willing to grant it to another.[4]

Keep the context of the biblical parable in mind. Peter is asking Jesus, "How many times should we forgive?" Jesus responds that we are to forgive seventy times seven—that is, an unlimited number of times. Jesus

---

[3]Ibid., 451.
[4]Ibid.

understood that the disciples might think it unreasonable to be expected to forgive so many times. With this parable, Jesus was teaching that *whatever someone has done to offend us always pales in comparison to what we have done to offend God*. The Christian who will not forgive is like a guy who will not forgive a few-thousand-dollar debt when he has himself been forgiven billions.

It goes without saying; human beings do horrible things to one another. And the point is not that these are small offenses. Some of them are huge. However, they *are* small in comparison to what we have done to offend God.

What Should Be Said to Those Who Won't Forgive?

Let's go back to the questions with which we began the chapter. What should be said to the person who cannot or will not forgive? This is not a theoretical question. Many are quite comfortable saying they will not forgive. In a 1988 Gallup poll on forgiveness, 94 percent of respondents indicated that it is important to forgive. But only 48 percent said they make it a practice to forgive.[5] What should be said to the 46 percent who don't forgive?

At this point we need to look at the parable in dead earnest. This is the most serious of subjects. Jesus said that the unforgiving servant would be turned over to "jailers" to be punished until he could repay the amount. The word translated "jailers" is better translated "torturers."[6] And given the unforgiving servant could never repay the huge amount he owed, the deliberate indication of the parable is that he would be eternally tortured.

Jesus' point is clear. *Those unwilling or unable to forgive should fear for their salvation.* Jesus stressed the importance of forgiveness elsewhere. After teaching the disciples to pray, Jesus said:

> *"For if you forgive others their trespasses, your heavenly Father will also forgive you, but if you do not forgive others their trespasses, neither will your Father forgive your trespasses." (Matthew 6:14–15)*

And again, in Matthew 7:1–2,

> *"Judge not, that you be not judged. For with the judgment you pronounce you will be judged, and with the measure you use it will be measured to you."*

[5]Quoted from Randall O'Brien, *Set Free by Forgiveness: The Way to Peace and Healing* (Grand Rapids, MI: Baker, 2005), 143.
[6]R.T. France, *The Gospel of Matthew*, ed. Gordon D. Fee, The New International Commentary on the New Testament (Grand Rapids, MI: Eerdmans, 2007), 708.

For each of us, the thought of what it means to refuse to forgive some-one should make us shudder. If you are reading this and you say either "I cannot forgive" or "I will not forgive," then I plead with you to consider the reality of hell more carefully. Are you so unwilling to forgive that you would choose *eternal* punishment?

Read these words from a sermon preached by Jonathan Edwards that carried the title "The Eternity of Hell's Torments." Those unwilling to forgive should force themselves to read these words more than once:

> Do but consider how dreadful despair will be in such torment. . . . After you shall have worn out the age of the sun, moon, and stars, in your dolorous groans and lamentations, without rest day and night, or one minute's ease, yet you shall have no hope of ever being delivered. After you shall have worn a thousand more such ages, you shall have no hope, but shall know that you are not one whit nearer to the end of your tor-ments. . . . Your souls, which shall have been agitated with the wrath of God all this while, will still exist to bear more wrath. Your bodies, which shall have been burning all this while in these glowing flames, shall not have been consumed, but will remain to roast through eternity, which will not have been at all shortened by what shall have been past.[7]

You might respond, "You say that if I won't forgive, I should fear for my soul. This sounds like salvation by works. Was Jesus saying that we have to earn our salvation by forgiving people?"

The answer to that question is clearly no. Jesus was not teaching that we must forgive others in order to be saved. Rather, he was teaching that people who have genuinely received grace are characterized by a willing-ness to give grace to others.

Think of it this way: holding apples in your hands does not make you an apple tree. But it is indeed characteristic of apple trees to bear apples. Forgiving people will not make you a Christian, but Christians do forgive.

Or here is another one. Wherever you are while reading this book, do your best imitation of a duck. If you are on an airplane, you won't be able to waddle or flap anything, so just mutter "quack, quack!" under your breath. After you have done this, look into a mirror. You are still not a duck, right?

On the other hand, ducks do quack. If you find a creature somewhere that *will not* quack, then it is extremely likely that this creature is not a duck.

Forgiving will not make you a Christian. If you are not already a

---

[7]Jonathan Edwards, "The Eternity of Hell's Torments"; http://www.biblebb.com/files/edwards/eternity.htm.

Christian, you might forgive the worst interpersonal offenses that have ever been committed, but that will get you no closer to being a Christian. However, if someone is a genuine Christian, he or she will be both willing and able to forgive others.

There are many stories about people who have demonstrated a remarkable ability to forgive others after becoming Christians. Let me conclude this chapter with one such story about two men who fought in World War II, one for Japan and the other for the United States. They received God's grace and became willing and able to forgive others.

The Story of Jacob DeShazer and Mitsuo Fuchida

To appreciate the story of Jacob DeShazer and Mitsuo Fuchida, we need to reflect on the hatred between Japan and the United States during World War II. I was born well after World War II. I never participated in the deep animosity between our countries, though I did have the opportunity to work directly with a Japanese company. Before I was a pastor, I worked in new product development for a research-based company. In the late eighties we entered into a joint venture with Konica Corporation. From the beginning, individuals in both our companies enjoyed getting to know the other culture. There was virtually no tension between our two groups.

But emotions were far different during and immediately after World War II. It is hard to describe the depths of the mutual hatred. About the war in the Pacific, historian Stephen Ambrose said:

> It was the worst war that ever was . . . [because of] the extent of the mutual hatred of the Japanese for the Americans, and the Americans for the Japanese. . . . The outrages they committed are surpassed only by the holocaust. . . . In the Pacific War, both Japanese and Americans did things to each other that are unspeakable. Atrocities included routinely cutting off a dead man's private parts and sticking them in his mouth, extracting gold teeth, urinating in the open mouth of a dead man. . . . Only hatred as intense as the heat at the core of an active volcano could have caused that.[8]

Nowhere was the deep hatred more evident than for those in Japanese prisoner of war camps. Prisoners were starved and beaten. Their hands were crushed in vises. They were hung by their thumbs and buried alive.[9]

---

[8]Stephen Ambrose, *To America: Reflections of an Historian* (New York: Simon & Schuster, 2002), 101, 102, 103.
[9]Charles Colson and Harold Fickett, *The Good Life: Seeking Purpose, Meaning and Truth in Your Life* (Wheaton, IL: Tyndale House, 2005), 147.

They were forced to work beyond what any of us can imagine. Japanese commanders ordered that under no circumstances should their prisoners survive. A typical order read like the one translated below:

> Whether they are destroyed individually or in groups, and whether it is accomplished by means of mass bombing, poisonous smoke, poisons, drowning, or decapitation, dispose of them as the situation dictates. It is the aim not to allow the escape of a single one, to annihilate them all, and not to leave any traces.[10]

Both Mitsuo Fuchida and Jacob DeShazer were in the thick of all this mutual hostility. Fuchida was the combat general officer who gave the final order to bomb Pearl Harbor. Years later Fuchida recounted:

> Like a hurricane out of nowhere, my torpedo planes, dive bombers and fighters struck suddenly with indescribable fury. As smoke began to billow and the proud battleships, one by one, started tilting, my heart was almost ablaze with joy. . . . It was the most thrilling exploit of my career.[11]

On the other side of the ocean at an army base in Oregon, Jacob DeShazer was on KP duty when he heard that Japan had bombed Pearl Harbor. He hurled a potato at the wall and said, "Jap, just wait and see what we'll do to you!"[12]

DeShazer took the first opportunity to fight against Japan. Four months after Pearl Harbor he served on the crew of one of the bombers led by Jimmy Doolittle. When the plane he was on ran out of fuel, DeShazer was captured by the Japanese. He endured forty horrific months as a prisoner of war. Some of his friends were executed instantly. The rest starved slowly. He hated the Japanese intensely. Anger ate away at the core of his being.

Finally, due in part to the testimony of a Christian POW who had died, DeShazer decided to turn to Scripture for answers. DeShazer wrote:

> I was gripped with a strange longing to examine the Christian's Bible to see if I could find the secret. I begged my captors to get a Bible for me. At last, in the month of May, 1944, a guard brought the Book, but told me I could have it for only three weeks.

---

[10]Hampton Sides, *Ghost Soldiers: The Forgotten Epic Story of World War II's Most Dramatic Mission* (New York: Doubleday, 2001), 24.
[11]Mitsuo Fuchida, "From Pearl Harbor to Calvary"; this can be read on various websites, including http://www.christianitytoday.com/history/newsletter/2001/jun01a.html.
[12]Ibid.

I eagerly began to read its pages. Chapter after chapter gripped my heart. . . . On June 8th, 1944, the words in Romans 10:9 stood out boldly before my eyes: "If thou shalt confess with thy mouth the Lord Jesus, and shalt believe in thine heart that God hath raised Him from the dead, thou shalt be saved." In that very moment God gave me grace to confess my sins to Him, and He forgave me all my sins and saved me for Jesus' sake, even as I later found that His Word again promises so clearly in 1 John 1:9: "If we confess our sins, He is faithful and just to forgive us our sins, and to cleanse us from all unrighteousness."

How my heart rejoiced in my newness of spiritual life, even though my body was suffering so terribly from the physical beatings and lack of food. But suddenly I discovered that God had given me new spiritual eyes, and that when I looked at the Japanese officers and guards who had starved and beaten me and my companions so cruelly, I found my bitter hatred for them changed to loving pity.[13]

At last, on August 20, 1945 parachutists dropped into the prison camp and freed the prisoners from their cells. DeShazer was nearly dead physically, but he was a new man spiritually. He returned to the United States and attended Bible college. His heart now overflowed with such love that he decided to become a missionary to Japan.

DeShazer wrote out his story and distributed it in Japan. One of the people who read it was Mitsuo Fuchida, who was gripped by DeShazer's story. He wrote:

[DeShazer's testimony] was something I could not explain.

Neither could I forget it. The peaceful motivation I had read about was exactly what I was seeking. Since the American had found it in the Bible, I decided to purchase one myself, despite my traditionally Buddhist heritage.

In the ensuing weeks, I read this book eagerly. I came to the climactic drama—the Crucifixion. I read in Luke 23:34 the prayer of Jesus Christ at His death: "Father, forgive them; for they know not what they do." I was impressed that I was certainly one of those for whom He had prayed. The many men I had killed had been slaughtered in the name of patriotism, for I did not understand the love which Christ wishes to implant within every heart.

Right at that moment, I seemed to meet Jesus for the first time. I understood the meaning of His death as a substitute for my wickedness, and so in prayer, I requested Him to forgive my sins and change me

---

[13]Jacob DeShazer, "The Untold Story of Pearl Harbor"; http://www.thesoulwinner.org/pearl_harbor.htm.

from a bitter, disillusioned ex-pilot into a well-balanced Christian with purpose in living.

That date, April 14, 1950—became the second "day to remember" of my life. On that day, I became a new person. My complete view on life was changed by the intervention of the Christ I had always hated and ignored before.[14]

Were it not for Christ, hatred and bitterness would have consumed both Fuchida and DeShazer. With Christ, the Japanese officer who gave the final order to bomb Pearl Harbor and a tortured American prisoner of war were filled with love for one another. The Lord Jesus Christ was glorified. DeShazer and Fuchida found everlasting joy.

Conclusion

If you are someone who says that you cannot or will not forgive, then you should fear for your soul. Saying, "I cannot or will not forgive," is essentially another way of saying, "I am thinking about going to hell." Why do I say that? Jesus said, "For if you forgive others their trespasses, your heavenly Father will also forgive you, but if you do not forgive others their trespasses, neither will your Father forgive your trespasses" (Matthew 6:14–15).

It is not forgiving others that saves us or merits our salvation. Rather, it is characteristic of those who have received grace that they are willing to share it with others. Quacking doesn't make you a duck, but ducks do quack. Forgiving does not make you a Christian, but Christians do forgive.

Discussion Questions

Complete this sentence: "Whatever someone has done to offend me pales in comparison . . ."

How should someone who is unwilling to forgive be warned?

Does forgiving others earn salvation?

How does the saying, "Quacking doesn't make you a duck, but ducks quack" relate to the content of this chapter?

Read 1 John 2:1–6. Should the person who is unwilling to do what God commands in the area of forgiveness be confident of his or her salvation?

Write out a prayer for someone who is unwilling or unable to forgive a person who has offended him or her.

---

[14]Fuchida, "From Pearl Harbor to Calvary"; http://www.christianitytoday.com/history/newsletter/2001/jun01a.html.

chapter eleven

How Should I Respond to the Unrepentant? Two Principles

They cried out with a loud voice, "O Sovereign Lord, holy and true, how long before you will judge and avenge our blood on those who dwell on the earth?"
    REVELATION 6:10

"Don't you think I am forgiven?" "Goodness, no," Reverend Emmett said briskly. Ian's mouth fell open. He wondered if he'd misunderstood. He said, "I'm *not* forgiven?"
    ANNE TYLER[1]

The Question

What should be done in the case of an *unrepentant* offender? How should we respond to those who take no responsibility for evil?

You might picture any number of terrorism-related tragedies when considering this question: the Holocaust, Oklahoma City, Columbine, Rwanda, 9/11, or Virginia Tech perhaps. But chances are, you have an even more personal story. For every Columbine covered on CNN, there are tens of thousands of unknown stories: young girls assaulted by their mother's boyfriends, boys molested by friends of older brothers, those who endure the pain and humiliation of an unfaithful spouse.

How should a young mother remember her father who repeatedly

---

[1]Anne Tyler, *Saint Maybe* (New York: Fawcett Books, 1991), 122.

molested her, never took any ownership of his offenses, and is now dead? How should parents remember their child's killer who never took responsibility? How should New Yorkers remember the terrorists of 9/11?

The need for a careful Christian answer to the question of how to deal with unrepentant offenders is increasingly evident. There have been too many irresponsible opinions sounded in recent days. The following website opinion about the Virginia Tech shootings is becoming typical fare: "Cho Seung-Hui deserves to be 'respectfully and lovingly remembered just like the rest of the victims.'"[2]

However well-intentioned, such sentiments are maddeningly misguided. Indeed, it is not too much to say that they are sinful. It is wrong to argue that Cho Seung-Hui should be remembered in the same way as those he murdered.

Christians who insist on such trite, glib answers should consider what Holocaust survivor Elie Wiesel said about responding to evil. After describing what it was like being imprisoned at Auschwitz—where he had to decide whether or not to continue giving his father food or to assume that his father was not going to live and to eat the food himself[3]—Wiesel reflected:

> Sometimes I am asked if I know "the response to Auschwitz"; I answer that not only do I not know it, but that I don't even know if a tragedy of this magnitude *has* a response. What I do know is that there is "response" in responsibility. When we speak of this era of evil and darkness, so close and yet so distant, "responsibility" is the key word.[4]

Wiesel is right. We must speak to these questions *responsibly*. For the Christian, this means reflecting deeply on what the Bible teaches and following through in obedience. Romans 12:17–21 offers a great place to begin.

Principle #1: Resolve Not to Take Revenge

In Romans 12:17–21 Paul speaks directly to how Christians should respond to evil. Three principles from this passage provide the framework for a responsible Christian response to evil and unrepentant offenders. Below I have presented the biblical text in a way that draws attention

---

[2]Quoted in "Compassion: Students Forgive Virginia Tech Killer," CBS News, 2007; http://wcbstv.com/topstories/local_story_107170729.html (accessed April 18, 2007).
[3]Wiesel, *Night*, 110–112.
[4]Ibid., xv.

to the literary structure of the passage and to the first of these three principles:[5]

> [17] **Repay no one evil for evil,**
>> but give thought to do what is honorable in the sight of all. [18] If possible, so far as it depends on you, live peaceably with all.
>>> [19] **Beloved, never avenge yourselves,** but leave it to the wrath of God, for it is written, "Vengeance is mine, I will repay, says the Lord."
>> [20] To the contrary, "if your enemy is hungry, feed him; if he is thirsty, give him something to drink; for by so doing you will heap burning coals on his head."
> [21] **Do not be overcome by evil,** but overcome evil with good.

With repeated emphasis, we see the first principle: believers cannot take revenge. Paul admonishes his readers in verse 17, "Repay no one evil for evil." In verse 19 he says in a way that is at once tender and firm, "Beloved, never avenge yourselves." In verse 21 we read, "Do not be overcome by evil, but overcome evil with good."

To take revenge means "to retaliate in kind or degree" or "to inflict injury in return." The Bible forbids it.

Surely the reason that Paul is so emphatic in forbidding revenge is that it seems so right. In fact, there are people and cultures that see revenge as virtuous. One website (I am intentionally not giving the address) is entirely dedicated to encouraging women to take revenge on men. The site offers eleven basic rules for revenge. Here is an excerpt:

> 1. Get mad . . . then get even. It's justice, plain and simple. 2. Revenge is healthy. Don't listen to those mealy-mouths who tell you otherwise. You're teaching people to behave better. At the same time you're getting icky poisonous feelings out of your system once and for all. What could be healthier? . . . 4. Revenge is excellent self-therapy. It's far cheaper than a therapist and much healthier than pigging out on a box of donuts. . . . 6. Always aim your revenge where it hurts the most. Go right for the jugular.

John Grisham's novel *A Time to Kill* builds a more compelling case. The story begins with the brutal rape of a ten-year-old girl. It is hard

---

[5]For this literary understanding of the passage, see Douglas Moo, *The Epistle to the Romans*, ed. Gordon Fee, The New International Commentary on the New Testament (Grand Rapids, MI: Eerdmans, 1996), 769ff. Moo in turn points to D. A. Black, "The Pauline Love Command: Structure, Style and Ethics in Romans 12:9–21," *Fiologia Neotestamentaria* (1989).

fiction to read: "Billy Ray Cobb . . . sat on the tailgate drinking a beer, smoking a joint, watching his friend Willard take his turn with the black girl."[6]

A few pages later, the father, Carl Lee, arrives home from work aware that something is wrong but not knowing what.

> As he opened the front door he heard Gwen [his wife] crying. To his right in the small living room he found a crowd huddled above a small figure lying on the couch. The child was covered with wet towels and surrounded by crying relatives. As he moved to the couch the crying stopped and the crowd backed away. Only Gwen stayed by the girl. She softly stroked her hair. He knelt beside the couch and touched the girl's shoulder. He spoke to his daughter, and she tried to smile. Her face was bloody pulp covered with knots and lacerations. Both eyes were swollen shut and bleeding. His eyes watered as he looked at her tiny body, completely wrapped in towels and bleeding from ankles to forehead.
>
> Carl Lee asked Gwen what happened. She began shaking and wailing, and was led to the kitchen by her brother. Carl Lee stood and turned to the crowd and demanded to know what had happened.
>
> Silence.
>
> He asked for the third time. The deputy, Willie Hastings, one of Gwen's cousins, stepped forward and told Carl Lee that some people were fishing down by Foggy Creek when they saw Tonya lying in the middle of the road. She told them her daddy's name, and they brought her home.
>
> Hastings shut up and stared at his feet.
>
> Carl Lee stared at him and waited. Everyone else stopped breathing and watched the floor.[7]

I have two daughters. At the time of this writing, one is four years old, and the other is thirteen. It is hard for me to fathom what it would be like as a father to walk through the door of my home and learn that one of them had been brutally molested. Each time I read those paragraphs, I am Carl Lee. Each time I feel anger, rage even.

As the story unfolds, the father, played by Samuel L. Jackson in the movie, finds out who did this to his little girl. He buys a machine gun on the black market, and he kills the men who harmed his daughter with a hail of bullets. The balance of the book is about whether or not Carl Lee will be convicted of murdering the men who molested his daughter. A jury must decide.

---

[6]John Grisham, *A Time to Kill* (New York: Dell, 1989), 1.
[7]Ibid., 7.

How would you have voted if you were on the jury? Clearly the father broke the law in killing the two men who molested his daughter. But should there be a place in society for a father to avenge the assault of his ten-year-old little girl?

Too often fathers face such situations in real life. Grisham explained how as a young lawyer he came up with the idea of *A Time to Kill*.

> One day I stumbled upon a horrible trial in which a young girl testified against the man who had brutally raped her. It was a gut-wrenching experience for me, and I was only a spectator. One moment she was courageous, the next pitifully frail. I was mesmerized. I could not imagine the nightmare she and her family had been through. I wondered what I would do if she were my daughter. As I watched her suffer before the jury, I wanted personally to shoot the rapist. For one brief yet interminable moment I wanted to be her father. I wanted justice.[8]

We understand how Grisham felt, yet our emotions must not prevail. There may be questions about how you or I would vote if we were on such a jury. Even if the man clearly broke the law in taking revenge, we might be tempted to acquit him. But there is no question about how Jesus would vote. Revenge is not an option. No matter how horrible the offense—and the book of Romans was written to Christians who would face the most horrible kinds of violence—revenge is un-Christian. It is not honorable. It is not romantic. And it is not "a time to kill." Read the words again: *"Repay no one evil for evil. . . . Beloved, never avenge yourselves. . . . Do not be overcome by evil."*

Thankfully, the circumstances in which we consider revenge are not normally so violent. But we are tempted nonetheless. There is a garden-variety revenge that many cultivate regularly:

- A spouse is rude and insensitive. Affection is withheld, and the silent treatment is implemented.
- An insensitive cousin is greeted with an icy reception at a family dinner.
- A pastor behaves irresponsibly. Phone wires burn as the offended tells his or her story to others.
- A boss is harsh and unreasonable. Frustrated employees talk viciously about him to one another.
- A father disciplines his son, not because he is trying to teach, but because he resents the inconvenience his son has caused him.
- Parents resent their adult children changing churches. Over the years they make small hurtful remarks designed to show disapproval.

---

[8]Ibid., ix–x.

If you are honest, you can surely identify small ways you have been tempted to take revenge. We feel entitled to just a little payback when we are hurt. Small acts of revenge seem right. But each act of revenge is wrong; it is sin.

The tragedy of revenge is that so often it is the warm gulf waters over which hurricanes of violence will circle. Small winds of injustice, whether real or perceived, swirl about, each increasing and bringing about more retaliation. One act of revenge leads to another. With each rotation, the cycle picks up speed, and a full-scale storm begins. Before you know it, more are sucked into the violence, and the cycle gets bigger.

There is a sense in which Grisham's *A Time to Kill* makes the case for revenge. I cannot imagine watching the movie hoping that the father would be convicted for killing the men who raped his little girl, even though I am persuaded that revenge is wrong. On that level, *A Time to Kill* argues against biblical teaching, in spite of the biblical allusion in its title.

But if Grisham builds a case for revenge, he is at least honest with the collateral damage that revenge can cause. Throughout the story he shows how Carl Lee's revenge wreaked havoc on the lives of nearly everyone involved. Carl Lee's family suffered financially. His children missed their father during the trial. A deputy's leg is amputated because Carl Lee accidentally shot him while taking the lives of the men who abused his daughter. More people died. The cycle of violence continued to grow.

We must never take revenge. Not even in small ways. Revenge seems right, but the Bible clearly prohibits it.

Perhaps the Holy Spirit is convicting you right now about a time when you took revenge. Confess your sin to God and ask for his forgiveness. Then seek forgiveness from the person against whom you retaliated. Don't attempt to justify your actions. Don't explain why you felt driven to do what you did. Humbly ask forgiveness.

If revenge is wrong, what then should be the proper response? How should Grisham's Carl Lee have dealt with the two men who raped his ten-year-old daughter? This takes us to principle #2.

Principle #2: Proactively Show Love

[17] Repay no one evil for evil,
> but give thought to do what is honorable in the sight of all. [18] If
> possible, so far as it depends on you, live peaceably with all.

> [19] Beloved, never avenge yourselves, but leave it to the wrath of God, for it is written, "Vengeance is mine, I will repay, says the Lord."
>
> **[20] To the contrary, "if your enemy is hungry, feed him; if he is thirsty, give him something to drink; for by so doing you will heap burning coals on his head."**
>
> [21] Do not be overcome by evil, but overcome evil with good.

To fully grasp this point, we need to study the verses in context. This section of Romans 12 begins in verse 9 where Paul gives an overarching command: "Let love be genuine." These verses elaborate on how love should be genuine.[9]

Paul's point here is that love should show itself in our lives even when we are wronged. Christlike love actively seeks and offers peace: "Give thought to do what is honorable in the sight of all. If possible, so far as it depends on [us], live peaceably with all" (Romans 12:17b–18).

When Paul says, "give thought," he uses a word that carries the idea of actively planning. Christians should dream of how they can pursue peace even with their enemies.[10] Rather than lying in bed picturing how we might retaliate, we are to use our mental energy creatively to plan a response that will end the cycle of violence. Theologian John Murray summarized, "By well-doing we are to be the instruments of quenching the animosity and the ill-doing of those who persecute and maltreat us."[11]

Of course, the biblical emphasis on love is not unique to Paul's writings. Jesus said that the first and greatest commandment is to love God completely, and the second commandment is inextricably linked to the first one: "Love your neighbor as yourself" (Matthew 22:37–40). Building on this, Jesus taught:

> *"You have heard that it was said, 'An eye for an eye and a tooth for a tooth.' But I say to you, 'Do not resist the one who is evil. But if anyone slaps you on the right cheek, turn to him the other also. And if anyone would sue you and take your tunic, let him have your cloak as well. And if anyone forces you to go one mile, go with him two miles. Give to the*

---

[9]See Douglas Moo, *The Epistle to the Romans*, ed. Gordon Fee, The New International Commentary on the New Testament (Grand Rapids, MI: Eerdmans, 1996), 774. Paul's emphasis on love in Romans continues on into chapter 13. Notice especially Romans 13:8–10.

[10]The word translated "give thought to" appears two other places in the Greek New Testament—2 Corinthians 8:21 and 1 Timothy 5:8. In the former, Paul describes his team's ongoing plans for ministry and evangelism, in which they "aim at what is honorable not only in the Lord's sight but also in the sight of man." The latter verse refers to providing for one's family.

[11]John Murray, *The Epistle to the Romans*, ed. Ned B. Stonehouse, The New International Commentary on the New Testament (Grand Rapids, MI: Eerdmans, 1990), 144.

one who begs from you, and do not refuse the one who would borrow from you.'" (Matthew 5:38–42)

So, how might a Christian in the place of Grisham's Carl Lee have acted to make peace with the men who assaulted his daughter? How could he have proactively and lovingly showed grace instead of vengeance? Could he have written them a heartfelt letter explaining his pain and offering them forgiveness if they would only accept? Could he have reached out to the families of the men who assaulted his little girl? Could he have offered them financial assistance? Such thoughts seem almost inconceivable, but this is the stunning implication of Paul's teaching. We should use all our mental energy to love those who harm us and to live at peace with them: let your love be authentic; give thought to do what is honorable; so far as it depends on you, live at peace with all people.

Paul amplifies the point in verse 20 by saying that we should see to the refreshment of our enemies even though they have injured us. He explains that kindness to our enemies may be the means God uses to bring them to repentance.[12] "'If your enemy is hungry, feed him; if he is thirsty, give him something to drink; for by so doing you will heap burning coals on his head'" (Romans 12:20).

There is, perhaps, no better recent example of showing love and kindness in the face of evil than that of the Amish community in 2006 when five of their daughters were murdered.

The Amish at Nickel Mines, Pennsylvania

Numerous reports opened a window to what the school day looked like on October 2, 2006 at the Amish school in Nickel Mines, Pennsylvania. It was a clear, sunny, September day. Students walked into a bright classroom with a sign on the blackboard that said, "Visitors brighten our days."[13] To begin school, their twenty-year-old teacher, Emma, led them in Bible reading and prayer. In German, the students sang about the frailty of life:

---

[12]There has been quite a lot of discussion about Paul's intent with the use of this quotation from Proverbs. The consensus is that it may be what God uses to bring them to repentance. Moo summarizes, "Acting kindly toward our enemies is a means of leading them to be ashamed of their conduct toward us and, perhaps, to repent and turn to the Lord whose love we embody." Moo, *Epistle to the Romans*, 789.

[13]For the details of the Nickel Mines School shooting, I am particularly indebted to Donald B. Kraybill, Steven M. Nolt, and David L. Weaver-Zercher, *Amish Grace: How Forgiveness Transcended Tragedy* (San Francisco: Jossey-Bass, 2007), 17–28. See also John L. Ruth, *Forgiveness: A Legacy of the West Nickel Mines Amish School* (Harrisonburg, VA: Vision Publishers, 2007), Harvey Yoder, *The Happening: Nickel Mines School Tragedy* (Harrisonburg, VA: Vision Publishers, 2007).

Think, O man about the end,
Think about your death,
Death often comes quickly;
Today you may be healthy and ruddy,
But tomorrow, or sooner,
You may have passed away.
Keep this in mind, O sinner!
Be ready to die each day.[14]

Their teacher led them through morning lessons, and the children were dismissed to play outside for recess. Some of the boys played softball. Maybe the little girls played with dolls, though that is speculation on my part.

If the students had looked closely in the right direction, they would have seen a man four hundred yards or so away, sipping a pop. Up close, some of the students would have recognized Charles Carl Roberts IV as the trucker who picked up milk from their farms. But nothing would have warned them of his evil intent. Before Roberts stopped to buy a soda at the vending machine, he had left suicide notes behind for his wife and children and loaded his truck with guns, ammunition, binoculars, and lubricating jelly. He planned to molest and murder.

Roberts made his move at about 10:15 A.M. after the students came in from recess. He backed his truck up to the front porch of the school and ordered everyone inside. One of the first persons Roberts sent out of the school was the young teacher. Eventually Roberts dismissed all the boys and any adults present.

Once they were alone, Roberts threatened the girls who remained by saying, "I'm angry at God and I need to punish some Christian girls to get even with him."[15] Proverbs 19:3 reads, "When a man's folly brings his way to ruin, his heart rages against the LORD." That was Roberts.

He told the girls that if one of them let him do what he wanted to do, he would let the others go. One of the younger girls offered to help. But the older girls quickly warned in Pennsylvania Dutch, "Duh's net! Duh's net! (Don't do it! Don't do it!)."[16]

By this time, Emma, the teacher, had run to get help at a nearby farm. They called 911, and within nine minutes state troopers began to arrive.

Realizing that the police were already present, Roberts told the girls

---

[14]Yoder, *The Happening*, 35.
[15]Kraybill, Nolt, and Weaver-Zercher, *Amish Grace*, 25.
[16]Ibid., 24.

he was going to make them pay for his daughter, who had died as an infant. The book *Amish Grace* describes what happened next.

> Marian, one of two thirteen-year-olds in the room quickly assumed leadership of the younger girls, doing everything she could to help protect them. Realizing he planned to kill them, she said, "Shoot me first," hoping to save the others and fulfilling her duty to watch over the little ones in her care.
>
> At about 11:05 A.M. the police heard three shotgun blasts followed by rapid-fire pistol shots. A shotgun blast, fired through the window by the main door, narrowly missed several officers. Troopers rushed the building, smashing windows with batons and shields. The killer turned the pistol on himself and fell to the floor as troopers broke through the windows. In execution style, he had gunned down the lineup of girls on the floor. Five would die. The other five, critically injured, had survived by rolling around and burying their heads in their arms.[17]

The horrible reality of what Charles Roberts did was worse than John Grisham's fiction in *A Time to Kill*. He murdered defenseless little girls and then took his own life, unrepentant to the end.

Yet the beauty and loveliness of Christ reflected in the lives of the Amish in how they responded to Roberts. There was never a thought of revenge. They showed love proactively and creatively. First, there was the thirteen-year-old, Marian, who asked Roberts to shoot her first. "Greater love has no one than this, that someone lay down his life for his friends" (John 15:13). God bless Marian.

The families continued what Marian began. When donations began to pour in to help with the expenses, the Amish immediately offered assistance to the family of the man who had murdered their daughters. One Amish elder explained:

> Who will take care of their family? It's not right if we get $1,000 and they get $5. We must set something up for these children's education.[18]

The stories of Amish grace and love after the shooting can only be highlighted here. More than half of the people who attended the funeral for Charles Roberts were Amish. Parents of the slain children invited Roberts's widow, Marie Roberts, to attend the funeral for their daugh-

[17]Ibid., 25–26.
[18]Tracie Mauriello, "Amish Extend Hand to Family of Schoolhouse Killer," *Pittsburgh Post-Gazette*, October 7, 2006; http://www.post-gazette.com/pg/06280/728083-85.stm (accessed April 6, 2007).

ters.[19] Overwhelmed by such love and grace, Marie Roberts wrote to the Amish, "Your love for our family has helped to provide the healing we so desperately need. Your compassion has reached beyond our family, beyond our community, and is changing our world."[20]

Conclusion

How should Christians respond to unrepentant offenders? We have examined two principles thus far:

- Principle #1: Resolve not to take revenge.
- Principle #2: Proactively offer love.

These principles are not simply for the Amish. All Christians are called to embody these. Revenge is never an option. We must resist the temptation to retaliate, even in small ways. And we must lovingly and proactively reach out to those who have injured us with the quality of grace that the Amish extended to the widow and children of Charles Roberts.

But these two principles are not a complete answer to how Christians should respond to unrepentant offenders. One more important principle remains. The next chapter will develop it.

Discussion Questions

What are the first two guidelines for responding to unrepentant offenders?

Why is revenge so tempting?

How did the Amish live out the first two guidelines for responding to unrepentant offenders?

Read 1 Peter 2:21–25. How did Jesus live out the principles outlined in this chapter? What is Peter's purpose in the context of 1 Peter for including the example of Jesus (see 1 Peter 2:13–3:7).

Can you describe a time when someone you know showed creativity in loving in a proactive way?

This chapter cautioned that most of us are tempted to take revenge in small and subtle ways. What are some everyday ways that you see yourself or others taking revenge?

---

[19]Kraybill, Nolt, and Weaver-Zercher, *Amish Grace*, 43–44.
[20]Quoted in Stan Guthrie, "The Scandal of Forgiveness," *Christianity Today*, January 2007; http://www.christianitytoday.com/ct/2007/january/15.58.html (accessed March 3, 2008).

chapter twelve

How Should I Respond to the Unrepentant? A Third Principle

Alexander the coppersmith did me great harm; the Lord will repay him according to his deeds. Beware of him your-self, for he strongly opposed our message.

2 TIMOTHY 4:14–15

. . . it is only when God's wrath and vengeance are hang-ing as grim realities over the heads of one's enemies that something of what it means to love and forgive them can touch our hearts.

DIETRICH BONHOEFFER IN A LETTER TO EBERHARD BETHGE[1]

Even John Grisham's title *A Time to Kill* attempts to build a case for revenge. Presumably, the title is a reference to the book of Ecclesiastes:

> For everything there is a season, and a time for every matter under heaven: a time to be born, and a time to die; a time to plant, and a time to pluck up what is planted; a time to kill, *and a time to heal . . . a time for war, and a time for peace. (Ecclesiastes 3:1–8)*

Grisham's fiction implied that Carl Lee's "time to kill" was after his daughter had been molested. In the previous chapter of this book, I dis-cussed Carl Lee's passion for revenge in light of the Bible's clear mandate

---

[1]Dietrich Bonhoeffer, *Letters and Papers from Prison*, ed. Eberhard Bethge (New York: Simon & Schuster, 1971), 157.

against revenge. Vengeance belongs to God. That was the first principle stressed in responding to unrepentant offenders.

The second principle we discussed raised the standard even higher. Christians are called to show love proactively, even to their enemies. In Carl Lee's case, this meant that he should have sought to love even the men who molested his young daughter.

Still, we must ask if more needs to be said in formulating a Christian response to unrepentant offenders. What about justice? If we were to take our analysis of Romans 12:17–20 no further than these two principles, Christians might legitimately be accused of throwing justice out the window. We would be susceptible to the charge that there is no accountability or responsibility for evil. But Principle #3 completes a balanced Christian response that neither suspends nor dismisses justice.

Principle #3: Don't Forgive the Unrepentant, but Leave Room for the Wrath of God

[17] Repay no one evil for evil,
> but give thought to do what is honorable in the sight of all. [18] If possible, so far as it depends on you, live peaceably with all.
>> [19] **Beloved, never avenge yourselves, but leave it to the wrath of God, for it is written, "Vengeance is mine, I will repay, says the Lord."**
>> [20] To the contrary, "if your enemy is hungry, feed him; if he is thirsty, give him something to drink; for by so doing you will heap burning coals on his head."
[21] Do not be overcome by evil, but overcome evil with good.

Jesus told his followers that we ought to forgive people as many times as they ask for forgiveness (Luke 17:3b–4). But what of those who do *not* ask for forgiveness? How should we respond to them? Should we automatically forgive? Remember, the biblical definition of forgiveness includes the condition that the one receiving the forgiveness is repentant:

> Forgiveness is a commitment by the offended to pardon graciously the repentant from moral liability and to be reconciled to that person, although not all consequences are necessarily eliminated.

In Grisham's *A Time to Kill*, should Carl Lee have pardoned those who assaulted his daughter, even though they were unrepentant? The answer to that is no. Rather, Paul wrote that we are to "leave it to the wrath of God" (Romans 12:19), trusting that God will appropriately accomplish justice when and how he deems to do so.

In that verse, Paul quoted Moses from Deuteronomy 32. In this passage Moses encouraged Israel to rejoice in the truth that God will make sure that justice is done.

> *Vengeance is mine, and recompense, for the time when their foot shall slip; for the day of their calamity is at hand, and their doom comes swiftly. . . . Rejoice with him, O heavens; bow down to him, all gods, for he avenges the blood of his children and takes vengeance on his adversaries. He repays those who hate him and cleanses his people's land. (Deuteronomy 32:35, 43)*

Read those verses carefully. This principle of leaving room for God's wrath is how Israel was equipped to deal with those who would do evil against them. And the summary of that passage is that God does *not* forgive everyone and that Israel should rest in the truth that God will "avenge the blood of his children."

Ultimately, this means that those who have been unrepentant should understand that offenders do face hell. That truth deserves close, sober consideration. No one can properly unpack forgiveness without interacting with the biblical truth that some will spend eternity in everlasting torment. I shudder even in writing that sentence. The reality of hell is nearly unthinkable. It is beyond me that some will be tormented for a billion years and yet still be no closer to the end of their time in hell. I have said from the pulpit that if it were up to me, I would give Hitler only a billion years. Then I would just make him cease to exist. But it is not up to me. And it was not me against whom he sinned.

Of course, Hitler is one thing. And I have read enough about the Holocaust that I could be persuaded rather easily to change my opinion that a billion years would be enough. But the knowledge that some in our community who are considered "good people" will spend eternity in everlasting torment is jolting.

This is what Paul has in mind in Romans 12:19. And the reality of hell is why Paul legitimately encourages his audience not to take revenge. God will handle it. And we can be sure that God's justice will be infinitely more severe than anything we might have administered.

Second Timothy 4 offers an example of how Paul personally lived out this third principle of leaving room for God's wrath:

Alexander the coppersmith did me great harm; the Lord will repay him according to his deeds. Beware of him yourself, for he strongly opposed our message. (2 Timothy 4:14–15)

It is not recorded that Paul ever forgave Alexander. He did not pardon his behavior. On the contrary, Paul told Timothy that he was resting in the truth that God would repay Alexander for his deeds, and he warned Timothy simply to "beware" of Alexander.[2]

As I described in the last chapter, I believe the Amish community of Nickel Mines glorified God in how they proactively and lovingly offered grace to the family of the man who murdered their daughters. They were so exemplary in their love amid such awful circumstances that one hesitates to differ with their response in any way. And yet because their actions were widely represented as a model of how Christians should respond to evil, it is appropriate to consider if their response could have been more balanced.

So far as I am aware, and I have not done an exhaustive study, there was little or no mention by the Amish of the justice of God. From the beginning they automatically forgave Roberts. An Amish woman said on television that they had to forgive if they wanted God to forgive them.[3] The grandfather of a victim said, "We shouldn't think evil of the man who did this."[4]

It is true that Christians must not be overcome by hatred. Yet, Christians must also *warn* an onlooking world about the justice of God. Christians should most explicitly point people to the cross when evil is darkest. There is a way to lovingly remind people that God's judgment is certain (Hebrews 9:27).

There is not room here to dialogue thoroughly with the Amish position. Several quick points, however, can be made.

• The Amish *do* practice conditional forgiveness with their own members. They shun those who breach their order and do not receive them back into fellowship unless they are repentant.

• The Amish *do* believe in hell and eternal judgment. While they may say that they forgive an unrepentant offender, they believe God will deal justly with him or her.

---

[2]When Paul expresses his confidence in the justice of God, he uses a phrase that appears several times in the Old Testament and refers to the vengeance of God. George W. Knight, *The Pastoral Epistles: A Commentary on the Greek Text*, New International Greek Testament Commentary (Grand Rapids, MI: Eerdmans, 1992), 467. See 2 Samuel 3:39; Psalm 28:4; 62:12; Proverbs 24:12.

[3]Donald B. Kraybill, Steven M. Nolt, and David L. Weaver-Zercher, *Amish Grace: How Forgiveness Transcended Tragedy* (San Francisco: Jossey-Bass, 2007), 45.

[4]Ibid.

• The Amish are *not* evangelistic. While a rare event such as Nickel Mines may draw attention to Amish faith, it is hard to square their radical separation from culture to Jesus' commandment to go into all the world to make disciples (Matthew 28:18–20). Amish passivity is not effective in calling people to faith and repentance.

●   ●   ●

I have preached and taught this material on a number of occasions. Two questions almost always come up. First, whenever it is argued that forgiveness should be preceded by repentance, some will counter, "Isn't it true that Jesus forgave those who crucified him?" They allude to the crucifixion account in Luke 23.

> *And when they came to the place that is called The Skull, there they crucified him, and the criminals, one on his right and one on his left. And Jesus said, "Father, forgive them, for they know not what they do."* (Luke 23:33–34)

The short answer to that question is no. Jesus did not forgive them. If you think carefully about this passage, you will see this is the case. Jesus prayed that those who crucified him would be forgiven in the future—he did not thank God that they were already forgiven. If they had already been forgiven, such a prayer would have been superfluous.

Jesus surely *could have* forgiven them on the spot himself, had they been repentant on the spot. We know from elsewhere in Scripture that Jesus had authority to forgive sins. Indeed, there were times when he told people that their sins were forgiven (for example, Luke 5:20–24; 7:49).

Notice also that on the cross, in exactly the same context where Jesus prayed that his killers would be forgiven, Jesus does grant forgiveness to someone else! There were two criminals hanging with Jesus, and one of them repented. Jesus forgave him immediately: "Today you will be with me in paradise" (Luke 23:43). He did not say, "I pray that you will be forgiven." He forgave him. And Jesus' forgiveness promised a new relationship: "Today you will be with me in paradise."

Stephen's prayer for those who stoned him closely parallels the interceding prayer of Jesus on behalf of his tormentors.

> *And falling to his knees he [Stephen] cried out with a loud voice, "Lord, do not hold this sin against them." And when he had said this, he fell asleep.* (Acts 7:60)

I would not be the first to observe that the apostle Paul's conversion was an answer to Stephen's prayer. Paul, who stood nearby holding the garments of those who stoned Stephen (v. 58), was later saved. But again it could be pointed out that Stephen did not say to those stoning him, "I forgive you." Paul was not forgiven until he repented on the road to Damascus. Hypothetically speaking, if Paul had lost his life in a chariot accident during the time period between Stephen's death and his own conversion, Paul would not have gone to heaven.

Others argue that elsewhere in Scripture Jesus does not seem to include repentance as a condition for forgiveness (Matthew 6:12, 14–15; 18:21–22). It is true in these verses that Jesus does not explicitly utter a condition of repentance. However, the requirement is implicit. In Matthew 6, Jesus told the disciples to forgive as God forgives. He does not explicitly mention this in Matthew 6, but we learn from other passages that God's forgiveness is indeed conditional. The emphasis of Matthew 6 is to forgive as God forgives, which is another reiteration that we ought to forgive only repentant offenders.

In Matthew 18:21–22 Jesus does not explicitly include repentance as a prerequisite for forgiveness. However, the conditional nature of forgiveness is certainly assumed in the context of the chapter. Both in the teaching on church discipline in Matthew 18:15–20 *and* in the parable that follows in Matthew 18:23–35, Jesus describes situations in which people should be forgiven *when* they repent.

Forgiveness is conditional. The great Reformed theologian John Murray summarized this truth as follows:

> Forgiveness is a definite act performed by us on the fulfillment of certain conditions. . . . Forgiveness is something actively administered on the repentance of the person who is to be forgiven. We greatly impoverish ourselves and impair the relations that we should sustain to our brethren when we fail to appreciate what is involved in forgiveness.[5]

Objections

Won't Conditional Forgiveness Lead to Bitterness?

Some would argue that automatic forgiveness is the key to avoiding bitterness. In part, the argument here goes back to the matter of defining forgiveness. Those who argue for automatic forgiveness generally define

---

[5]John Murray, "A Lesson in Forgiveness," in *The Collected Writings of John Murray* (Carlisle, PA: The Banner of Truth Trust, 1982), 191.

forgiveness psychologically or therapeutically. And if that is your definition, then the only way to avoid bitterness or negative feelings is to forgive. But in the previous chapters I have laid out for you why I think this definition is the wrong definition. The Bible always presents forgiveness as something that happens between two parties.

Contrary to the conventional understanding, I believe that the notion of automatic forgiveness itself fosters bitterness. We are created with a standard of justice written on our hearts. When we forgive someone who is not repentant, we are acting in a way that is unjust. Deep down we are saying that forgiveness must sometimes happen at the expense of justice.

On the other hand, when we recognize that those who have offended us will face the vengeance of God, at that point we will begin to feel true love and compassion for them.

Whether we are talking about the Amish families grieving for their daughters in Pennsylvania or the families of the 9/11 victims or the families hurt by the Columbine tragedy, the Bible teaches that God's people who were involved should all trust God to deal justly with the perpetrators.[6]

Remembering that vengeance belongs to God also removes the temptation to take revenge. After all, those who pursue revenge are basically saying that God cannot do his job.[7] But when we remember that God will accomplish justice, we will be less tempted to take revenge.

Christians should offer grace to all people. We should wrap up forgiveness as a present and make it available to anyone who will accept, regardless of the offense. But it is not the offense that conditions forgiveness but the repentant heart. Whether or not they unwrap the present and accept the gift so that forgiveness takes place is up to them.

Isn't This Just a Matter of How We Use Words?

Some people might reconcile their thinking with mine this way: "Oh, now that I understand your position, I think we're on the same page. You just like to say, '*Offer* grace and forgiveness unconditionally,' while I prefer just to say, '*Forgive* unconditionally.'"

Well, no. We are not on the same page. The problem with that approach is that it redefines a biblical word—forgiveness. This leads to the problems I described in Chapter 5.

---

[6]See also "Faith in Future Grace vs. Bitterness," in John Piper, *Future Grace* (Sisters, OR: Multnomah, 1995), 261–271.
[7]Rob Bell, *Luggage 007*, Nooma series (Grand Rapids, MI: Zondervan, 2005), 8. Bell writes (on DVD jacket), "If we take revenge when we get hurt, do you think it's like saying to God, 'I think I can handle this better than you'?"

Scott and Janet Willis: Grace through Flames

On November 8, 1994, Scott and Janet Willis were driving through the Milwaukee area on I-94 with their six youngest children in a minivan. They had left a couple of hours before from Chicago. They had fun singing and laughing together on the first part of the trip. But after they stopped and got gas, they encouraged the children to get some sleep. Three older children were not with them.

When he was able, Scott Willis described what transpired on I-94 that November day.

> I was looking at the road and was alert. Our little baby was behind us; Ben was behind us on the other side. In the back were the other four children; they were all buckled in. I saw the object (a metal brace, 6"x30", 30 lbs.). I thought it was one of those blocks that maybe came off a flatbed truck. The car in front of me swerved, and I knew I couldn't miss hitting the object. I thought if I took it on the tire I might roll the car. It was a split-second decision.
>
> When we hit the object, the rear gas tank exploded, taking the car out of control. I was able to grip the wheel and take the car out of the slide. When we were sliding and the flames were coming around the seat, it was a shock—a surprise—like, 'What is this?' It was just roaring flames coming up on both sides. I was yelling to get out of the car. Janet and I had to consciously put our hands into the flames to unbuckle the seat belts and reach for the door handles.
>
> Janet fell out the door while the car was still moving. [Our son] Benny was in the midst of the burning; his clothes were mostly burned off by the time he got out. The five youngest children, who had been asleep, died instantly. No sound was heard by Janet or me as we struggled to get out of the van. An unknown man took his shirt off his back to soak Benny's wounds, and another beat out the burning clothes on Janet's back. Benny died in intensive care around midnight.[8]

If possible, the tragedy got even worse for Scott and Janet Willis. They had found some comfort in knowing that their children had died instantly. But months later they learned that there were signs that some of the children struggled to get out of the van. Their son Benny lost consciousness at the scene. They assumed he had not regained it before he died. But a hospital worker told them he was alive and alert at the hospital. He had asked her to hold his hand, but she was unable to do so because of his burns. He had asked her to pray with him.

---

[8]*Through the Flames: The Willis Family Story* (gospel tract) (Wheaton, IL: Good News Publishers, 2000), http://www.gnpcb.org/product/663575724360 (accessed March 29, 2007).

Then Scott and Janet Willis learned that the driver of the semi had obtained his license illegally because of corruption under George Ryan, future governor of Illinois, at that time Secretary of State. Licensing facilities had accepted bribes that allowed unqualified drivers to receive licenses. These bribes became a part of Ryan's campaign fund. Ironically, Janet Willis had voted for Ryan the very morning of the accident.

On the morning of the accident, the driver ignored repeated warnings from other drivers that a large piece of metal was going to fall off the back of his truck.

It all seemed so senseless, so preventable.

So Scott and Janet Willis had to decide how to relate to a driver who should have heeded warnings, who should not have been on the road in the first place. They had to decide how to treat a politician whose corrupt values had played a part in their children's deaths.

In the short run, it would have been easiest to gravitate to one of two extremes. They could have been angry and vindictive; they could have hated the politicians who allowed unqualified drivers to get a license through a bribe. *Or* they could have granted automatic forgiveness. This would have meant that there would be no accountability for actions. Instead of either of these extreme choices, the Willis family chose to live out the principles of Romans 12. This is evident from letters that they sent to a U.S. District Judge, including this one written recently by Janet:

> My husband and I have prayed and asked God to keep us from bitterness and to help us be faithful to him and he has. We tried to honor God by not complaining.
>
> But there is a time to speak. I am sharing these facts only because I believe if justice rules, wrongdoing will be deterred. I have learned "when [God's] judgments come upon the earth, the people of the world learn righteousness. Though grace is shown to the wicked, they do not learn righteousness; even in a land of uprightness they go on doing evil" (Isaiah 26:9, 10).[9]

Scott Willis added his thoughts to her letter:

> Janet and I are ordinary people. Not powerful, not forceful. Our children brought great joy to us. Benjamin, Joseph, Samuel, Hank, Elizabeth and Peter were like anybody else's kids: playful, happy, mopey, energetic. The

---

[9] Scott Willis and Janet Willis, "Corruption and Providence: Letters Scott & Janet Willis Sent to U.S. District Judge Rebecca Pallmeyer," *World* Magazine (September 14, 2006); http://www.worldmag.com/webextra/12246 (accessed April 6, 2007).

boys loved reading and sports. Elizabeth was her mom's shadow and her doll's mom. We love them. We miss them. We do not despair. We live with a God-promised hope in Jesus Christ.

Almost 12 years have passed since Nov. 8, 1994. The heartache remains but has softened. Janet and I have prayed to not have a bitter or revengeful spirit. These feelings have only occasionally flared up but have not consumed or dominated our thoughts and are not the motive for this letter.

Our thoughts are not on punishment. That is for the court to decide. The real tragedy is that no reconciliation has yet been attained between George Ryan and Janet and me. My wife and I have a strong desire to forgive Gov. Ryan but it must be on an honest basis: sorrow and admission. Even a 6-year-old boy knows when he's done wrong he needs to be truly sorry, and admit it. Then forgiveness and mercy can be graciously offered. That would be our joy.[10]

Notice how the Willis family lived out the principles of Romans 12:9–21.

Fig. 12.1 Scott & Janet Willis and Forgiveness

Forgiveness Principle	How the Willises Demonstrated This Principle
Principle 1: Resolve not to take revenge.	"My husband and I have prayed and asked God to keep us from bitterness and to help us be faithful to him and he has." "Janet and I have prayed to not have a bitter or revengeful spirit. These feelings have only occasionally flared up but have not consumed or dominated our thoughts and are not the motive for this letter."
Principle 2: Lovingly and proactively offer grace.	"The real tragedy is that no reconciliation has yet been attained between George Ryan and Janet and me. My wife and I have a strong desire to forgive Gov. Ryan but it must be on an honest basis: sorrow and admission. Even a 6-year-old boy knows when he's done wrong he needs to be truly sorry, and admit it. Then forgiveness and mercy can be graciously offered. That would be our joy."
Principle 3: Don't forgive the unrepentant, but leave room for the wrath of God.	"But there is a time to speak. I am sharing these facts only because I believe if justice rules, wrongdoing will be deterred. I have learned 'when [God's] judgments come upon the earth, the people of the world learn righteousness. Though grace is shown to the wicked, they do not learn righteousness; even in a land of uprightness they go on doing evil' (Isaiah 26:9, 10)."

[10]Ibid.

Conclusion

Romans 12:17–21 gives a framework for responding to evil. (1) Resolve not to take revenge. Do not even allow yourself to rehearse it in your mind. (2) Lovingly and proactively offer grace to your enemies. Although love and grace are undeserved, creatively consider what you might do to live at peace with all people, even those who may have murdered your own family. (3) Do not forgive the unrepentant. Leave room for the wrath of God. He will deal justly with all wrongs. When we consider that those who do not know Christ will spend eternity in an everlasting hell, we can move beyond bitterness to compassion, even in the most awful circumstances.

On an emotional level, it may seem like too much to suggest that John Grisham's Carl Lee should not have avenged the man who molested his daughter. But then we remember the example of our Lord. I am writing these words on the Saturday between Good Friday and Resurrection Day. And I consider Peter's exhortation that all Christians are to follow our Lord's example.

> *For to this you have been called, because Christ also suffered for you, leaving you an example, so that you might follow in his steps. He committed no sin, neither was deceit found in his mouth. When he was reviled, he did not revile in return; when he suffered, he did not threaten, but continued entrusting himself to him who judges justly. He himself bore our sins in his body on the tree, that we might die to sin and live to righteousness. By his wounds you have been healed. (1 Peter 2:21–24)*

The Lord took no revenge. He prayed that his killers would be forgiven. He entrusted himself to him who judges justly. The Word become flesh (John 1:14), Christ is *the* example of how we should respond to evil.

Discussion Questions

What is the third principle for responding to unrepentant offenders?

How does a failure to implement this principle undermine evangelism?

How can an understanding of what the Bible teaches about hell help us avoid bitterness?

Read 2 Thessalonians 1. Why did Paul say he was boasting about the Thessalonians? How did Paul seek to comfort the Thessalonians in the midst of their suffering?

Paul stressed that Christians should leave room for the wrath of God (Romans 12:19). How might someone misapply this principle or take the verse out of context?

Ron and Sue are Christians. Their only son, Brett, was killed by a drunk driver who refuses to accept any responsibility, even though he was convicted of manslaughter charges. Ron and Sue say they could never feel any compassion for this man who killed their son and is now unrepentant. What would you say to them?

chapter thirteen

How Can I Conquer Bitterness?

Fret not yourself because of evildoers; be not envious of wrongdoers!

PSALM 37:1

The assurance of God's ultimate justice (then) frees radical love (now).

JOHN N. DAY[1]

No one sets out to be a bitter person. Nor do we encourage others to pursue bitterness. Bitterness is bad. Everyone agrees on that.

People often appeal to this common goal when debating about forgiveness. Whenever I teach that forgiveness should not be automatic, someone inevitably plays the trump card, "But *that* approach would lead to bitterness." Their underlying premise is, "If I can establish that your position causes bitterness, I will have proven you wrong."

Of course, bitterness is bad. But conditional forgiveness (*not* automatically forgiving) does not spawn bitterness. As I have already said, we must follow the example of God, who does not forgive everyone but who does *offer* forgiveness to all. The offer of forgiveness to *everyone*, regardless of the offense, is no more bitter than the father who wraps presents and puts them under the Christmas tree hoping that his child will accept the gifts. Forgiveness, and a restored relationship, is what offenders will find inside if they choose to open the package.

---

[1]John N. Day, *Crying for Justice: What the Psalms Teach Us About Mercy in an Age of Terrorism* (Grand Rapids, MI: Kregel, 2005), 99.

But I digress. The point here is that bitterness is to be avoided like the bubonic plague.

And yet there are so many bitter people. In fact, one of the reasons we agree that bitterness is bad is because we witness what it does to people. We all know sour people who kick dogs, yell at children cutting through their yards, and shout with red faces at church business meetings about insignificant issues. They are cynical at work. They are unappreciative of how they have been blessed, and they resent the successes of others.

The Wicked Witch of the West, for instance, was bitter. If nothing else, her vendetta against Toto gives her away: "I'll get you, my pretty—and your little dog too!" Bitter.

But before we begin to feel too self-righteous because *we* do not terrorize munchkins or light scarecrows on fire, we need to remember that even a little bitterness is bad. We have all stewed about some injustice. And thus bitterness begins. After an offense, few of us would hop on a broomstick or hire a bunch of flying monkeys, at least not immediately. But a little pouting is the seed from which a root of bitterness germinates. And bitterness kills.

When I was in junior high, some friends and I discovered mercury. We were in an out-of-control science class, and we had too-easy access to the chemical cabinet. We started experimenting with different chemicals, and mercury was our favorite. It is an amazing substance. It is physically dense. Even a small container of mercury weighs a lot. It is shiny, like liquid aluminum foil. And it has a high viscosity (surface tension). You can slide mercury around on a piece of paper, break it into little droplets, and then put it back together—unless everyone decides to keep some of it, which they did (except for me since I was planning to become a pastor).

We were fascinated by mercury, and we were extremely foolish. Much later, as a chemistry major, I learned that mercury is highly toxic. Get mercury in your system, and it will go to your brain and make you crazy (literally). The Wikipedia article on mercury poisoning says:

> Mercury damages the central nervous system, endocrine system, kidneys, and other organs, and adversely affects the mouth, gums, and teeth. Exposure over long periods of time or heavy exposure to mercury vapor can result in brain damage and ultimately death.[2]

Other than that, mercury's great for you.

[2]"Mercury Poisoning," Wikipedia, 2008; http://en.wikipedia.org/wiki/Mercury_poisoning (accessed April 9, 2008).

Bitterness is like mercury. It is tempting to play with it. We can stew for hours on end thinking about how we have been treated unfairly and how we hope that someday justice will be done. We slide bitterness around in our minds and slip some of it into our pockets. And we are oh so foolish because all the while it is attacking our bones (Proverbs 14:30).[3] Fooling around with bitterness is like drinking poison and hoping that someone else will die.[4]

So, what we really need to do with bitterness is to deal with it as soon as possible. And the Bible is where we find answers. In Psalm 73, Asaph[5] shared the story of his battle with bitterness. This Psalm is both real in its wrestling and timeless in the solution it offers. Psalm 73 will help us understand how bitterness works and will help us know how, with God's help, we can beat it.

If you are struggling against bitterness, the best thing would be for you to put this book aside and read Psalm 73 through four or five times. Look for the answer to two questions: First, what is bitterness like? Second, how did Asaph beat bitterness?

Know How to Beat Bitterness

First, wait for God's justice, and trust his providence.

The nature of bitterness is to complain. "It isn't fair." This is the first thing we notice about Asaph's struggle in Psalm 73. He felt like evil people were rewarded. He admitted, "For I was envious of the arrogant when I saw the prosperity of the wicked" (v. 3).

Asaph spent a lot of time reviewing in his mind the unfairness of the whole thing.

For they have no pangs until death; their bodies are fat and sleek. They are not in trouble as others are; they are not stricken like the rest of

---

[3]Proverbs 14:30 reads, "A tranquil heart gives life to the flesh, but envy makes the bones rot." The word translated "envy" might also be translated "hot passion." Waltke summarizes, "Inward excitation, a resentful mind, which cares only for itself and which gets worked up, is like bone cancer that rots the most firm components of the body and shortens a person's life" (Bruce C. Waltke, *The Book of Proverbs 1–14*, ed. R. K. Harrison and Robert L. Hubbard Jr., The New International Commentary of the Old Testament [Grand Rapids, MI: Eerdmans, 2005], 606–607).

[4]Credit to Nancy Leigh DeMoss for this phrase. She used it in reference to "unforgiveness." I think it is more precise to say this in reference to bitterness given that there are times when unforgiveness is appropriate. Nancy Leigh DeMoss, *Choosing Forgiveness: Your Journey to Freedom* (Chicago: Moody, 2006), 50–51.

[5]The title of Psalm 73 contains the line, "A Psalm of Asaph." Scholars are not sure if this means that Asaph wrote this Psalm or that he led the choir that sang it. Peter C. Craigie, *Psalms 1–50*, ed. David A. Hubbard and others, 52 vols., Word Biblical Commentary, Vol. 19 (Nashville: Word, 1983), 31–35. However, like Spurgeon, I am comfortable reflecting on the Psalm believing that Asaph wrote it. See C. H. Spurgeon, *The Treasury of David: An Expository and Devotional Commentary on the Psalms: 1–89* (Grand Rapids, MI: Baker, 1984), 338.

mankind. Therefore pride is their necklace; violence covers them as a garment. Their eyes swell out through fatness; their hearts overflow with follies. They scoff and speak with malice; loftily they threaten oppression. They set their mouths against the heavens, and their tongue struts through the earth. (vv. 4–9)

Ever been there? Ever find yourself thinking over and over again how unfair something is?

The more Asaph thought about the prosperity of the wicked, the madder he got. He began to wonder if it was even really worth it to honor God. "All in vain have I kept my heart clean and washed my hands in innocence" (v. 13). Asaph said in essence, "I tried to live for God, and it didn't get me a thing."

Now, it is not wrong to notice that we have been treated unjustly. The question is, how should we deal with being treated unjustly? Those who process it wrongly will become bitter.

Esau, who is something of a biblical poster child for bitterness (Hebrews 12:15–17), also complained that life had not been fair to him (Genesis 27:36–38). Esau had a point. His mother favored his twin brother, which must have been horribly painful. Worse yet, his father favored Esau (Genesis 25:28). What's so bad about that? No child deserves the burden of having a parent center too much on him. In addition to being treated unfairly by his parents, Esau had a twin brother who conned him out of both his birthright and his blessing (Genesis 25–27).

How did Esau respond to the unfairness of life? He gave in to bitterness. He married a foreign woman just to spite his parents, vowed to kill his brother, and brought tremendous grief to his parents (Genesis 27:41; 28:6–9). Esau was not responsible for how his parents treated him. But he chose to be bitter.

In this context, we find a key insight. If bitterness is a wrong response to injustice or perceived injustice, then the first step in beating bitterness is to recognize that when we have been treated unjustly, we are particularly vulnerable to bitterness.

So ask yourself, is there some aspect of your life where you focus on injustice done to you? Maybe you try not to think about it, but over and over you find yourself haunted by some wrong.

- "I cannot believe I was passed over for that promotion after all I have done for this company."
- "How could my father possibly leave more to her for an inheritance?"
- "I will never forgive him for leaving me for her. It wasn't fair."

- "My parents have ruined my life."
- "I might have expected such treatment from non-Christians, or even people at church, but not from my pastor."

To the extent that that you may have been wronged, you are at risk for bitterness. The essence of bitterness is that it is a sinful response to injustice or perceived injustice.

You might say, "I know I am on the verge of bitterness. But how can I possibly move past it? How can I forget that I was abused? How can I forget that I was cheated?"

Asaph gives us the answer. The turning point in Psalm 73 happened when Asaph stopped thinking about himself and the injustice of evil people having an easier life and started centering on God.

> *. . . until I went into the sanctuary of God; then I discerned their end. Truly you set them in slippery places; you make them fall to ruin. How they are destroyed in a moment, swept away utterly by terrors! . . . For behold, those who are far from you shall perish; you put an end to everyone who is unfaithful to you. (vv. 17–27)*

In centering on God in Psalm 73:17, Asaph recognizes that the Lord will deal with evil people in his timing. Verse 17 is the hinge on which the whole Psalm swings. Asaph is comforted by the justice of God. Evil people do not get away with it. God is just. He *always* acts in accordance with what is right.[6] God will deal with wicked people. If someone has wronged you, you can be sure that God will deal with the matter. Be comforted by this.

Numerous other passages tell believers they can be protected from bitterness by remembering that God will deal with the wicked. Proverbs 24:19–20 reads:

> *Fret not yourself because of evildoers, and be not envious of the wicked, for the evil man has no future; the lamp of the wicked will be put out.*

Old Testament theologian Bruce Waltke summarized, "Keeping the extinction of [evildoers'] lamp in view will extinguish burning envy."[7]

This is one of the reasons that I believe the doctrine of automatic forgiveness is damaging. By teaching that we ought to forgive automatically,

---

[6]Wayne Grudem, *Systematic Theology: An Introduction to Biblical Doctrine* (Grand Rapids, MI: Zondervan, 1994), 203–205.
[7]Bruce C. Waltke, *The Book of Proverbs 15–31*, The New International Commentary of the Old Testament (Grand Rapids, MI: Eerdmans, 2005), 285–286.

regardless of repentance, we distance our pain from the justice of God. And this is precisely the opposite of what the Bible does.

John Piper writes this on the topic:

> What I find in the New Testament is that one powerful way of overcoming bitterness and revenge is to have faith in the promise that God will settle accounts with our offenders so that we don't have to.[8]

Here we need to see that confidence in the justice of God is connected to a firm grasp of God's providence. Theologians use the word *providence* to describe the truth that God is directly involved in history and is working all things together to accomplish his purposes.[9] Paul said in Romans 8:28, "And we know that for those who love God all things work together for good, for those who are called according to his purpose."

So it is not simply that God will see that people face justice. Along with that, God is so great that he is sovereign over the evil that people do. This means that ultimately he works out evil intentions against his people to accomplish the best for his people and his purposes.

This idea of providence brings us to the most important paragraph in this chapter and one of the most important in the whole book:

If you feel yourself wrestling with bitterness, then focus more intently on our glorious God. Savor the providence of God. He is in control of all things. He is perfectly just and cannot be unjust. Bitterness begins when we have been treated unfairly. But if we believe that God will accomplish justice, and if we are simultaneously confident that God is working all things together for our good, if that is our center, then we will beat the stuffings out of bitterness every time. Derek Kidner brilliantly summarizes:

> An obsession with enemies and rivals cannot be simply switched off, but it can be ousted by a new focus of attention; note the preoccupation with the Lord himself.[10]

Do you doubt that God—who is so committed to justice that he sent his only begotten Son to the cross—do you doubt that he will bring justice to its rightful fruition in the end? Do you have any question that God—who spoke all things into existence, numbers the hairs on your

---

[8]John Piper, *Future Grace* (Sisters, OR: Multnomah, 1995), 261.
[9]Millard Erickson, *Christian Theology* (Grand Rapids, MI: Baker, 1990), 387–388; Grudem, *Systematic Theology*, 315.
[10]Derek Kidner, *Psalms 1–72*, ed. D. J. Wiseman, Tyndale Old Testament Commentaries, Vol. 14a (Downers Grove, IL: InterVarsity Press, 1973), 149. Kidner makes this comment in reference to Psalm 37, which is also a wonderful resource for conquering bitterness.

head, and determines the times set for you and the exact places where you live—do you have any question that this God will work all things together for your good?

Asaph is nothing if not honest. Consider how he describes his bitterness toward God: "I was brutish and ignorant; I was like a beast toward you [the Lord]" (Psalm 73:22).

We think of bitterness in emotional categories. But bitterness begins between our ears. It is a mental skid that, left unchecked, quickly ruins our ability to think clearly. Bitter people will not listen. In the midst of his bitterness, Asaph said that he was "brutish and ignorant." In *The Message,* Eugene Peterson paraphrases Asaph's self-evaluation, "I was totally ignorant, a dumb ox."[11]

Asaph says he was like a dumb ox. As a farm kid, I can tell you that animals in the bovine family can be gloriously dumb. I once had this stupid 4-H calf. My job was to train it to be led by a rope in a show at the county fair. The calf should have been my biggest fan. I fed and watered it and treated it better than any steer has a right to be treated. I did not participate in the operation that moved it from being a bull to being a steer. So it should not have held that against me. True, he did figure into our family's fall barbeque plans, but there was no way he could have known.

This steer should have spent his days wanting to follow me with the devotion of Mary's little lamb. But I couldn't for the life of me get that stupid calf to budge an inch. Finally, when I was trying to get it ready for the fair, it took a single step—honest; this is true!—and stepped right on my foot, smashing my toenail. Otherwise, it was about as ambulatory as the Washington Monument. Eleven hundred pounds of anchored beef. In the end, to teach him to be led, I had to hook him to a tractor and pull him around our property.[12] There was no other way. That stubborn inertia is how Asaph describes his bitterness that made him brutish and ignorant toward God. Unwilling to move.

Remember Cain, who killed his brother Abel? His is one of the most tragic stories in all of Scripture. Sin was crouching at Cain's door (Genesis 4:7) even as God sought to reason with him. But Cain was too brutish and ignorant. He was unwilling to listen, angry because he believed he had been treated unfairly.

---

[11]Eugene Peterson, *The Message: Psalms* (Colorado Springs: NavPress, 1994), 104.
[12]For the record, it was a Hereford steer. It performed miserably at the fair. Those who are experts in raising beef might suggest that I did not begin soon enough to train it to be led. I continue to blame the steer.

Those who are battling bitterness tend to avoid using the word *bitterness* to describe what they are feeling. Instead they talk about how badly they have been hurt. Based on the depth of their hurt, they talk about what they can or cannot do. "I can never be around that kind of person again."

But do you see how such thinking has turned inward? Rather than trusting in who God is and what he can do, people begin to trust in the barricades they themselves have erected. They develop a protective callus over their hurts. They believe they deserve their self-diagnosis, that they need to arrange their own protection. Their whole thought process and orientation has become distorted.

Keeping in mind, then, how muddled and brutish our thinking can become when we are struggling with bitterness, let's discuss a second key strategy for conquering it.

Second, listen to wise people.

If you find yourself on the verge of bitterness, if you know you have been treated unfairly and you feel yourself giving in, understand that it is very likely you are losing your ability to think objectively about the situation. It is very possible that the instruments of your mind are giving you incorrect readings. And if you try and fly by your own thought processes and ideas, you are heading for destruction.

At this point, you need to talk with your pastor, an elder, or some very godly person soon. Proverbs 19:20 says, "Listen to advice and accept instruction, that you may gain wisdom in the future."

I met recently with Lisa (not her real name) who had suffered some of the worst circumstances growing up that a little girl could face. Her father was evil. Now, years later, she is still battling bitterness. I understand why. Humanly speaking, the easiest thing for her to do would be to develop a callous heart and to close herself off from the memories and pain of what she's endured. But she knows that this would be wrong before God and that it would also harm her marriage and her children.

Lisa's battle is far from over. But I think she is going to defeat bitterness. In fact, I believe the worst part of her battle will be over within the year. My optimism is based in part on her willingness to listen to the scriptural counsel that I give her. I suggested to her at one point that she might be trusting in the barricades she puts up rather than in God and who he is. Though I said it as gently as I possibly could, that must have been so hard to hear. And yet she listened to it and processed it and tearfully determined to keep growing.

Third, pursue God's blessing for yourself and those close to you.

Bitterness harms everyone involved. Psalm 73:15 says, "If I had said, 'I will speak thus,' I would have betrayed the generation of your children." It might be easy to glide past this verse when reading Psalm 73. It is worded in a way that today's reader might not easily understand. But its truth is one of the most important warnings in the entire Psalm, and universal to all its readers. Claiming and doing this verse will help us win the battle with bitterness.

Asaph's point is that to be bitter is to "betray" the family, meaning not only actual family but also God's people.[13] Bitter people betray the people closest to them.

Returning to the example of Esau, this is exactly the warning of Hebrews 12:

See to it that no one fails to obtain the grace of God; that no "root of bitterness" springs up and causes trouble, and by it many become defiled; that no one is sexually immoral or unholy like Esau, who sold his birthright for a single meal. For you know that afterward, when he desired to inherit the blessing, he was rejected, for he found no chance to repent, though he sought it with tears. (vv. 15–17)

A root of bitterness can ruin not only the life of the bitter person but many others'. As I have already said, the turning point in Psalm 73 is verse 17, when Asaph begins to be God-centered. But he begins to turn this corner in verse 15 when he admits that if he continues his bitterness, he will ruin the lives of other people.

If you are stubbornly holding onto some wrong done against you, remember that those who continue in bitterness will damage the lives of many other people.

A lady called me once because she had questions about our church. But we ended up talking about a horrible ordeal she had been through—her daughter came down with cancer. In the midst of her cancer, she was attending a church where they promised that if she did certain things she would be healed. The memory is a little fuzzy, but I think it involved her giving money to that church. So this lady's daughter gave money, they prayed over her—and she died.

Is that not an awful story? How horrible that any church would make such a promise. In the aftermath, the lady with whom I was talking

---

[13]Derek Kidner, *Psalms 73–150*, ed. D. J. Wiseman, Tyndale Old Testament Commentaries, Vol. 14b (Downers Grove, IL: InterVarsity Press, 1975), 261.

was raising her grandchildren, her daughter's bereaved children. You can understand why she would be vulnerable to bitterness. In describing her bitterness to me she said, "I used to take my grandchildren to [a different church, not the one who had misled her daughter]. But I don't think I will ever take them again."

I responded by telling her how sorry I was that someone representing himself as a pastor had promised her daughter she would be healed. But I went on to say, "I know of this other church you mentioned. It is a fine church. I know their pastor, and he is not like the pastor who made that irresponsible promise to your daughter. You must not stop taking your grandchildren to church." I continued, "Listen, it may be that the very reason you are on Earth right now is so someone will take your grandchildren to church."

I do not know what happened with that grandmother. I never met her face-to-face, nor do I know whether she ended up taking her grandchildren to church. I do not know if she ever won her battle against bitterness. But if she lost that battle, I guarantee that her grandchildren suffered as well. For your sake and the sake of people close to you, you cannot afford to lose any battles with bitterness.

Fourth, call bitterness what it is.

It may seem like stating the obvious to say that bitterness is sin. But it needs to be said. Most bitter people were treated unfairly. They become very adept at defending their bitterness, because they reason that their situation was so unfair. Usually they won't even admit that they are bitter. Bitter people feel that if others knew how unfairly life has treated them, others would certainly concede their right to be bitter. But *sin* is never justifiable, regardless of unfairness. Bitterness is not something done to us. Others may create a situation that tempts you to be bitter, but if you live with bitterness, you do so because you have invited it to be your houseguest.

You can defeat bitterness in these ways:
- Trust God's justice and providence.
- Listen to wise people.
- Love those people to whom you are close.
- Decide not to sin.

Beat bitterness, or it will beat you.

Bruce Murakami: Winning the Battle over Bitterness

Bruce Murakami's story is an example of how bitterness can be defeated. Bruce and his wife, Cindy, lived in the sunshine, literally and figuratively.

They met in Hawaii. Cindy had walked into an Oahu car dealership where Bruce was working as a salesman. She bought a car, and he bought her dinner. A year later they were married.

Cindy already had a five-year-old son when they got married. They soon had another son, and a few years later they adopted a little girl named Chelsea. More sunshine.

After Hawaii, they moved to Florida, the Sunshine State. Bruce started a construction business. They joined Without Walls International Sunday School Class and taught a class on parenting.

But the sunshine did not last.

On November 18, 1998 the Murakamis' world turned pitch-black when a teenager named Justin Cabezas killed Cindy and eleven-year-old Chelsea.

It was not intentional. Cabezas was street-racing when he collided with the van in which Cindy and Chelsea were riding. They both died at the scene of the accident.

Bruce Murakami described how he found out about the tragedy:

> As I was leaving our home, I noticed the smoke from the wreck billowing above the houses in my neighborhood, so I decided to drive by and see what had happened. Actually, something inside pulled me there. When I came upon the crash and realized it was my family trapped inside the van, I was devastated. I literally blacked out, and when I came to, I was numb. For months after that, I went through the motions of each day in a zombie-like state not caring much about life.[14]

After the accident Murakami focused his energy on two goals. He wanted to clear Cindy's name by proving that the accident was not her fault. And he wanted to bring justice to the person who killed her.

Murakami was especially consumed with seeing Cabezas charged. When no charges were filed against Cabezas, Murakami hired attorneys and threatened action against the Florida Highway Patrol. He filed a suit against a rental car company involved and met repeatedly with the prosecutor's office.[15] "What happened to our so-called [justice] system?" he asked.[16]

Even though prosecutors claimed there was not enough evidence, Murakami was relentless. Finally Murakami's persistence won out. In 2002 charges were brought, and Cabezas pleaded guilty to manslaughter. Justice was about to be served.

---

[14]Bruce Murakami, "Founder Bruce Murakami's Story"; http://www.safeteendriver.org/story-bruce murakami.htm (accessed September 4, 2007).
[15]Kathryn Wexler, "Case Closed, but Not for Grieving Spouse," *St. Petersburg Times*, November 19, 2000.
[16]Ibid.

But then sunshine broke through the dark clouds again. Rather than asking the judge to give Cabezas the maximum penalty, Murakami asked the judge for leniency in sentencing Cabezas. He said, "I believe Justin is remorseful. He is a young man. I believe in giving him a second chance."[17]

The judge was lenient. Although Cabezas could have been sentenced to up to thirty years in prison (sentencing guidelines called for twenty-two years), he was sentenced to house arrest for two years, probation for eight years, and three hundred hours of community service.

Why the sudden change of heart? Bruce Murakami described in his own words why he asked the judge to be lenient:

> I read voraciously and sought counsel with my pastor. I wanted to know what I could do to move on. Finally, I realized that the only way I could really move on was to forgive Justin. . . . So, in an emotional and painful meeting, I talked with Justin. It was just the two of us face-to-face for the first time. And when Justin apologized, I realized he was in as much pain as I was.[18]

But the best was yet to come. Murakami began to pray about how he could do what was honorable and overcome evil with good. Again in his words:

> Then, this seemingly crazy idea came into my head—an idea so crazy that I couldn't even believe it at first. I started thinking about what might happen if Justin and I talked to teenagers together about driving and responsibility. I started thinking that maybe we could teach them about responsibility behind the wheel of a car and in life.[19]

Murakami's idea was to begin an organization called Safe Teen Driver. Among other things, he and Justin Cabezas would go to school assemblies and share what the consequences of unsafe driving can be.

Seven years later, Justin Cabezas reflected on what had happened between him and Bruce Murakami:

> In my heart, I always had wanted to talk with Bruce. . . . But somewhere behind all that, there had always been that desire to atone. I think I probably went through a hundred different things I was going to say. But when I got there, nothing really came out rehearsed. I was too emotional

---

[17]Quoted in Joshua B. Good, "Grief Gives Way to Compassion," *Tampa Tribune*, July 25, 2002.
[18]Murakami, "Founder Bruce Murakami's Story."
[19]Ibid.

for that. . . . [Today] Bruce is a great friend. He is somewhat like family. He knows the worst thing I've ever done in my life and has forgiven me for it.[20]

Review the key points of how Bruce Murakami forgave Justin Cabezas:
- He could have easily become bitter—he lost his wife and daughter.
- At first he was nearly consumed with the injustice of the situation.
- He sought the counsel of wise people.
- Bruce Murakami and Justin Cabezas reconciled. They met together. Justin was repentant, Bruce forgave him, and they began a new relationship.
- Rather than give in to bitterness, Bruce Murakami thought creatively about how to move forward. Out of the darkness of losing his wife and daughter came the light of a new organization, Safe Teen Driver.[21]

Conclusion

When we have been deeply and unjustly hurt, it is tempting to give in and be bitter. That is a battle that we cannot afford to lose. Center your attention on God. He is perfectly just. Rest in his providence. Listen to wise counsel. Remember that if you fail, others will be harmed too. Follow through with those things, and you will win your battle with bitterness, just as Asaph did in Psalm 73.

Discussion Questions

What is bitterness?

In what situation are people most vulnerable to bitterness?

What is meant by the providence of God?

How will understanding and believing in the providence of God help us defeat bitterness?

Read Psalm 37. What help do you find for defeating bitterness in this chapter?

Can you describe a situation where someone conquered bitterness by trusting in the providence of God?

---

[20]"An Interview with Justin Cabezas," ParentGuide.com, March–April 2005; http://www.safeteendriver. org/images/parentguide-safeteendriver.pdf (accessed September 4, 2007).
[21]The Hallmark movie *Crossroads: A Story of Forgiveness* (2007) tells the story of Bruce Murakami and Justin Cabezas.

chapter fourteen

How Can I Stop Thinking about It?

And we all, with unveiled face, beholding the glory of the Lord, are being transformed into the same image from one degree of glory to another. For this comes from the Lord who is the Spirit.

2 CORINTHIANS 3:18

An obsession with enemies and rivals cannot be simply switched off, but it can be ousted by a new focus of attention.

DEREK KIDNER[1]

The Mental Gerbil Wheel

Finding mental peace can be the most difficult aspect of unpacking forgiveness and avoiding bitterness. It is one thing to know what the Bible teaches about how we should respond to those who have hurt us. It is quite another to stop thinking about what happened. Silencing the memories can be nigh unto impossible.

My friend Tom calls this "the mental gerbil wheel." When we have been deeply offended, we may find ourselves thinking over and over about what happened. We mentally run in place. The more we think about it, the faster our thoughts go, and the faster we go *nowhere*.

---

[1]Derek Kidner, *Psalms 1–72*, ed. D. J. Wiseman, Tyndale Old Testament Commentaries, Vol. 14a (Downers Grove, IL: InterVarsity Press, 1973), 149.

A biography of Chevy Chase shared how he struggled to get off his own mental gerbil wheel. Depending on your level of exposure to entertainment, you may associate Chase more with the *Vacation* movies than with serious reflection. But there is nothing comedic about Chase's childhood. His mother abused him repeatedly. She locked him in a closet for hours at a time and would wake him up in the night to slap him in the face. Fifty years later, Chase has said he still cannot shake off the memories of what his mother did, even after her death.[2]

Christians are certainly not exempt from mental battles. In his book *The End of Memory*, theologian Miroslav Volf described his fight against the memory of being interrogated as a suspected spy. Volf said:

> My mind was enslaved by the abuse I had suffered. It was as though [the person who wronged me] had moved into the very household of my mind, ensconced himself right in the middle of its living room, and I had to live with him.[3]

Can you relate? Do you have memories that barge in and seat themselves in your living room, boisterously refusing to leave? Perhaps your spouse was unfaithful. You rehearse it—the events leading up to it, the discovery and confrontation, everything about it, real or imagined—repeatedly in your mind. How could she do that to you? What did you do wrong? How could you have prevented it? What would you say to the other man if you were to meet him on the street? You keep replaying the tape in your mind, imagining what you would say or do if given the chance, savoring the thought of the person who hurt you getting hurt, too.

This Is a Battle We Must Not Lose

It is tempting to stay on the mental gerbil wheel. You may feel that you are vindicating yourself for whatever breach of trust took place. You convince yourself that you have the right to stew. Besides, you reason, it won't hurt me to think about it.

Or you may claim that you can't help but think about it. You say, "I want to quit thinking about it, to move on. But I simply cannot. I am a prisoner of my own thoughts."

Whatever the reason you continue running on the mental gerbil wheel, know this—you cannot afford to stay there. If you give in to the

[2]Rena Fruchter, *I'm Chevy Chase . . . and You're Not* (London: MPG Books, 2007), 3–16.
[3]Miroslav Volf, *The End of Memory: Remembering Rightly in a Violent World* (Grand Rapids, MI: Eerdmans, 2006), 7.

memories and allow your mind to spin them over and over, they will even-tually destroy you. Bitterness and anger will wear a rut in your heart and soul. You will be like the Holocaust survivor who said he had become so consumed by bitterness that if you were to lick his heart, it would poison you.[4]

The seriousness of these mental battles is driven home when we con-sider that one of Satan's favorite tactics is to use unresolved relational issues. When Paul exhorted the Corinthians that it was time to forgive, he followed up with the reminder that they should be aware that unresolved differences are one of Satan's favorite strategies to divide and destroy God's people (2 Corinthians 2:5–11; Ephesians 4:25–27).

If you catch yourself brooding about a wrong done to you, be aware, too, that Satan prowls around like a roaring lion. He would love to crush your spiritual neck between his jaws when you are most vulnerable (1 Peter 5:8). You cannot lose this battle for your mind.

I recently read the heart-wrenching story of what happened to a woman named Anne Coleman. She lived every parent's worst nightmare when she received a phone call to tell her that her daughter, Frances, had been murdered in her car. Anne described going with her son Daniel to pick up Frances's car.

> They hadn't really prepared us for what we would see when we picked up the car from the pound. Frances had bled to death in her car. The bul-lets had passed through her aorta, her heart, both lungs. She had choked on her own blood.[5]

More sorrow was to come. Anne's grief was compounded by how her son dealt with the loss of his sister. Daniel was consumed. He could not, or would not, stop thinking about the murder. He kept remembering the trip to pick up Frances's car.

> [When we picked up the car], it stank. That smell never left Daniel's mind, and he wanted vengeance in the worst way. . . . Over the next two-and-a-half years I saw Daniel go downhill, and then I stood alongside his sister's grave to watch him being lowered into the ground. He had finally taken revenge—on himself. I saw what hatred does: It takes the ultimate toll on one's mind and body.[6]

---

[4]Claude Lanzmann, director, *Shoah* (1985).
[5]Johann Christoph Arnold, *The Lost Art of Forgiving: Stories of Healing from the Cancer of Bitterness* (Farmington, PA: The Plough Publishing House, 1998), 20.
[6]Ibid.

Such are the consequences of losing the battle of the mind. Determine that you are not going to be mentally defined by something done to you. You may feel like giving in. Don't do it.

Winning the Battle of Your Mind Will Be a Process

But how can we get off the mental gerbil wheel? The first thing to realize is that it will be a process.

In theological categories, the questions of how to forgive and stop dwelling upon past wrongs fall into the area of sanctification. *Sanctification* refers to the process by which we become increasingly like our Lord and Savior. The key to Christlike responses, the key to winning a mental victory over bitterness and hurt, is to fix our eyes on Jesus Christ himself, day in and day out.

Jesus, of course, dealt perfectly with those who offended him. "When he was reviled, he did not revile in return; when he suffered, he did not threaten, but continued entrusting himself to him who judges justly" (1 Peter 2:23). Jesus did not run on the mental gerbil wheel. Rather, he entrusted himself to the justice of God the Father. He was at peace. Our goal ought to be to become like him.

We do not become like Jesus in an instant. The Bible teaches that sanctification is a process. As we fix our eyes on Christ, we are transformed into his likeness from one degree to another, often in small and incremental steps.

> *And we all, with unveiled face, beholding the glory of the Lord, are being transformed into the same image from one degree of glory to another. For this comes from the Lord who is the Spirit. (2 Corinthians 3:18)*

One of the reasons that people become so discouraged by the mental gerbil wheel is that they expect an instant solution, a magic switch to help them stop thinking about a wrong done to them. While God does sometimes give immediate victories, it is usually slow in coming, a matter of striving day after day to focus on Jesus Christ rather than focusing on ourselves and those who have inflicted our pain.

We read in Scripture that we ought to "strive for peace with everyone, and for the holiness without which no one will see the Lord" (Hebrews 12:14). The word translated "strive" means to pursue with intensity of effort.[7] Scripture paints the picture of believers laboring after Christ-likeness. We strain toward it. The battle for your mind will not be won easily or instantaneously. C. S. Lewis described how long it took him to win one mental battle. In his book *Letters to Malcolm* he wrote, "Last week, while at prayer, I suddenly discovered—or felt as if I did—that I had really forgiven someone I have been trying to forgive for over thirty years."[8]

It may take thirty years to feel that you have won the victory in a mental war. It is critical to avoid giving in or allowing yourself to be defined by bitter and vindictive thoughts. Don't let bitterness wear a rut in your soul. Give no place to Satan. He would love nothing better than to use your mental battle to ruin your life.

Specifics for Winning the Battle for Your Mind

How precisely are we to go about winning this war? Where mental battles are concerned, the Christian's work to be increasingly Christlike should take place in some very specific ways. Paul said in 2 Corinthians 10:4 that the weapons we fight with are not the weapons of the world. On the contrary, our "weapons" have divine power to demolish "strongholds." And that includes strongholds in the mind. Here are some specific directions for getting yourself ejected off the mental gerbil wheel.

Burn into your mind what the Bible teaches about forgiveness.

If you have stuck with this book, you should understand an outline of what the Bible teaches about forgiveness. Make it a goal for these truths and principles to be burned into your mind.

• The most basic forgiveness principle is that Christians should forgive others as God forgave them. (See Matthew 6:12; 7:2; Ephesians 4:32.)

• Christians should have an attitude or disposition of grace toward all people even as God offers forgiveness to all who receive it. God does not forgive all people, but he does offer grace and forgiveness to all. (See John 1:12; 3:16; Ephesians 2:8–9.)

• Therefore, Christians must be willing to forgive all who ask for forgiveness. (See Luke 17:3–4.) Remember: whatever anyone has done to offend you will always pale in comparison to what you have done to offend God.

• Christians can conquer bitterness by trusting in the justice and providence of God. God is just. Vengeance belongs to him. He will repay. God providentially works all things together for good for those who know him. This includes the

---

[7]J. P. Louw and Eugene Albert Nida, *Greek-English Lexicon of the New Testament: Based on Semantic Domains*, Electronic Version, second edition, 2 vols., Vol. 1 (New York: United Bible Societies, 1989).
[8]C. S. Lewis, *Letters to Malcolm: Chiefly on Prayer—Reflections on the Intimate Dialogue Between Man and God* (Orlando, FL: Harcourt, 1992), 106.

acts of people who intend to harm us. You are not ultimately a victim. (See Romans 12:19; 8:28; Genesis 45:5–7.)

• Never excuse bitterness or an unwillingness to forgive. Those unable or unwilling to forgive should question their salvation. Read this sentence aloud: *Saying "I cannot or will not forgive" is another way of saying "I am thinking about going to hell."* (See Matthew 6:14–15; 18:21–35.)

Take a long look at Christ in his Word.

If you want to get off the mental gerbil wheel, stop scrutinizing your own situation. Take your eyes off yourself, and fix them on Christ (see Hebrews 12:1–3).

> *I lift up my eyes to the hills. From where does my help come? My help comes from the LORD, who made heaven and earth. (Psalm 121:1–2)*

You will not find relief by constantly reviewing what happened. Psalm 77 is the journal of one struggling to get off the mental gerbil wheel. In verse 3 the psalmist writes that he "meditated." But because he meditated in the wrong way, "his soul refuse[d] to be comforted" (v. 2). So he began to question the goodness of God. He asked:

> "Will the Lord spurn forever,
> And never again be favorable?
> Has his steadfast love forever ceased?
> Are his promises at an end for all time?
> Has God forgotten to be gracious?
> Has he in anger shut up his compassion?" (vv. 7–9)

You see the danger of allowing this mental turmoil to continue unchecked. If we persist in wrong patterns of thought, we can even begin to question the character of God.

The psalmist also shared how he was finally delivered. He turned his attention to who God is and what God had done.

> Then I said, "I will appeal to this,
> to the years of the right hand of the Most High."
> I will remember the deeds of the LORD;
> yes, I will remember your wonders of old.
> I will ponder all your work,
> and meditate on your mighty deeds. (vv. 10–12)

The most important thing you can do to gain victory in your mind is to fix your "meditations" on Christ. Stop analyzing your personal situation and your personal pain. Look instead to the Savior as he is revealed in the Bible. Prayerfully spend time with Christ in the pages of his Word. Savor his perfection and loveliness in all things. And as you meditate on him, you will find that you are increasingly like him.

Pray, pray, pray.

Another key strategy for clearing our minds of turmoil is to pray. I am not talking about occasionally throwing up a petition to God in your car on the way to work or rolling over in bed, muttering, "God, just help me stop thinking about this." Rather, put yourself in an environment where you can really be focused in your prayer. I go about this in different ways. Sometimes I go into our church sanctuary when no one else is there, get down on my knees, and bury my face in the front pew. Other times I take long prayer walks. Find what works best for you.

We see this emphasis on prayer in Philippians. This letter was written to a group of Christians who were experiencing conflict and turmoil in relationships. Immediately after speaking to some involved in a conflict (4:2–3), Paul challenged the Philippians to stop being anxious and to start praying instead.

> *Rejoice in the Lord always; again I will say, Rejoice. Let your reasonableness be known to everyone. The Lord is at hand; do not be anxious about anything, but in everything by prayer and supplication with thanksgiving let your requests be made known to God. And the peace of God, which surpasses all understanding, will guard your hearts and your minds in Christ Jesus. (4:4–7)*

This passage promises that when believers pray, God's peace will guard their hearts and minds.

I have learned to journal my prayers. When I am struggling against lingering hurt and bitterness, it can be difficult to stay with the prayer. Far too easily, my thoughts veer back to a spirit of turmoil and anxiousness. If I write out my prayers, however, the discipline of writing helps me engage mentally with God's truth and forces me to think about my circumstances in light of that truth.

Giving thanks should be central in your prayers. Notice in this same passage in Philippians that Paul wrote, "But in everything by prayer and supplication with thanksgiving let your requests be made known to God" (v. 6). Thanking God gives him the glory he deserves for his provision in your life. It will also shape how you think. Thanksgiving will take your mind off what is troubling you and turn your attention to Christ. None of us should have any problem journaling pages and pages of ways we are thankful.

If you have been treated unfairly, it is also legitimate to pray for justice (Revelation 6:10), as Jesus taught in the parable of the persistent widow (Luke 18:1–8). Praying for justice is also a frequent emphasis in the Psalms.[9] As I stressed in Chapter 13, a confidence in the justice of God is vital to conquering bitterness.

Say and do the right things.

When we have been treated unfairly, it is a great temptation to state our case to other people. Of course, there are legitimate times to talk to others. You may need counsel from someone or you may want to ask for prayer.

But remember this: what you say and what you do are *formative*. Talking about a wrong done to you will make it far more difficult to stop thinking about the matter. Instead of rehearsing to others, even to those you trust, what has happened to you, expend your energy in positive ways. Get involved in serving people. Encourage others. Reach out to someone else who has been hurt.

Participate in the God-given means of grace.

As I stressed in Chapter 1, Jesus offers rest to those who are mentally weary. But he did not bid us to come to him and *sleep*. Instead, Jesus said, "Take my yoke upon you, and learn from me" (Matthew 11:29). The way we assume Christ's yoke is through labor: studying and listening to his Word, fellowshipping with his people, engaging in worship, praying, and so on.

Chuck Colson's Victory over the Mental Gerbil Wheel

On July 8, 1974, Chuck Colson laid down for the first time on a prison cot. Physically, he was miserable. The temperature in his cell was over a hundred degrees. It was stifling. Even breathing seemed like hard work.

But Colson's physical suffering was nothing compared to his mental and emotional battle. Only a couple of years before, Colson had been

---

[9]This brings up the controversial area of the imprecatory Psalms (psalms that declare a desire for God's just vengeance to call upon enemies). See, for instance, Psalm 58. In theologian and pastor John N. Day's excellent book *Crying for Justice: What the Psalms Teach Us About Mercy in an Age of Terrorism* (Grand Rapids, MI: Kregel, 2005), 10, 115–116, he argued that there is a legitimate application of the imprecatory Psalms for New Testament Christians. He writes, "When God's people find themselves suffering from gross or sustained injustice, they are in principle justified in calling for divine justice and appealing to divine vengeance." But Day is careful to balance his position with the New Testament emphasis on enemy-love.

serving as chief counsel on the Nixon White House staff. He had been one of the most influential men in the world. Now Colson thought he would never have any opportunity to make a meaningful contribution with his life. He had gone from power to oblivion. Colson wrote:

> The most shattering thing about prison was the thought that I would never again do anything significant with my life. . . . The story I had been living had come apart, and I couldn't find the ghost of a theme that might continue. My future seemed imprisoned—for life. True, I had thought of success in material terms—power, money, fame, security. But I had also seen success as doing things that affected how people lived. How could I ever achieve this now? I would always be a marked man, an ex-convict, a disgraced public official.[10]

Nearing his forty-fourth birthday, Colson felt like life was over.

Colson's suffering was not completely his own fault. While he was guilty of some offenses, he had also been treated terribly unfairly at other points by the media and judicial system. Understandably, he sought to defend himself and President Nixon over Watergate. Colson shared how he initially tried to build a case:

> In fact, during the first two years after Watergate, I assembled a massive file of information, attempting to establish that the CIA had been involved in the fall of the Nixon presidency.[11]

So, Chuck Colson's mental battle was a mixture of regrets over his own mistakes, how he was treated unjustly, and his fear that he would never make a meaningful contribution.

But Chuck Colson couldn't have been more mistaken when he thought his opportunity to make a difference was over. On January 31, 1975, he was released from prison after serving seven months. By the summer of 1976, only two years after that sweltering first night in prison, Colson founded Prison Fellowship. He has now written numerous books and has spoken all around the world. He also founded the Wilberforce Forum, a conservative Christian political and social think tank. His daily radio broadcast, *Breakpoint*, is heard across the country. He has received thirteen honorary doctorates. In 1993 the once-convicted felon Chuck Colson received the Templeton Prize, a cash gift of over one million dol-

---

[10]Charles Colson and Harold Fickett, *The Good Life: Seeking Purpose, Meaning and Truth in Your Life* (Wheaton, IL: Tyndale House, 2005), 22.
[11]Ibid., 101.

lars given each year by the Templeton Foundation to the one person in the world who has done the most to advance the cause of religion. (Colson donated the money to Prison Fellowship.) Today he is one of the most influential Christian leaders in the world.

Chuck Colson is living proof that we can have victory over mental turmoil. One cannot help but marvel at how God turned his life around and delivered him from the mental quicksand. But even as we give God the glory for how he has used Chuck Colson's leadership, it is critical to understand that Colson's victory over the mental gerbil wheel was not instantaneous. It was not as though the moment Chuck Colson became a Christian he stopped battling his destructive thought life. There was not a magic switch that made a quick end of his pain. In fact, he was already a Christian when he felt that his life was over that first night in prison.

Rather, Chuck Colson fought his way out of the mental quicksand. He refused to give in to the temptation to be bitter and angry over what had happened to him. From the beginning, he determined not to give in to bitterness.

> When I arrived in prison, my caseworker told me, "Just settle in, accept it. This is where you live now. Don't think about your home." Reading Bonhoeffer convinced me to do just the opposite. . . . I drove myself to work as hard as I could. My entire day was consumed with writing, studying, doing my job in prison laundry, exercising, and helping other inmates. I seldom allowed myself any recreation. More than anything else, I feared doing nothing.[12]

Chuck Colson centered on Christ and on saying and doing the right things. In a few years he moved from the mental despair of that first night in prison to a significant position of Christian leadership.

Today Colson is thankful for his seven months in prison. He knows God used those miserable days to prepare him for a great ministry. His time in prison made it possible for him to begin Prison Fellowship. Now he thanks God for the circumstances he faced that put him in prison.

> I thank God for Watergate. Not only did prison radically transform my view of life, but the experience also gave me the one thing I thought I would never have again—an opportunity to serve others in significant ways. In my case that service has been a ministry to prisoners around the world.[13]

---

[12]Ibid., 84.
[13]Ibid., 23.

Conclusion

It is hard not to dwell on wrongs done to us. In fact, *not dwelling* may seem impossible. Like Chuck Colson, we are all tempted to build files of defense material, either literally or figuratively. We feel a need to prove we have been treated unfairly. The more we have been hurt, the more we are tempted to stew on it in our minds.

Through the power of the Holy Spirit, however, you can get off the mental gerbil wheel. You do not have to be held hostage by your thoughts. Understand that you probably will not see instantaneous victory. You will need to fight your way out of the mental rut. This means each morning you must get up and fix your eyes on Jesus once again.

Read his Word. Pray biblically. Attend church. Say and do the right things. Then one day you will realize that you are no longer fighting that same mental battle. You will even thank God for how he has further shaped and strengthened you through the hurt you suffered.

The battle for your mind is one that you must not lose. Over time, unresolved anger and bitterness will wear a rut in your heart and soul. Given the chance, Satan will use it to his advantage. He prowls around like a roaring lion looking for someone to devour. This is a battle you must not lose. The stakes are too high.

Discussion Questions

What was meant in this chapter by "the mental gerbil wheel"?

Is getting off the mental gerbil wheel accomplished in a moment, or is it usually a process?

What specific steps did this chapter suggest for getting off the mental gerbil wheel?

Did Chuck Colson have immediate mental peace when he was sentenced to prison? How did he go about finding it?

Read Psalm 77 several times. How does the psalmist move off the mental gerbil wheel? Notice especially verses 10–12.

Suppose someone told you that he is struggling not to think bitterly about an offense. After some discussion, the individual decided to memorize Scripture. Would you counsel that person to memorize verses specifically related to the situation? Why or why not?

chapter fifteen

What If Christians Cannot Agree?

And there arose a sharp disagreement, so that they separated from each other. Barnabas took Mark with him and sailed away to Cyprus, but Paul chose Silas and departed, having been commended by the brothers to the grace of the Lord.

ACTS 15:39–40

In fact, it is with great confidence that I can predict: You will face relational conflict in your future. Not only your distant future, but your immediate future. . . . For as sinners living in a fallen world, conflict is inevitable and in fact, is heading your way right now. You can count on it.

C. J. MAHANEY[1]

In a perfect world, Christians would resolve all conflicts. If we all followed God's Word completely, we would resolve our differences and move forward together.

The reality is, it does not always work that way. There are times when trying to achieve resolution seems to make matters worse. People remember what has already taken place differently. And they disagree about how to move forward. It is an impasse, a hopelessly complicated knot. Despite

---

[1]C. J. Mahaney, "Cravings and Conflict," *Reformation 21: The Online Magazine of the Alliance of Confessing Evangelicals*; http://www.reformation21.org/Counterpoints/Counterpoints/342/vobId__6296/ (accessed July 31, 2007).

prayer, despite efforts, despite meeting after meeting, reconciliation seems impossible.

These impasses can begin calmly enough. But when lines are drawn and people align on one side or another, the situation takes on a life of its own. E-mails fly. If it is in a church setting, out-of-town ministry authorities may be contacted "for advice." Some people, even those who have not read the Bible for years, begin to search for relevant verses. Others organize "prayer" meetings. Laymen are tempted to gossip or to accuse leadership of being overly controlling. Leaders are tempted to issue accusations of gossip and mutiny. Some talk about holding high a banner of "truth." Others dismiss doctrinal issues to major on "love."

Almost always, there is more to a conflict than the obvious issues. Soon enough these other matters are dredged up, and the knot is tied tighter still. Well-intentioned attempts to defuse the situation are taken the wrong way.

The damage from these interpersonal cycles of violence is horrific. Sometimes local churches never recover. Young believers are hurt. Pastors are burned out. Joy is taken away. God is not glorified by his people.

How do we move beyond an impasse? What do we do when people simply cannot reconcile with one another or agree on a solution? In such cases it seldom works to simply walk through the steps of Matthew 18:15–17. This is not because there is any deficiency in God's Word. It is because we are fallen people who do not always think alike. And sometimes we do not know how to come to resolution.

We find a great deal of help in addressing impasses from studying a conflict that took place in the early church between Paul and Barnabas. It was a major disagreement between two key leaders. It was tremendously painful and resulted in the parting of ways. Yet in the end, healing happened, and God's Word went forward. To those struggling with an impasse, this story from Acts offers wisdom and hope.

Paul and Barnabas's Impasse

Luke summarizes Paul and Barnabas's impasse in six verses:

> And after some days Paul said to Barnabas, "Let us return and visit the brothers in every city where we proclaimed the word of the Lord, and see how they are." Now Barnabas wanted to take

with them John called Mark. But Paul thought best not to take with them one who had withdrawn from them in Pamphylia and had not gone with them to the work. And there arose a sharp disagreement, so that they separated from each other. Barnabas took Mark with him and sailed away to Cyprus, but Paul chose Silas and departed, having been commended by the brothers to the grace of the Lord. And he went through Syria and Cilicia, strengthening the churches. (Acts 15:36–41)

To the casual reader of those six verses, Paul and Barnabas's disagreement may not seem so bad. But Luke says that they had "a sharp disagreement." This is a rare word in the Greek New Testament, and it refers to the kind of conflict that may have included shouting.[2] Whatever happened, they parted company over it, though by that time they had known each other for twelve years.[3] How tragic. The first missionaries of the early church—Barnabas ("son of encouragement") and Paul ("the apostle to the Gentiles")—split up and went their markedly separate ways. What happened?

Other Factors that Pressured Paul and Barnabas's Relationship

To understand what happened, we must be aware that other factors pressured Paul's relationship with Barnabas. As is often the case, there was more to it than the matter immediately in view (whether or not to take John Mark with them on their next trip). A number of other factors put pressure upon the relationship between Paul and Barnabas. Any one of these would have upped the stakes considerably. Together they made for an incredibly tense situation.

• *A major rift at Antioch.* The last eighteen months had witnessed an angry debate over circumcision. It exploded at Antioch when Paul blasted Peter and Barnabas openly for their public cowardice. Looking back on it, Barnabas knew that Paul had been right. He and Peter had been wrong, hypocritical even, to be cozy with the Gentiles but then later to distance themselves when they feared

---

[2]παροξυσμός/*paroxysmos*. This word appears only here and in Hebrews 10:24, where it is used in the positive sense of stirring one another to love and good works. It is closely related to words that mean "anger." H. C. Hahn, "Anger, Wrath," in *The New International Dictionary of New Testament Theology*, ed. Colin Brown (Grand Rapids, MI: Zondervan, 1971), 110. Outside of the Bible, it is used to refer to a severe fit or disease. This was a major disagreement between Paul and Barnabas. See William F. Arndt, F. Wilbur Gingrich, and others, *A Greek-English Lexicon of the New Testament and Other Early Christian Literature (Electronic Version)*, third edition (Chicago: University of Chicago Press, 2000).

[3]H. Wayne House, *Chronological and Background Charts of the New Testament* (Grand Rapids, MI: Zondervan, 1981), 124–125.

how it would look to the Jewish leaders. Paul rebuked Peter publicly (see Galatians 2:11–14).[4]

• *Family relationships were involved.* Barnabas and John Mark were cousins (see Colossians 4:10), and Barnabas *really* wanted to take John Mark along (see Acts 15:37).

• *Disappointment.* Paul and Barnabas must have both been especially excited about their next chapter in ministry. After going through terrible persecution while opening new mission fields, they were now planning to visit the churches in every city where they had proclaimed the Word of God so they could see how the believers were doing (Acts 15:36). It must have been especially disappointing for both of them to see this complication come up.

• *Silas was forced to take sides.* Neither Paul nor Barnabas probably wanted that to happen, but it was the nature of the thing. Silas chose to go with Paul (Acts 15:40).

• *Barnabas and Paul both knew that Barnabas had once stood up for Paul.* It was because of Barnabas that Paul was first allowed to meet with the leadership in Jerusalem (Acts 9:26–27). Also, John Mark had merely deserted them, but Paul stood by and approvingly held the garments of the people who stoned Stephen (Acts 7:58; 8:1; 22:20) and sought to undermine the gospel by wiping out the Christians (Acts 9:1ff.).

• *Barnabas was one of the largest financial backers of the early church* (Acts 4:36–37). I am not for a minute suggesting that Barnabas would have leveraged this in his relationship with Paul. Nor do I think that Paul would have let it affect him. Still, it shows the kind of passion and commitment that Barnabas had for the Lord's work. *Perhaps* part of Paul's argument in not taking John Mark was that it would not be good use of God's money. And *if* Paul did make that point, then perhaps Barnabas thought about how sacrificially he had given.

So these things go. While one particular issue may be in view (in this case it was whether or not Paul and Barnabas would take along John Mark), other factors contribute. If you are involved right now in an unresolved conflict, you can probably list three or more other factors at work that may include previous conflicts, family relationships, disappointment, and money issues.

What We Can Learn

Happily, this is not the end of the story for Paul, Barnabas, or John Mark. Paul later referred fondly to Barnabas (1 Corinthians 9:6). Even more

---

[4]New Testament scholar F. F. Bruce believed that tension over the circumcision debate was behind some of the disagreement about John Mark. He wrote, "It is a pity that the dispute was allowed to generate such bitterness; it might not have been so but for the memory of the incident at Antioch when 'even Barnabas,' as Paul says, followed Peter's example in withdrawing from the society of Gentile Christians (Galatians 2:13). After that, it is doubtful if Paul and Barnabas could ever be so happy in their association as they had once been. The old mutual confidence had been damaged and could not be restored: 'never glad confident morning again.'" F. F. Bruce, *The Book of the Acts*, revised edition, The New International Commentary on the New Testament (Grand Rapids, MI: Eerdmans, 1988), 302.

encouraging, at the end of his life Paul spoke positively of John Mark on multiple occasions. Read Paul's own words:

> *Aristarchus my fellow prisoner greets you, and Mark the cousin of Barnabas (concerning whom you have received instructions—if he comes to you, welcome him). (Colossians 4:10)*

> *Epaphras, my fellow prisoner in Christ Jesus, sends greetings to you, and so do Mark, Aristarchus, Demas, and Luke, my fellow workers. (Philemon 23–24)*

> *Luke alone is with me. Get Mark and bring him with you, for he is very useful to me for ministry. (2 Timothy 4:11)*

What can we learn from Paul and Barnabas in this scene? First, the point of this text is surely not to lay blame. The Bible does not indicate that either Barnabas or Paul was right. F. F. Bruce wrote:

> Luke does not relate the dispute in such a way as to put Paul in the right and Barnabas in the wrong. In view of Luke's restraint, it is idle for the reader to try and apportion the blame.[5]

While it was sad that Paul and Barnabas parted company in this manner, and while they may not have handled the situation perfectly, it is significant that they both continued on for Christ. The Lord's work went forward.

There are a number of specific lessons to consider from this conflict that happened in the early church.

Accept it: impasses do happen.

It happened. The first missionaries in the history of the church disagreed sharply with one another and parted company.

If you or I were recording the beginning of the church, we might have omitted the conflict between Paul and Barnabas. We might have been tempted to present an idyllic picture of leaders who worked through things without ever raising their voices. But Luke's goal was not to glorify Paul and Barnabas. Rather, Luke wanted to describe how the beginning of the church and the advancement of the Word was a gracious work of the Holy Spirit. The church and the Word moved forward not *because of* people but *in spite of* them.

---

[5]Ibid., 301.

If this kind of conflict could happen to the likes of Paul and Barnabas, then be assured it will happen to us as well. Don't be surprised. Impasses happen.

Fix your eyes on Jesus, and continue forward.

Perhaps Paul and Barnabas themselves never considered throwing in the towel in their ministry. But I'll bet that John Mark felt like quitting for good. Can you imagine being the source of the conflict between Paul and Barnabas? If John Mark had never messed up in the first place, his restoration would never have been necessary. How easy it would have been for John Mark to say, "Oh, just forget the whole thing."

Have you ever felt like quitting the Christian life because of a conflict with another Christian? You may be there right now. Hurt by the sin of others, discouraged by your own failures, and unsure how much is your fault and how much isn't, you want to say, "Oh, just forget it."

It's not really that you want to completely renounce your faith. Rather, you wish you could unplug yourself from any commitments in a local church or that you could simply cut off all contact with someone who once was close to you.

If you are discouraged because of conflict, I can relate. There have been several times since I have become a pastor that it was so discouraging not to be able to see people agree with one another and reconcile. I remember one situation where a group of people disagreed strongly with our elders on several issues. The elders arranged a meeting to try to resolve the conflict. I can still picture what I saw when I walked by them on my way into the building that evening: the people who opposed the elders were standing in the church's parking lot, praying. Like Paul and Barnabas, they too were convinced that they were the ones in the right. But we certainly never found agreement that evening in the meeting.

It still hurts to think about that time. I wish the outcome had been different. But we cannot allow such setbacks to stop us from wholeheartedly serving Christ in his church. Hear the encouragement of Hebrews 12:2–3:

> *Looking to Jesus, the founder and perfecter of our faith, who for the joy that was set before him endured the cross, despising the shame, and is seated at the right hand of the throne of God. Consider him who endured from sinners such hostility against himself, so that you may not grow weary or fainthearted.*

Jesus endured less than ideal circumstances and relationships, and so must we. No quitting. No unplugging. Keep on for Christ.

Say less: without gossip, a quarrel dies down.

Whenever we face conflicts that are not easy to resolve, there is a powerful temptation to present the particulars of our case favorably before other people. We have a remarkable ability to justify what the Bible calls "whispering" or "gossip." But tragically, when we rationalize gossip, we provide fuel that keeps the conflict burning. So many interpersonal fires would be doused if people would simply stop talking about them (Proverbs 26:20). See the earlier discussion "Keep the Circle Small," page 109.

Submit: respect God-ordained authority structures.

One of the first questions that we ought to ask when facing an impasse is, what authority structures are already in place? A teenager and his parent might find themselves at an impasse about whether or not the teen should have a cell phone. The reasons teens present for having a phone are often quite compelling, at least in the eyes of the teen. I have personally been on the receiving end of brilliant explanations why teenagers should have their own cell phones.

However, some parents out there, wise parents even, may not be swayed easily by their teens' rationale. And in that case the Bible clearly states a resolution to the impasse: children are to obey their parents (Ephesians 6:1–2). As long as the parents are not demanding something that goes against God's revealed commands, the teen's final answer in that case is that he ought to submit to his parents' wishes.

Similarly, there are God-given authority structures in place in a local church. God has called some to lead and others to submit to their leadership (Hebrews 13:17). Of course, this does not mean that leaders should abuse their authority or lord it over people (see 1 Peter 5:3). But it *does* mean there are times when the leaders must make a decision so the work can move forward, even though agreement is not unanimous. When leaders have to make decisions like that, people who have submitted themselves to their leadership should submit themselves to those decisions (unless, of course, they are asked to disobey God; cf. Acts 5:29).

Be hopeful and wait: time heals what reason and emotions cannot.

We should always strive to settle our differences before the sun sets. But when we are unable to achieve resolution, we should be hopeful for the future. This side of heaven, Christians should always dream that time and distance may provide ample enough space for eventual healing and a clearer understanding of the situation. So often it is true that when we cannot find resolution by reasoning with one another, time and distance will allow us to heal and mature to a point where resolution does become possible.

If you come to an impasse and simply cannot resolve it, continue to pray and hope. Time heals wounds that emotions and reason cannot. You may be amazed at the healing you may find as both parties continue to grow in Christ.

Soften: there'll always be something to admit.

Less of a man than Paul might not ever have been willing to pay John Mark a compliment, lest it come across as though he were admitting his earlier stance was an error. But Paul did not let his pride stand in the way of acknowledging what God had done to change John Mark into a profitable servant. Perhaps Paul realized that earlier he had been too hard on John Mark. Later, when John Mark had proven himself over time, Paul spoke of him both publicly and affectionately. Do not allow a bitter difference you have had with someone to keep you from ever again demonstrating respect and care. The cause of Christ is too dear for us to hold onto old offenses. If you were treated unfairly or the situation leading to a conflict was unjust, leave the matter to God. Be willing to admit that others might change over time, showing themselves to be the real deal.

Conclusion

Christians must make every effort to resolve all differences. But we should not be surprised when we come to an impasse. We live in a fallen world, and imperfect people cannot always sort everything out. When we do come to an impasse, we should:

- Accept that impasses happen. If Paul and Barnabas came to one, then we might as well.
- Fix our eyes on Jesus and continue on. We must not quit.
- Say less. Without gossip a quarrel dies down.
- Submit. We must respect God-ordained authority.
- Wait. Time heals wounds that emotions and reason cannot.

Discussion Questions

Why did Paul and Barnabas decide to go different directions?

What other pressures had there been on Paul and Barnabas's relationship?

How do you think Paul and Barnabas felt when they parted company?

Why is gossip such a temptation when two parties cannot come to agreement about something?

Read Matthew 18:5–9 again. How do these verses and the material covered in Chapter 7 relate to this chapter? What do you think would have happened to the early church if Paul and Barnabas had been unwilling to part company, yet continue to move forward for Christ?

Can you think of a time in your life when time has healed wounds that reason could not heal in the short run?

chapter sixteen

Final Thoughts

And we know that for those who love God all things work
together for good, for those who are called according to
his purpose.

ROMANS 8:28

All their life in this world and all their adventures in Narnia
had only been the cover and the title page: now at last they
were beginning Chapter One of the Great Story, which no
one on earth has read: which goes on for ever: in which
every chapter is better than the one before.

C. S. LEWIS[1]

I began Chapter 1 with one of my favorite recent stories on forgiveness—how Ronald Cotton forgave Jennifer Thompson when her false
testimony had sent him to prison for a crime he never committed.

Let me end this book with one of my favorite ancient forgiveness
stories—the true Old Testament story of how Joseph forgave his brothers. It happened almost four thousand years ago in northern Africa. No
matter how well you know that Scripture passage, you would do well to
read it again and marvel (Genesis 37–50). If you are struggling to unpack
forgiveness, immerse yourself in it.

Here is the story in broad strokes. Joseph's ten older brothers hated
him. This went way beyond the normal sibling rivalry (the kind where

---

[1]C. S. Lewis, *The Last Battle* (New York: Macmillan, 1970), 184.

one brother pushes another brother off the bunk bed)—Joseph's brothers plotted to kill him. At the last minute they backed away from outright murder, but just barely. Instead they sold him into slavery.

Granted, Joseph was not a perfect brother. He told his older brothers that they would one day bow down to him, a surefire way for a younger brother to create friction with older brothers. But he did not deserve to be sold into slavery. To say that he was treated unjustly is an understatement.

Slavery is seldom an ideal situation. It was especially tough for Joseph. He lived on an emotional roller coaster. Every time he saw a glimmer of hope, he got blindsided by some setback.

Joseph had been gaining an honorable reputation in his new position when the boss's wife made false accusations of the worst kind against him, landing him in prison. There he interpreted a dream for a fellow inmate who was well-connected. The guy promised to put in a good word for him if all went well. Again there was a speck of daylight. The guy was released, and Joseph had good reason to expect that he would help him out. But his well-connected friend forgot him.

Finally Joseph was miraculously released, and Pharaoh put him in charge of the Egyptian food reserve. At this point, the tables turned providentially on Joseph's brothers. Because of a famine, they were forced to trek down to Egypt and beg for food. The brothers had no idea they would run into Joseph, much less that he would be the vice president of Egypt's food reserves.

They did not recognize Joseph because so many years had passed by and perhaps also because he was speaking to them through an interpreter. Rather than reveal himself immediately, Joseph kept his identity hidden until his brothers' repentance was clear.[2]

Finally the moment came when Joseph could no longer keep his identity a secret. Now get the picture—Joseph's brothers *destroyed* his life. They considered killing him and sold him into slavery. He had lost the best years of his life in an Egyptian prison and had been deprived of sharing the growing-up years of his younger and only full brother, Benjamin.

---

[2]See Derek Kidner, *Genesis: An Introduction and Commentary*, ed. D. J. Wiseman, Tyndale Old Testament Commentary Series, Vol. 1 (Downers Grove, IL: InterVarsity Press, 1967), 199. Judah, in particular, showed a change in character. On Judah, see Victor P. Hamilton, *The Book of Genesis: Chapters 18–50*, ed. R. K. Harrison and Robert L. Hubbard Jr., The New International Commentary on the Old Testament (Grand Rapids, MI: Eerdmans, 1995), 567–570, 657–658. For a more technical analysis of forgiveness in this passage, see David J. Reimer, "Stories of Forgiveness: Narrative Ethics and the Old Testament," in *Reflection and Refraction: Studies in Biblical Historiography in Honour of A. Graeme Auld*, ed. Robert Rezetko, Timothy H. Lim, and W. Brian Aucker (Leiden: Brill, 2007), 368–369.

They cut him off from his aging father, who could have died in the interim years. Joseph had been uprooted from the Promised Land and planted in a strange place. He had every reason to be bitter.

But Joseph refused to give in to bitterness. Read what he said:

> *So Joseph said to his brothers, "Come near to me, please." And they came near. And he said, "I am your brother, Joseph, whom you sold into Egypt. And now do not be distressed or angry with yourselves because you sold me here, for God sent me before you to preserve life. For the famine has been in the land these two years, and there are yet five years in which there will be neither plowing nor harvest. And God sent me before you to preserve for you a remnant on earth, and to keep alive for you many survivors. So it was not you who sent me here, but God. He has made me a father to Pharaoh, and lord of all his house and ruler over all the land of Egypt. Hurry and go up to my father and say to him, 'Thus says your son Joseph, God has made me lord of all Egypt. Come down to me; do not tarry. You shall dwell in the land of Goshen, and you shall be near me, you and your children and your children's children, and your flocks, your herds, and all that you have. There I will provide for you, for there are yet five years of famine to come, so that you and your household, and all that you have, do not come to poverty.' And now your eyes see, and the eyes of my brother Benjamin see, that it is my mouth that speaks to you. You must tell my father of all my honor in Egypt, and of all that you have seen. Hurry and bring my father down here." Then he fell upon his brother Benjamin's neck and wept, and Benjamin wept upon his neck. And he kissed all his brothers and wept upon them. After that his brothers talked with him. (Genesis 45:4–15)*

If there ever was any question about the sincerity of Joseph's forgiveness, it had to have been cleared up seventeen years later, when Jacob died.[3]

> *When Joseph's brothers saw that their father was dead, they said, "It may be that Joseph will hate us and pay us back for all the evil that we did to him." So they sent a message to Joseph, saying, "Your father gave this command before he died, 'Say to Joseph, Please forgive the transgression of your brothers and their sin, because they did evil to you.' And now, please forgive the transgression of the servants of the God of your*

---

[3]Reimer writes, "Here we wonder at the brothers for their continued suspicion and fear of reprisals from Joseph given their teary embraces in Genesis 45. Nonetheless, there is—as perceived on their part—a life-threatening situation: their 'evil' actions (v. 17) against Joseph may end with his vengeance against them. But their abasement is met with further tears and assurances of peace between brothers and well-being for the clan. Again a life-long situation of conflict is brought to final resolution with the assurance of life displacing the threat of death." "Stories of Forgiveness," 369.

father." Joseph wept when they spoke to him. His brothers also came and fell down before him and said, "Behold, we are your servants." But Joseph said to them, "Do not fear, for am I in the place of God? As for you, you meant evil against me, but God meant it for good, to bring it about that many people should be kept alive, as they are today. So do not fear; I will provide for you and your little ones." Thus he comforted them and spoke kindly to them. (Genesis 50:15–21)

I gave the following definition for biblical forgiveness in Chapter 4:

Forgiveness—a commitment by the offended to pardon graciously the repentant from moral liability and to be reconciled to that person, although not all consequences are necessarily eliminated.

Consider how Joseph put this into practice.

• Joseph made a *commitment* to pardon his *repentant* brothers, and he stood by that commitment the rest of his life.

• He forgave them *graciously*. There is no way that Joseph's brothers could have purchased forgiveness, no way they could have paid him back. He offered forgiveness as a free gift.

• Joseph was *reconciled* to his brothers. He did not issue a pardon and then tell them to get out of his sight. He committed to providing for his brothers and their families. He spoke tender words.

Maybe what stands out most is how Joseph defeated bitterness. He believed deeply in the providence of God. (On providence, see the section, "On Justice and Providence" in Chapter 13, page 155.) Even though his brothers intended to harm him, he knew that God is so powerful and in control that he can weave even the threads of others' evil intentions into the glorious tapestry of his plan for his people.

●   ●   ●

Joseph unpacked forgiveness. He centered on God and his truth. He understood what that truth meant as applied to forgiving his brothers. And then he put that truth into practice. He forgave his brothers and was reconciled to them. What a beautiful story.

Now, I am praying for more stories. How much more should we who live on this side of the cross, who hold in our hands the completed Scripture, how much more should we be renewing our minds with the truth and seeking to live out the good, pleasing, and perfect will of God (Romans 12:1–2)?

If you are worn out from the baggage of broken relationships, accept Christ's invitation. Take his yoke upon you, and learn from him (Matthew 11:29). There is nothing you could imagine that you would want in a Savior that you will not find in him. In him you will find rest for your soul. His yoke is easy, and his burden is light. Don't fear following Christ in the area of forgiveness. Be confident that the more you unpack forgiveness, the more you will reflect and showcase the brilliant beauty of Christ, finding your maximum joy and happiness in him.

Discussion Questions

Why is the idea of providence so important to understanding Joseph's willingness to forgive his brothers?

How did Joseph demonstrate that his forgiveness included reconciliation?

Read Genesis 37–50 (including Genesis 38). How did Joseph's brother Judah change from the time of the brothers' selling Joseph into slavery until Jacob's final blessing?

Chapter 1 of this book told the story of how Ronald Cotton forgave Jennifer Thompson. What parallels do you see between Ronald Cotton's story and Joseph's?

In a quote shared in Chapter 1, Ronald Cotton told Jennifer Thompson, "We were both his victims." In what sense can a Christian be a victim? In what way can a Christian never be a victim (see Romans 8:28–39)?

More Forgiveness Questions

His divine power has granted to us all things that pertain
to life and godliness, through the knowledge of him who
called us to his own glory and excellence.

2 PETER 1:3

Anybody who thinks hard about forgiveness will start a lot
more rabbits than he can catch.

CORNELIUS PLANTINGA JR.[1]

Here are some additional questions that often come up when I
preach and teach on forgiveness.

How can I be sure that God has forgiven me?

This is *the* most critical forgiveness question. Indeed, it is the most
critical question, period. Nothing can be more important than knowing
that God has forgiven your sins and that you will spend eternity in perfect
fellowship with him and his people.

We must be careful that we do not falsely assume we are forgiven by
God when, in fact, we are not. As I said in the Introduction, Jesus taught
that a group of people has a false assurance of salvation. Similarly, James
said there is a kind of faith that is "dead" faith (James 2:14–17).

But don't be discouraged. Even as the New Testament exhorts us to
evaluate our salvation, it also teaches that there is a proper basis for assur-

---

[1]Cornelius Plantinga Jr., "Rehearsing Forgiveness: Practicing the Hard Parts Till We Get Them Right,"
Christianity Today, April 29, 1996, 31; http://www.christianitytoday.com/ct/1996/april29/6t5031.
html?start=1 (accessed March 6, 2008).

ance of salvation. You *can* be sure that you will not be one of the people who hears, "I never knew you; depart from me" (Matthew 7:23). Indeed, God *wants* his people to have assurance of eternal life. The entire book of 1 John in the New Testament outlines the proper basis for assurance of salvation. For example:

> *I write these things to you who believe in the name of the Son of God that you may* know *that you have eternal life. (1 John 5:13)*

So, how can you be sure you are truly a Christian? You can evaluate whether you are forgiven by God by asking yourself three questions. Each of these questions is of vital importance. Don't ask yourself just one of them, but all three.

First, do you presently have faith in the Lord Jesus for salvation?

Do you *presently* trust in Christ, and in him alone, for eternal life? You may be able to identify a time when you turned in faith to Christ. Looking back on that point when you put your faith and trust in Jesus ought to be a great blessing. But the more important question is, do you trust Jesus *today* for eternal life? True, saving faith is not something that comes and goes. If we truly have faith, we will *continue* to have faith (1 Corinthians 15:1–2; Colossians 1:23; Hebrews 3:14). Wayne Grudem writes:

> Therefore a person should ask him or herself, "Do I have trust in Christ to forgive my sins and take me without blame into heaven forever? Do I have confidence in my heart that he has saved me? If I were to die tonight and stand before God's judgment seat, and if he were to ask me why he should let me into heaven, would I begin to think of my good deeds and depend on them, or would I without hesitation say that I am depending on the merits of Christ and am confident that he is a sufficient Savior?"
>
> This emphasis on *present* faith in Christ stands in contrast to the practice of some church "testimonies" where people repeatedly recite details of a conversion experience that may have happened 20 or 30 years ago. If a testimony of saving faith is genuine, it should be a testimony of faith that is active this very day.[2]

Second, does the Holy Spirit testify with your spirit that you are a Christian?

---

[2]Wayne Grudem, *Systematic Theology: An Introduction to Biblical Doctrine* (Grand Rapids, MI: Zondervan, 1994), 803.

The Bible says in Romans 8:16, "The Spirit himself bears witness with our spirit that we are children of God." If you are truly a Christian, then the Holy Spirit will give you an inner confidence that you know Christ.

This question is the most difficult to answer. You could drive yourself crazy asking, is that the Spirit testifying with my spirit? Do I truly have a sense of the presence of Christ in my life?

Yet if you are a Christian, the Bible says, God has poured his love into your heart (Romans 5:5). Douglas Moo wrote:

> The confidence we have for the day of judgment is not based only on our intellectual recognition of the fact of God's love, or even only on the demonstration of God's love on the cross . . . but on the inner, subjective certainty that God does love us . . . and it is this internal, subjective, yes, even emotional, sensation within the believer that God does indeed love us—love expressed and made vital in real, concrete actions on our behalf—that gives to us the assurance that "hope will not disappoint us."[3]

If you are truly forgiven, then you are a new creation in Christ (2 Corinthians 5:17,) and the Spirit will testify with your spirit.

Third, does my conduct give evidence that I am a Christian?

If you are truly a Christian, you should act like it. John said:

> *And by this we know that we have come to know him, if we keep his commandments. Whoever says "I know him" but does not keep his commandments is a liar, and the truth is not in him. (1 John 2:3–4)*

Now, let us be clear. Acting like a Christian *does not make you* a Christian. However, true Christians do act like Christians. As I said in Chapter 10, quacking doesn't make you a duck, but ducks do quack. Holding pears in your hands does not make you a pear tree, but pear trees do hold pears. And acting like a Christian does not make you one, but Christians do act like Christians. "Even a child makes himself known by his acts, by whether his conduct is pure and upright" (Proverbs 20:11).

Whatever you profess to believe, and whatever experience of God you may think you have had, if your conduct is not honoring to Christ, you should question your salvation. Let's say you profess to be a Christian, yet you are content to live your life with no consistent local church involvement. Let's say you are unwilling to identify with Christ in baptism, or

---

[3]Douglas Moo, *Romans 1–8*, ed. Kenneth Barker, The Wycliffe Exegetical Commentary (Chicago: Moody, 1991), 312–313.

perhaps you persist in habitual sin. If these things characterize you, then you should seriously, *seriously* question whether you are truly forgiven by God.

So, in order to evaluate whether or not you are truly a Christian, ask yourself those three questions:

1. Do I have present faith in the Lord Jesus Christ for salvation?
2. Does the Holy Spirit testify with my spirit that I am a Christian?
3. Is there evidence in my life that I am different because of my faith?

Now, at this point you may be saying, "Well, I've tried to evaluate myself in each of those three areas, and yet I'm still unsure. What do I do next?"

First, I would encourage you to talk with someone who is a mature, Bible-believing Christian. Beyond that, the best thing you can do if you are unsure about your salvation is get busy living the Christian life. Don't sit around thinking in circles. Get involved in a Christ-centered, Bible-believing church. Start reading the Bible. Pray consistently. Ask God to give you confidence in your salvation. Take Jesus' yoke upon you, and learn from him.[4]

What if I need to forgive God?

As I argued in Chapter 5, it is wrong to presume that we would *ever* need to forgive God. God is perfect and holy and has never and will never do anything that requires our forgiveness. It is never appropriate to think of God as someone who needs our forgiveness.

So why does this question even come up? One reason is that some people are blaming God for their own sins. Proverbs 19:3 says, "When a man's folly brings his way to ruin, his heart rages against the LORD."

Another reason we might raise this question is that we cannot understand why we face difficult tragedies or trials. In that case, we must remember that our finite minds cannot understand the plan of God. Think of the biblical example of Joseph. It is not for us to make sense of it all. Again, our minds cannot understand the plan of God (Deuteronomy 29:29; Isaiah 55:8). But we can rest in the assurance that God loves us so much that he gave his only begotten Son to pay the penalty for the sins

---

[4]Jonathan Edwards said, "And although self-examination be a duty of great use and importance, and by no means to be neglected, yet it is not the principal means by which the saints do get satisfaction of their good estate. Assurance of salvation is not to be obtained so much by *self-examination* as by *action*." Jonathan Edwards, *The Religious Affections* (Carlisle, PA: The Banner of Truth Trust, 1997), 123, emphasis his.

of those who put their faith and trust in him. Those who trust him will spend eternity in his glorious presence, in a place where there is no more death, mourning, crying, or pain (Revelation 21:3–5).

If you are going through a time of great pain and need further reading, I would point you to Jerry Bridges's book *Trusting God Even When Life Hurts*.[5]

How can I forgive myself?

If you are asking, "How can I forgive *myself?*" it is probably in reference to mistakes you have made in your life. You know that your choices have caused yourself and others great pain. You want to know how you can move beyond your regret.

While it is a good thing to want to move beyond your mistakes and the consequences they have reaped, there are fundamental problems with even raising this question. As I have stressed throughout this book, forgiveness is something that must occur between two parties. In light of that truth, it makes no more sense to talk about forgiving yourself than it does to talk about shaking your own hand.

More important, our great need in life is not forgiveness from ourselves. Rather, we need God's forgiveness. When it comes to regrets and lingering guilt, we need to ask God to forgive our sins, knowing that Christ already paid the penalty for our sins on the cross. Paul talked about this very point in 2 Corinthians 7:10 where he said that godly grief brings about true repentance that leads to salvation. Nancy Leigh DeMoss said, "Forgiveness isn't something you can give yourself. It is something [God] has purchased for you."[6]

You might respond, "Maybe you're right. Maybe *forgiveness* is not the word I should use. But how do I get past this? How do I move beyond my feelings of regret?" The short answer to that question is that you must be increasingly centered on the cross. You must live in the glory of the gospel. The more you focus on Christ and the truth of his gospel, the more you will find joy in your salvation and victory over guilt and bitterness.

What is the unforgivable sin?

Troubled people often raise this question after reading Jesus' words in Matthew 12:

> *"Therefore I tell you, every sin and blasphemy will be forgiven people,*
> *but the blasphemy against the Spirit will not be forgiven. And whoever*

[5]Jerry Bridges, *Trusting God Even When Life Hurts* (Colorado Springs: NavPress, 2008).
[6]Nancy Leigh DeMoss, *Choosing Forgiveness: Your Journey to Freedom* (Chicago: Moody, 2006), 115.

speaks a word against the Son of Man will be forgiven, but whoever speaks against the Holy Spirit will not be forgiven, either in this age or in the age to come." (vv. 31–32)

I have a friend, Steve (not his real name), who once got very frustrated about something. Even though he was not a believer at the time, he asked God for help. When God did not answer his prayer in the way that he wanted, Steve became so furious that he cursed God. Later, when he shared concern about the incident, someone with just enough Bible knowledge to be dangerous told Steve that he had committed "the unpardonable sin" and that he could not hope that God would ever forgive him.

A few years later, Steve turned in repentance from his sin and put his faith in Christ for salvation. But the thought of those verses in Matthew 12 still made him anxious. Had he committed the unforgivable sin Jesus described? The answer to that question is no.

When Jesus gave this stern warning in Matthew 12, he was not speaking about repentant people like my friend Steve. Rather, he was addressing a group of people who saw him perform miracles and yet still refused to believe that he was the Messiah. Even worse, they accused him of performing the miracles in the power of Satan (v. 24). Jesus' point was to warn people who refuse to believe in him even in the face of powerful, clear evidence.[7]

My friend Steve clearly was not guilty of what Jesus warned against in Matthew 12:31–32, and he eventually demonstrated that by his ongoing walk with Christ. The sin that Jesus was describing is characterized by an ongoing hardness of heart and an unwillingness to repent and turn to Christ.

If you are someone who has blasphemed God, but now you are sincerely repentant and have asked God for forgiveness, you need not fear that you have committed the unforgivable sin.

On the other hand, if you are someone who has heard the gospel many times, and yet you still refuse to bow your knee to Christ, you should realize that you are standing on very dangerous ground. There may come a time when it is too late for you. Turn to Christ now, today!

Do I need to ask God's forgiveness more than once?

The answer to this question depends on what the person asking it means by asking God for forgiveness of sins. If the question is, do I need

---

[7]See David L. Turner, "Matthew," in *Cornerstone Biblical Commentary*, ed. Philip W. Comfort (Wheaton, IL: Tyndale House, 2005), 175.

to ask God for forgiveness multiple times in order to be saved? the answer is no. At the moment a person has saving faith, he or she is justified or declared righteous by God. There is no condemnation for those who are in Christ Jesus (Romans 8:1).

Having said that, there is also a sense in which believers are continually seeking God's forgiveness for the sake of unblocked communion with him. Jesus taught the disciples in the Lord's Prayer that we are to ask God in an ongoing way for forgiveness. The apostle John wrote in 1 John 1:9, "If we confess our sins, he is faithful and just to forgive us our sins and to cleanse us from all unrighteousness." It is important for Christians to confess their sins in an ongoing way as a part of growing spiritually.[8]

Do you have any advice for parents of young children?

Yes!

Parents of young children will have many opportunities to teach their children about forgiveness. Here are a few brief tips:

Teach them to use the right words. The script is not that difficult.

"I am sorry [for the specific offense]. I was wrong. Will you please forgive me?"

"Yes, I forgive you."

Discourage the excuse words "if," "but," and "maybe."[9]

"I am sorry if I hurt your feelings when I destroyed your Lego castle, but you wouldn't play with me" is not acceptable.

Stress that when something is forgiven, it is over.

Begin teaching your children at an early age that once forgiveness has taken place, the matter is settled, and it does not need to be brought up again.

Example, example, example.

As my aunt has told me, the first three steps to effective parenting are example, example, example. One of the most important things a parent can do is to model repentance when it is appropriate. Show your children that you will own up to your sin without excuses, and ask for their forgiveness. I once had to ask my son Christopher for forgiveness. He was only three or four at the time. I had been grouchy at home, and I was convicted. I said, "Christopher, I am sorry that I was grouchy with you. Will you please forgive me?"

---

[8]See John MacArthur, *The Freedom and Power of Forgiveness* (Wheaton, IL: Crossway Books, 1998), 54–58.

[9]See Ken Sande, *The Peacemaker* (Grand Rapids, MI: Baker, 2004; reprint), 127–128.

Christopher responded, "It's okay, Daddy. You didn't mean to do it."

I said, "No, Christopher, I did mean to do it. Will you please forgive me?" He forgave me, and that was the end of it.

As resources go, the children's curriculum titled *The Young Peacemaker*, written by Corlette Sande,[10] is a great tool for teaching children about forgiveness. Janet Willis's book *A Dad's Delight* is a beautifully illustrated book aimed at young children.[11]

Must a person always stay married to a spouse who says he or she is repentant?

Suppose a husband is repeatedly unfaithful. Each time his infidelity comes out, he tearfully asks forgiveness. Two questions arise. Must his wife always forgive him? Must there always be reconciliation in the marriage?

This deserves a book all its own. I will give only the briefest of answers here. But the answer to the first question is that she should forgive him. Jesus taught clearly that we should forgive the one who repents an unlimited number of times (Luke 17:3–4). Of course, this assumes the person is repentant. If he is clearly insincere, then she should not forgive him. But here we must also be extremely careful in evaluating motives.

The second question—must there always be reconciliation?—is far more complex. As Chapters 3 and 4 argued, forgiveness does not necessarily mean the elimination of consequences. In the case of marriage, there are times when the Bible allows for divorce (Matthew 19:1–12; 1 Corinthians 7:10–16). So, in the situation described here, the wife might say to an unfaithful husband, "I do forgive you. But you have broken our marriage covenant repeatedly. I can't live any longer with someone I can't trust, so we can no longer be married."

Divorce is never God's *best*. God hates divorce. While he permits divorce in a fallen world, we must do all that we can to avoid divorce (Malachi 2:16) and the fallout it causes for all involved. If you are contemplating divorce, you can count on this: the divorce you imagine is not the divorce you will have; the cost of divorce is always greater than you thought it would be.

Deciding what to do when a spouse repeatedly commits a grave offense is a matter of spiritual wisdom and discernment that should be made only by a growing Christian in close interaction with a pastor and

---

[10]See http://www.peacemaker.net/site/c.aqKFLTOBIpH/b.958199/k.AFBE/Young_Peacemaker.htm (accessed March 6, 2008).
[11]This book can be ordered at www.adadsdelight.org.

other spiritual leaders. Scripture teaches that it is as we give ourselves as living sacrifices to the Lord that we are able to discern God's good, pleasing, and perfect will (Romans 12:1–2). And pastors are given as gifts to God's people so they can be equipped for what they face and for their service to him (Ephesians 4:11–12; 1 Peter 5:1–4). Learn from other mature believers at such times. "Listen to advice and accept instruction, that you may gain wisdom in the future" (Proverbs 19:20; cf. 18:1).

If you are in a situation where you believe you must consider divorce, my heart goes out to you. Be assured, God is a great God. He can heal your marriage. Even if you are convinced that you could never have feelings for your spouse again, God who spoke all things into existence can resurrect your marriage. If you must pursue divorce, do so only while you are growing as a Christian, involved in a Christ-centered, Bible-believing local church, and closely interacting with a pastor and spiritually mature people.

Should adultery always be confessed, even if it was a one-time offense and the spouse may never find out otherwise?

This is a question I have faced repeatedly in counseling sessions. I recall one conversation I had with a man who was wrestling over whether or not to tell his wife about unfaithfulness. It was a one-time offense, and it had occurred many years earlier. He reasoned that telling his wife would only hurt her.

At the time I was inclined to think he should tell his wife. But I did not strongly counsel him to do so. I understood his point that confession then would certainly have caused her pain. But I have reflected on this question now for a number of years. It is now my opinion that unfaithfulness should always be confessed, even if it was a one-time offense and the spouse does not have any apparent way of finding out. The fact remains that marriage vows were indeed broken. The Bible says, "Whoever conceals his transgressions will not prosper, but he who confesses and forsakes them will obtain mercy" (Proverbs 28:13).

In a book on forgiveness, John MacArthur explained why he believes that unfaithfulness should always be confessed:

> There is no doubt that in some cases confessing a sin may cause as much hurt as the offense itself. Nonetheless, I believe that in all cases the unfaithful party in a marriage relationship broken by adultery should confess the sin to his or her spouse.

Why? For one thing, it takes two people to commit adultery. The other party in the sin already knows about the offense. It compounds your unfaithfulness to share a secret with your cohort in sin but keep your spouse in the dark. The lack of total openness—the need to hide things and keep secrets—will continue to be a barrier to the proper unity of the marriage. Something as serious as a breach in the marital union cannot be repaired if the truth must be kept from your marriage partner. Failure to confess simply compounds lying and cover-ups. That sort of thing will eventually destroy the relationship, whether or not the adultery is repeated.

As difficult as it may be for both you and your spouse, you must deal honestly with a sin like this. If the offended spouse discovers the sin through other means, the hurt that is then caused will be drastically increased. You owe it to him or her to confess.[12]

National Football League star Mike Singletary humbly shared how he had to work through whether or not to confess to his wife that he had been unfaithful to her during their engagement. While Singletary did not break marriage vows, he still felt guilty. He said that at first he tried to let the matter stay between him and God. But the guilt that he felt continually gnawed at his conscience.

Every day I felt more guilty. I knew I should talk to Kim, but I didn't want to hurt her. And I didn't want to face the truth about myself. I was not what she thought I was. Not even close.[13]

Finally, Mike Singletary realized that he had to confess to his wife that he had been unfaithful during their engagement. She was deeply hurt, and it took time for him to win her trust back. But almost immediately, his spiritual life was different.

Having confessed to my wife, I felt a transformation in my heart. God began filling the void in me that had for so long been filled by my ego, sin, and guilt. I became open and honest with her. She would see me cry, hear my worries, fears, hopes, and dreams. I began to pray with Kim, to read Scripture with her, to talk to her constantly. We went to church as often as she wanted, because I wanted that now, too. I was finished running from God. I was running to him. Best of all, Kim forgave me. She loves God and she loves me. She makes our house a home, and there's no place on earth I'd rather be.[14]

[12]MacArthur, *The Freedom and Power of Forgiveness*, 186.
[13]Mike Singletary and Jerry Jenkins, "My Confession," *Moody Monthly*, December 1993, 30.
[14]Ibid.

If you are in this situation, the book *Rebuilding Your Broken World* by Gordon MacDonald[15] could prove a valuable resource.

What about restitution?

Whenever it is possible, Christians should make restitution for wrongs they have committed. This principle is seen in the Old Testament Law (see Exodus 22:1–15).

A child who breaks his neighbor's window should ask forgiveness. He and his parents should also make sure they pay the damages for the broken window.

Restitution may not always be monetary. The person who has spread a falsehood about someone should seek to communicate correct information just as widely as the false rumor has spread.

Of course, the person offended can choose to waive attempts at restitution. Once in a public meeting, a man said something about me that was false. I was able to prove that what he said was incorrect, and he asked me to forgive him. He also offered and (appropriately) to admit publicly that he had been wrong about me. At that point I declined. In that situation I believe it would have served only to drag the matter out unnecessarily.

Who should forgive?

Forgiveness should be granted only by the offended. You say, "Well, that is kind of obvious." I think so. But increasingly there seems to be confusion over this issue. Whether it is a school shooting in Kentucky or the Oklahoma City bombings, various Christian leaders or groups line up to offer their forgiveness. Often this forgiveness is offered regardless of whether or not the person being "forgiven" is truly repentant, and it is often offered by people who were not even directly offended. However well-intentioned such declarations may be, they reflect a profound misunderstanding of the nature of godly forgiveness. These declarations are also profoundly insensitive to the people who have actually been victimized.

Should I forgive people after they die?

If the person was unrepentant for what he or she did, then apply the principles of Chapters 11 and 12. (1) Do not relish thoughts of revenge toward the offender's memory or toward others involved with the situation. (2) Cultivate an attitude of grace and love toward the offender and toward his living loved ones. (3) Trust God to deal justly with the offender.

Perhaps it goes without saying, but if the offender was repentant before his death, you should have graciously and freely offered forgive-

---

[15]Gordon MacDonald, *Rebuilding Your Broken World* (Nashville: Thomas Nelson, 1990).

ness to him at that time. If the offender was repentant, yet you refused to forgive him or her before his death, then it is crucial for you to confess *your* sin to God and ask *him* for forgiveness.

What if someone I have offended will not forgive me?

The first thing you should do is, be sure you have truly repented before God and asked forgiveness from the person(s) you have offended. It may be that the other party does not believe you have truly taken ownership of your offenses. It may help you to review the section "Choose Your Words Carefully" on page 111.

Further, remember that forgiveness does not mean the elimination of consequences. Do not expect that when the other person forgives you, it means you will not have to face any consequences. This is not the case.

But if you know you have genuinely repented and clearly asked forgiveness, and yet the other person will not forgive you, then choose to leave the matter in God's hand. Rest in God's forgiveness of you, trust him to bring the other party to a point eventually where he or she might forgive you in this life, yet press on in following Christ. Regardless of whether or not the other party forgives you, God will forgive all those who come to him in faith and repentance.

Be sure to pray for the person you offended. Only the Holy Spirit can change hearts. You will not be able to persuade him or her on your own. And there is reason to be concerned for a person who will not forgive other people (see Chapter 10).

What Other Authors Say about Conditional Forgiveness

The idea of conditional forgiveness is so strange to many that I feel obliged to demonstrate that I am by no means the first to propose it. Here is a sampling of other theologians who have written in one way or another about the conditional nature of forgiveness.

Jay Adams

Jay Adams argues without qualification that forgiveness is conditional. Notice Adams's balance in stressing that Christians are obligated to try and bring an offender to repentance.

> What shall we say then? It is clear that forgiveness—promising another never to bring up his offense again to use it against him—is conditioned on the offender's willingness to confess it as sin and to seek forgiveness. You are not obligated to forgive an unrepentant sinner, but you are obligated to try to bring him to repentance. All the while you must entertain a genuine hope and willingness to forgive the other and a desire to be reconciled to him or her. Because this biblical teaching runs counter to much teaching in the modern church, it is important to understand it. Such forgiveness is modeled after God's forgiveness which is unmistakably conditioned on repentance and faith.[1]

---

[1]Jay Adams, *From Forgiven to Forgiving: Learning to Forgive One Another God's Way* (Amityville, NY: 1994), 37.

Ligon Duncan

In a roundtable discussion on forgiveness, Derek Thomas asked Ligon
Duncan the following:

> There is a connection between that question and a narrower question
> and that is the relationship between conditionality and forgiveness.
> There are two texts. One is Luke 17:3, "If your brother sins against
> you, rebuke him, and if he repents, forgive him," with the conditionality
> of repentance present in that case. Then in Matthew 6:14, 15, "If you
> forgive others their trespasses, your Heavenly Father will forgive you,
> but if you do not forgive others their trespasses, neither will your Father
> forgive your trespasses." What sort of response do you have to the idea
> that forgiveness must be unconditional?

Duncan responded:

> This is a question that many Christians have never thought through. I
> think that Christians who have themselves harbored unjustified bitter-
> nesses and have been unforgiving in places and in ways that they should
> have been forgiving, often when they are confronted with and gripped by
> the radical teaching of Christ on forgiveness, out of sorrow for their own
> sin, read Jesus' teaching on forgiveness in such a way that they under-
> stand it to mean that forgiveness is an automatic obligation in every
> circumstance, irrespective of the repentance of the other party. And,
> again, I think that that is a mistake. I believe that forgiveness always
> has in view reconciliation, and reconciliation is always two-sided. So if
> there is not a repentance corresponding to forgiveness, then very often
> there is an impossibility of reconciliation. I think that whatever we think
> about forgiveness, forgiveness is a component to what is a larger picture,
> and the larger picture is reconciliation. And reconciliation is necessarily
> two-sided. Consequently, I think it is important for us to talk about both
> forgiveness and readiness to forgive. There may be circumstances where
> a reconciliation is impossible, but a readiness to reconcile can still be
> present with a believer. Consequently, I would want to make that distinc-
> tion when I was counseling a believer who was in a circumstance where
> there was not a present possibility of reconciliation of the relationship.
> Instead of telling them that they need to forgive or they will become bit-
> ter, I think I would rather say that you need to be ready to forgive and
> not to be captured by your bitterness.[2]

---

[2]"A Roundtable Discussion on Forgiveness: Derek Thomas Interviews Ligon Duncan and Justin
Taylor," *Reformation 21*: The Online Magazine of the Alliance of Confessing Evangelicals;
http://www.reformation21.com/Upcoming_Issues/Forgiveness_Roundtable/354/ (accessed October
23, 2007).

In summary, Duncan would say that Christians must always demonstrate a willingness to forgive, but actual forgiveness takes place only when there is repentance.

L. Gregory Jones

The most thorough recent critique of recent thinking about forgiveness is given by L. Gregory Jones in his book *Embodying Forgiveness*. Although Jones is unfortunately vague about a precise definition of forgiveness,[3] he does brilliantly set forth the shallowness of much of what is espoused by Christians about forgiveness.

There is not space here to summarize all of Jones's thinking. However, a series of quotes highlight some of his points.

> People are mistaken if they think of Christian forgiveness primarily as absolution from guilt; the purpose of forgiveness is the restoration of communion, the reconciliation of brokenness.[4]

> Repentance and confession must be practiced in specific and concrete ways, as part of the larger craft of forgiveness, if they are to result in that truthfulness that empowers people for faithful discipleship to Jesus Christ. That is why Bonhoeffer stressed the importance of church discipline and why he insisted that forgiveness cannot be unconditional.[5]

> Underlying Smedes's internalization and privatization of forgiveness is its preoccupation with individual feelings and thoughts at the expense of analyses of culpability, responsibility, and repentance.[6]

> Therapeutic mind-sets and practices have overrun the contemporary Church, infecting our parishes, our seminaries, our ministerial workshops, conceptions of spirituality and the spiritual life. We will not be able to reclaim the significance of forgiveness for Christian life or Christian theology unless we abandon the therapeutic mind-set and begin the difficult yet more hopeful task of *embodying* forgiveness in specific habits and practices.[7]

---

[3]Reviewing this book, Plantinga writes, "Jones is plainly uneasy with the task of trying to define forgiveness." Cornelius Plantinga Jr., "Rehearsing Forgiveness: Practicing the Hard Parts Till We Get Them Right," *Christianity Today*, April 29, 1996.
[4]L. Gregory Jones, *Embodying Forgiveness: A Theological Analysis* (Grand Rapids, MI: Eerdmans, 1995), 5.
[5]Ibid., 19.
[6]Ibid., 50.
[7]Ibid., 66, emphasis his.

Rather than telling victims and those who are suffering that they ought to forgive, or that they ought to believe in a good and gracious God, the first task of the Church—as people struggle to embody God's forgiveness in the pursuit of holiness—is to show solidarity with and compassion toward those who find themselves *in extremis*. . . . If we can learn to live with the silences, to recognize that which cannot be said and should not be carelessly spoken, then our speech will be more spare and more richly charged with the redemptive power of the mystery of God.[8]

John MacArthur

Similar to the position developed in Chapter 8, "Should I Just Get Over It?" John MacArthur argues that for small matters there are times when forgiveness is unilaterally and unconditionally granted.[9] But MacArthur also states:

It is obvious from Scripture that sometimes forgiveness must be conditional. . . . There are times when it is necessary to confront an offender. In such cases, unconditional forgiveness is not an option. These generally involve more serious sins—not petty or picayune complaints, but soul-threatening sins or transgressions that endanger the fellowship of saints.[10]

John Piper

In a sermon on Matthew 6:7–15, John Piper pointed to the conditional nature of forgiveness.[11] While Piper allowed that at points Christians should forgive unconditionally he also added:

One last observation remains: forgiveness of an unrepentant person doesn't look the same as forgiveness of a repentant person.

In fact I am not sure that in the Bible the term forgiveness is ever applied to an unrepentant person. Jesus said in Luke 17:3–4, "Be on your guard! If your brother sins, rebuke him; and if he repents, forgive him. And if he sins against you seven times a day, and returns to you seven times, saying, 'I repent,' forgive him." So there's a sense in which full forgiveness is only possible in response to repentance.

---

[8]Ibid., 295–296, emphasis his.
[9]John MacArthur, *The Freedom and Power of Forgiveness* (Wheaton, IL: Crossway Books, 1998), 128.
[10]Ibid., 119, 128.
[11]John Piper, "As We Forgive Our Debtors: What Does Forgiveness Look Like?," Desiring God Ministries, 1994; http://www.desiringgod.org/ResourceLibrary/Sermons/ByDate/1994/868_As_We_Forgive_Our_Debtors/ (accessed September 19, 2007).

But even when a person does not repent (cf. Matt. 18:17), we are commanded to love our enemy and pray for those who persecute us and do good to those who hate us (Luke 6:27).

The difference is that when a person who wronged us does not repent with contrition and confession and conversion (turning from sin to righteousness), he cuts off the full work of forgiveness. We can still lay down our ill will; we can hand over our anger to God; we can seek to do him good; but we cannot carry through reconciliation or intimacy.

David J. Reimer

On an academic level, the most promising work done in recent years on forgiveness in the Old Testament is that of David Reimer at the University School of Divinity. Reimer's article "Stories of Forgiveness: Narrative Ethics and the Old Testament" is a concise gold mine on forgiveness narratives in the Old Testament.[12]

Reimer explains that in knowing Old Testament stories of forgiveness, our own understanding of forgiveness is "enriched and sustained."[13] He writes:

> Rather, we deal here with stories which invite us into their world, and as we enter it our own world is re-created. . . . To learn for ourselves how to be moral people as far as forgiveness is concerned means not simply to follow through certain obligations, but to allow our actions and our understanding of the world to be shaped by the Bible's stories of forgiveness as affirmation of life.[14]

In terms of whether or not forgiveness is automatic in Old Testament narratives, Reimer concludes, "These stories give no sense that the offended is under an obligation to forgive."[15] However, he does demonstrate that forgiveness is considered a matter of life and death.[16]

Ken Sande

Ken Sande agrees that there are times when a matter should be overlooked.[17] And he also concurs that ideally forgiveness should follow

[12]David J. Reimer, "Stories of Forgiveness: Narrative Ethics and the Old Testament," in *Reflection and Refraction: Studies in Biblical Historiography in Honour of A. Graeme Auld*, ed. Robert Rezetko, Timothy H. Lim, and W. Brian Aucker (Leiden: Brill, 2007).
[13]Ibid., 378.
[14]Ibid.
[15]Ibid., 377.
[16]Ibid., 374.
[17]Ken Sande, *The Peacemaker* (Grand Rapids, MI: Baker, 2004), 79–99.

repentance. Sande pictures forgiveness as a two-stage process. In his words:

> When an offense is too serious to overlook and the offender has not yet repented, you may need to approach forgiveness as a two-stage process. The first stage requires *having an attitude of forgiveness,* and the second, *granting forgiveness.* Having an attitude of forgiveness is unconditional and is a commitment you make to God. . . . By his grace you seek to maintain a loving and merciful attitude toward someone who has offended you. . . .
>
> Granting forgiveness is conditional on the repentance of the offender and takes place between you and that person. . . . When there has been a serious offense, it would not be appropriate to [make the promises of forgiveness] until the offender has repented.[18]

Justin Taylor

Justin Taylor summarizes his position:

> "Love your enemies" is something that we should do at all times and in all places. It is modeled after God's love for his enemies, whom he loves even when they are "unjust" and "evil" (Luke 6:35). At the same time, our forgiveness of others is likewise modeled upon God's forgiveness of sinners, whom he forgives *conditioned* upon their repentance. God does not forgive apart from repentance; neither should we. In major offenses, we are not to forgive the unrepentant.
>
> In the event of a tragedy that involves the loss of human life brought about by wanton human sin, it is therefore wrong for Christians to call upon immediate forgiveness in the absence of repentance. Such a call both cheapens and misunderstands the biblical doctrine of forgiveness.[19]

---

[18]Ibid., 210–211, emphasis his.
[19]Justin Taylor, "Is Forgiveness Always Right and Required?" January 10, 2007; http://theologica. blogspot.com/2007/01/is-forgiveness-always-right-and.html (accessed July 15, 2007). See also "A Roundtable Discussion on Forgiveness: Derek Thomas Interviews Ligon Duncan and Justin Taylor," emphasis his.

Biblical Words for Forgiveness

> Forgiveness takes the central place in Christian proclama-
> tion as the means whereby [the relationship between God
> and humanity] is restored. It stands as the action of God
> in the face of the sinful behavior of man, and is based on
> Christ. . . .
>
> H. VORLANDER[1]

It would be a mistake to imply that we can plumb the rich depths of biblical narrative and theological reflection through word studies by themselves. However, it is worthwhile to survey forgiveness words from the Scriptures even as we reflect on particular passages. The goal of this appendix is to help readers not equipped with the original language to better understand biblical forgiveness words and the contexts in which they appear.

The Bible uses three major word groups for *forgiveness*. One of these is in the Old Testament.[2] The other two are in the New Testament.

In the Old Testament

The Old Testament word סָלַח/*salah* means "to practice forbearance, pardon, or forgive."[3] It occurs forty-seven times and is found in Exodus 34:9;

---

[1] H. Vorlander, "Forgiveness," in *The New International Dictionary of New Testament Theology*, ed. Colin Brown (Grand Rapids, MI: Zondervan, 1971), 701.

[2] The amount of explicit discussion about forgiveness of sins is much smaller in the Old Testament than in the New Testament. McKeating notes, "The Christian who explores the idea of forgiveness in the Old Testament is likely to be surprised at first at the relative lack of interest which Old Testament writers show in the subject." He goes on to cogently argue that it was seen as a part of salvation as a whole. Henry McKeating, "Divine Forgiveness in the Psalms," *The Scottish Journal of Theology* 18 (1965): 69.

[3] J. P. J. Olivia, "Slh," in *The New International Dictionary of Old Testament Theology*, ed. William Van Gemeren (Grand Rapids, MI: Zondervan, 1997), 265. See also Francis Brown, S. R. Driver, and

Leviticus 4:20, 26, 31, 35; 5:10, 13, 16, 18; 6:7; 19:22; Numbers 14:19, 20; 15:25, 26, 28; 30:5, 8, 12; Deuteronomy 29:20; 1 Kings 8:30; 34, 36, 39, 50; 2 Kings 5:18 (2x); 24:4; 2 Chronicles 6:21, 25, 27, 30, 39; 7:14; Psalm 25:11; 86:5; 103:3; Isaiah 55:7; Jeremiah 5:1, 7; 31:34; 33:8; 36:3; 50:20; Lamentations 3:42; Daniel 9:19; Amos 7:2.

This word is usually translated "forgive" or "pardon" in the ESV.

Two things stand out about סלח/*salah*. First, it is used exclusively in connection to God forgiving or pardoning. It is not used relative to one person forgiving another. Second, God's forgiveness is conditioned upon repentance.[4] A cluster of uses of this word in Leviticus 4 illustrates both points.

> *Thus shall he do with the bull. As he did with the bull of the sin offering, so shall he do with this. And the priest shall make atonement for them, and they shall be forgiven. (Leviticus 4:20)*

> *And all its fat he shall burn on the altar, like the fat of the sacrifice of peace offerings. So the priest shall make atonement for him for his sin, and he shall be forgiven. (Leviticus 4:26)*

> *And all its fat he shall remove, as the fat is removed from the peace offerings, and the priest shall burn it on the altar for a pleasing aroma to the LORD. And the priest shall make atonement for him, and he shall be forgiven. (Leviticus 4:31)*

> *And all its fat he shall remove as the fat of the lamb is removed from the sacrifice of peace offerings, and the priest shall burn it on the altar, on top of the LORD's food offerings. And the priest shall make atonement for him for the sin which he has committed, and he shall be forgiven. (Leviticus 4:35)*

There are no Old Testament examples of God forgiving apart from faith or repentance on the part of the one being forgiven.

While not a *major* forgiveness word in the Old Testament, the word נשא/*nāśā'* is also translated "forgiveness." See for example, Genesis 50:17. In these contexts, it can be defined as "to take away guilt, iniquity, transgression."[5] For other examples, see Exodus 10:17; 23:21; 32:32; Isaiah 2:9.[6]

---

others, *A Hebrew and English Lexicon of the Old Testament: With an Appendix Containing the Biblical Aramaic: Based on the Lexicon of William Gesenius as Translated by Edward Robinson* (Oxford, UK: Clarendon Press, 1979), 699.

[4]Olivia, "Slh," 262.

[5]Brown, Driver, and others, *A Hebrew and English Lexicon of the Old Testament*, 671.

[6]See also Victor Hamilton, "Ns," in *The New International Dictionary of Old Testament Theology*, ed. William Van Gemeren (Grand Rapids, MI: Zondervan, 1997).

In the New Testament

In the New Testament the most common word for forgiveness is αφίημι/ *aphiēmi*. It occurs 143 times in the New Testament, 127 of the uses being in the Gospel accounts: Matthew 3:15 (2x); 4:11, 20, 22; 5:24, 40; 6:12 (2x), 14 (2x), 15 (2x); 7:4; 8:15, 22; 9:2, 5, 6; 12:31 (2x), 32 (2x); 13:30, 36; 15:14; 18:12, 21, 27, 32, 35; 19:14, 27, 29; 22:22, 25; 23:13, 23 (2x), 38; 24:2, 40, 41; 26:44, 56; 27:49, 50; Mark 1:18, 20, 31, 34; 2:5, 7, 9, 10; 3:28; 4:12, 36; 5:19, 37; 7:8, 12, 27; 8:13; 10:14, 28, 29; 11:6, 16, 25(2x); 12:12, 19, 20, 22; 13:2, 34; 14:6, 50; 15:36, 37; Luke 4:39; 5:11, 20, 21, 23, 24; 6:42; 7:47 (2x), 48, 49; 8:51; 9:60; 10:30; 11:4 (2x); 12:10 (2x), 39; 13:8, 35; 17:3, 4, 34, 35; 18:16, 28, 29; 19:44; 21:6; 23:34; John 4:3, 28, 52; 8:29; 10:12; 11:44, 48; 12:7; 14:18, 27; 16:28, 32; 18:8; 20:23 (2x); Acts 5:38; 8:22; 14:17; Romans 1:27; 4:7; 1 Corinthians 7:11, 12, 13; Hebrews 2:8; 6:1; James 5:15; 1 John 1:9; 2:12; Revelation 2:4, 20; 11:9.

This word has a *very* wide range of meaning and is often used in contexts other than those dealing with forgiveness. Hence, our English translations appropriately use different words to translate it depending on the usage.[7] For instance, in Matthew 4:20, 22 αφίημι/*aphiēmi* refers to Peter and Andrew leaving their nets behind.[8]

Vorlander summarizes:

> Oddly enough *aphiēmi* occurs only 45 times in the sense to forgive (17 times in Matt.; 8 times in Mk.; 14 times in Lk.-Acts; twice in John; and only once in Paul!). . . . In most cases, however, the NT uses *aphiēmi* in the original sense of to let (Mk. 1:34; 5:19, 37 par.; Acts 14:17, etc.); to dismiss, divorce, release (Matt. 13:36; 1 Cor. 7:11-13, etc.); to leave (Mk. 1:20; 10:28 par., etc.); to leave behind (Mk. 1:18 par., etc.); and to abandon (Mk. 7:8; Rom. 1:27, etc.).[9]

The closely related αφεσις/*aphesis* appears seventeen times in the New Testament. Fourteen of the seventeen occurrences are in the Gospels: Matthew 26:28; Mark 1:4; 3:29; Luke 1:77; 3:3; 4:18 (2x); 24:47; Acts 2:38; 5:31; 10:43; 13:38; 26:18; Ephesians 1:7; Colossians 1:14; Hebrews 9:22; 10:18.

---

[7]For instance, the NIV translates it twenty-eight different ways! See Edward W. Goodrick and John R. Kohlenberger III, *The NIV Exhaustive Concordance* (Grand Rapids, MI: Zondervan, 1990), 1692.
[8]William F. Arndt, F. Wilbur Gingrich, and others, *A Greek-English Lexicon of the New Testament and Other Early Christian Literature (Electronic Version)*, third edition (Chicago: University of Chicago Press, 2000). See also Vorlander, "Forgiveness."
[9]Vorlander, "Forgiveness," 700–701.

While this word is usually translated "forgive," in Luke 4:18 αφεσις/
aphesis appears twice, and the ESV translates it "liberty."

In the context of forgiveness, αφεσις/*áphesis* and αφίημι/*aphíēmi*
mean "to release from legal or moral obligation or consequence, to cancel,
remit, or pardon."[10] John uses the word αφίημι/*aphíēmi* in 1 John 1:9 and
stresses that forgiveness is conditioned on confession.

> *If we confess our sins, he is faithful and just to forgive us our sins and to*
> *cleanse us from all unrighteousness.*

Louw and Nida explain that forgiveness removes guilt.

> Some languages make a clear distinction between guilt and sin, and
> terms for forgiveness are therefore related to guilt and not to the wrong-
> doing. Therefore, 'to forgive sins' is literally 'to forgive guilt.' Though
> terms for 'forgiveness' are often literally 'to wipe out,' 'to blot out,' or
> 'to do away with,' it is obviously not possible to blot out or to wipe out
> an event, but it is possible to remove or obliterate the guilt.[11]

There is no sense in the New Testament in which someone could be
forgiven, yet still go to hell.

The other major word for forgiveness in the New Testament is
χαρίζομαι/*charizomai*. It is found twenty-three times in the New
Testament. Fifteen of the twenty-three occurrences are in Paul's writings.

This word is in the same family of words as the word translated
"grace." It can have the following connotations: (1) to give freely as a
favor, (2) to cancel a sum of money that is owed, (3) to show oneself gracious by forgiving wrongdoing.[12] The ESV translates it using forms of the
words *bestow, cancel, forgive, give,* and *grant.*

The word χαρίζομαι/*charizomai* appears twice in both Ephesians
4:32 and Colossians 3:13.

> *Be kind to one another, tenderhearted,* forgiving *one another, as God in*
> *Christ* forgave *you (Ephesians 4:32).*

> *. . . bearing with one another and, if one has a complaint against another,*
> forgiving *each other; as the Lord has forgiven you, so you also must*
> forgive *(Colossians 3:13).*

---

[10]Arndt, Gingrich, and others, *A Greek-English Lexicon of the New Testament and Other Early Christian Literature.*
[11]J. P. Louw and Eugene Albert Nida, *Greek-English Lexicon of the New Testament: Based on Semantic Domains (Electronic Version),* second edition, 2 vols., Vol. 1 (New York: United Bible Societies, 1989).
[12]Arndt, Gingrich and others, *A Greek-English Lexicon of the New Testament and Other Early Christian Literature.*

We might paraphrase "forgiving" in these verses as "graciously forgiving." God expects believers to extend grace to people in the same way it was extended to them.

Why Doesn't Paul Use the Same Forgiveness Words?

For those of us who get excited about such things, one of the more interesting aspects of studying biblical words for forgiveness is to notice the change in New Testament vocabulary. While extremely common in the Gospels, the two words αφεσις/*áphesis* and αφίημι/*aphíēmi* are endangered species in Paul's writings. With three exceptions (Ephesians 1:7; Colossians 1:14; Romans 4:7), Paul does not use the same forgiveness word in connection to salvation as the Gospels. And Romans 4:7 is a quotation of Psalm 32.

Granted, Paul does use the word sometimes translated "forgiveness," χαρίζομαι/*charizomai*, as shown above. Fifteen of the twenty-three times it appears in the New Testament are Paul's.[13]

This difference in vocabulary begs the question, why the change? A sliver of the reason that Paul does not use αφεσις/*áphesis* and αφίημι/*aphíēmi* may be that he prefers χαρίζομαι/*charizomai*. But there must be more to it than that. In the first place, Paul does not say too much explicitly about forgiveness. A different preference in vocabulary does not explain why Paul says so little directly about forgiveness. Why, for instance, do we not find Paul referring to forgiveness of sins over and over again in Romans, his grand presentation of salvation?

Is it because Paul does not believe that God pardons sin? Obviously not.

Or is it that Paul has a different theology of forgiveness than Jesus? Is Paul more grace-oriented than the Lord? The answer is, again, obviously no.

Or is it because the idea of forgiveness of sins is far from Paul's thoughts? Again, surely not. After all, Paul does summarize the gospel relative to forgiveness in both Ephesians 1:7 and Colossians 1:14.

Agreeing with Vorlander, I believe that the reason Paul so infrequently refers to forgiveness of sins is that he has broken the overarching concept of forgiveness down into a systematic presentation. Vorlander writes:

> In Paul the terms *aphíēmi* and *áphesis* virtually disappear. This is because
> the proclamation of forgiveness appears in Paul's writings as a thought-

---

[13]Luke 7:21, 42, 43; Acts 3:14; 25:11, 16; 27:24; Romans 8:32; 1 Corinthians 2:12; 2 Corinthians 2:7, 10 (3x); 12:13; Galatians 3:18; Ephesians 4:32 (2x); Philippians 1:29; 2:9; Colossians 2:13; 3:13 (2x); Philemon 22.

out and systematized doctrine. The fact that forgiveness is not merely a remission of past guilt, but includes total deliverance from the power of sin and restoration to fellowship with God, is expressed by Paul in his doctrine of justification . . . and of reconciliation . . . with God. This has taken place in Christ and is the center of the gospel. Forgiveness takes place because God gives himself completely in the sacrifice of his Son and so gives man a share in his own righteousness. Thus 'in Christ' man becomes a pardoned sinner and a 'new creature.' This teaching represents a summary and theological consolidation of the early Christian preaching of forgiveness.[14]

Vorlander's point is that Paul favors terms like *justification* and *reconciliation* because they facilitate a systematic understanding of forgiveness of sins. So, in 2 Corinthians 5:11–21 rather than referring to the gospel as "forgiveness of sins," Paul speaks of "the ministry of reconciliation." Paul did not intend that reconciliation would be understood as something apart from forgiveness or even in addition to it. Rather, reconciliation is a different facet of the many-splendored gospel.

Paul would not have accepted the notion that someone could be forgiven but not reconciled. Rather, he saw reconciliation as a component of forgiveness. This, of course, would extend to interpersonal relationships as well as salvation (Ephesians 4:32).[15]

Summary

Even a brief survey of the biblical vocabulary for forgiveness affirms the emphases of this book. Biblical forgiveness is not primarily a feeling. Rather, it is something that happens between two parties. Biblical forgiveness is conditioned on repentance and results in the elimination of guilt. God only forgives those who repent. While some consequences may remain, it would contradict biblical meaning to insist that God forgives everyone unconditionally or that someone forgiven could still go to hell. Still, while actual forgiveness is conditioned upon repentance, forgiveness should be graciously offered to all.

---

[14]Vorlander, "Forgiveness," 702.

[15]I reject on theological and hermeneutical grounds the solution to this question set forth by Shults and Sandage. Utilizing a "trajectory hermeneutic," they argue that the biblical presentation of forgiveness changes throughout the chronology of the Bible. For instance they write, "We have seen a trajectory in the Hebrew Bible that moves from an early interpretation of God as not at all forgiving, to a picture of God as easily angered." See F. LeRon Shults and Steven J. Sandage, *The Faces of Forgiveness* (Grand Rapids: Baker, 2003), 133.

Select Bibliography

This is not an exhaustive list. It is intentionally broad. I have included some websites. By listing a source here, I do not mean to imply that I am in complete agreement with it. "But test everything; hold fast what is good" (1 Thessalonians 5:21).

"A Roundtable Discussion on Forgiveness: Derek Thomas Interviews Ligon Duncan and Justin Taylor," *Reformation 21*: The Online Magazine of the Alliance of Confessing Evangelicals; http://www.reformation21.com/Upcoming_Issues/Forgiveness_Roundtable/354/.

Adams, Jay. *The Handbook of Church Discipline*, The Jay Adams Library. Grand Rapids, MI: Zondervan, 1986.

_____. *From Forgiven to Forgiving: Learning to Forgive One Another God's Way*. Amityville, NY: Calvary Press, 1994.

Bridges, Jerry. *Trusting God Even When Life Hurts*. Colorado Springs: NavPress, 1988.

_____. *The Discipline of Grace: God's Role and Our Role in the Pursuit of Holiness*. Colorado Springs: NavPress, 1994.

_____. *The Pursuit of Holiness*. Colorado Springs: NavPress, 1996.

Carrier, Chris. "I Faced My Killer Again: After 22 Years, I Found the Man Who'd Left Me for Dead." *Today's Christian*, 1998; http://www.christianitytoday.com/tc/8r1/8r1031.html (accessed July 9, 2006).

Colson, Chuck. "Capital Punishment: A Personal Statement." Prison Fellowship; http://www.prisonfellowship.org/article.asp?ID=523 (accessed July 7, 2006).

Colson, Charles and Harold Fickett. *The Good Life: Seeking Purpose, Meaning and Truth in Your Life*. Wheaton, IL: Tyndale House, 2005.

Day, John N. *Crying for Justice: What the Psalms Teach Us About Mercy in an Age of Terrorism*. Grand Rapids, MI: Kregel, 2005.

Dever, Mark. *Nine Marks of a Healthy Church*. Wheaton, IL: Crossway Books, 2004.

Edwards, Jonathan. *Altogether Lovely: Jonathan Edwards on the Glory and Excellency of Jesus Christ*, ed. Don Kistler. Morgan, PA: Soli Deo Gloria, 1997.

Guinness, Os. *Unspeakable: Facing up to Evil in an Age of Genocide and Terror*. San Francisco: Harper, 2005.

Jones, L. Gregory. *Embodying Forgiveness: A Theological Analysis*. Grand Rapids, MI: Eerdmans, 1995.

Jones, Robert D. "Anger against God." *The Journal of Biblical Counseling* 14, No. 3 (1996): 15–20.

Kraybill, Donald B. "Forgiveness the Amish Way." *Willow*, Winter 2007, 26–29.

Lewis, C. S. *The Weight of Glory and Other Addresses*, ed. Walter Hooper. New York: Simon & Schuster, Touchstone edition, 1996.

Lomax, Eric. *The Railway Man: A True Story of War, Remembrance, and Forgiveness*. New York: Ballantine, 1995.

Lundgaard, Kris. *Through the Looking Glass: Reflections on Christ That Change Us*. Phillipsburg, NJ: P&R, 2000.

MacArthur, John. *The Freedom and Power of Forgiveness*. Wheaton, IL: Crossway Books, 1998.

MacDonald, Gordon. *Rebuilding Your Broken World*. Nashville: Thomas Nelson, 1990.

Mahaney, C. J. "Cravings and Conflict." *Reformation 21*: The Online Magazine of the Alliance of Confessing Evangelicals; http://www.reformation21.org/Counterpoints/Counterpoints/342/vobId__6296/ (accessed July 31, 2007).

_____. *Humility: True Greatness*. Sisters, OR: Multnomah, 2005.

_____ and Kevin Meath. *The Cross Centered Life*. Sisters, OR: Multnomah, 2002.

Murakami, Bruce. "Founder Bruce Murakami's Story." Safe Teen Driver; http://www.safeteendriver.org/story-brucemurakami.htm (accessed September 4, 2007).

Piper, John. "What Does Forgiveness Look Like?" Desiring God Ministries, 1994; http://www.desiringgod.org/ResourceLibrary/Sermons/ByDate/1994/868_As_We_Forgive_Our_Debtors/ (accessed March 7, 2007).

_____. *Desiring God: Meditations of a Christian Hedonist*. Sisters, OR: Multnomah, 1996.

_____. *God's Passion for His Glory: Living the Vision of Jonathan Edwards*. Wheaton, IL: Crossway Books, 1998.

_____. *When I Don't Desire God: How to Fight for Joy*. Wheaton, IL: Crossway Books, 2004.

Powlison, David. "The Therapeutic Gospel." 9 Marks, 2007; http://www.9marks.org/partner/Article_Display_Page/0,,PTID314526%7CCHID598014%7CCIID2340064,00.html (accessed July 19, 2007).

Prager, Dennis. "The Sin of Forgiveness." *The Wall Street Journal*, December 15, 1997.

Reimer, David J. "Stories of Forgiveness: Narrative Ethics and the Old Testament." In *Reflection and Refraction: Studies in Biblical Historiography in*

Honour of A. Graeme Auld, ed. Robert Rezetko, Timothy H. Lim, and W. Brian Aucker. Leiden: Brill, 2007, 359–378.

Sande, Ken. *The Peacemaker*. Grand Rapids, MI: Baker, 2004.

Volf, Miroslav. *The End of Memory: Remembering Rightly in a Violent World*. Grand Rapids, MI: Eerdmans, 2006.

Wiesenthal, Simon. *The Sunflower: On the Possibilities and Limits of Forgiveness*. New York: Schocken, 1998.

Scripture Index

General Index